NIÇOISE

ROSA JACKSON

Photography by Jan Hendrik van der Westhuizen

NIÇOISE

Market-Inspired Cooking from France's Sunniest City

W. W. NORTON & COMPANY
Independent Publishers Since 1923

For Sam, with love

CONTENTS

⁕ ———————— ⁕

SPRING | 42

SUMMER | 114

FALL | 182

WINTER | 260

FOUNDATIONS | 332

⁕ ———————— ⁕

RECIPES

INTRODUCTION

Color was what struck me first about Nice after ten years in Paris: the deep turquoise, cloudless sky; the sea so transparent that from a distance you could spot a school of anchovies whizzing through; the scrubbed white facades along the Promenade, crowned by the Negresco hotel, with its voluptuous turquoise-capped pink dome; the ocher and pink buildings of the Old Town, glowing in the sunlight. And the markets! Acid-yellow local lemons plucked with their leaves and branches; stripy pale green zucchini with their wide-open golden flowers still attached; bouquets of baby artichokes, their jade-green leaves streaked with purple—in the Mediterranean sun, it all has a technicolor quality, and *fresh* has a different meaning here. When people ask me why I chose Nice, I often say, "I love color."

True as that might be, a Canadian does not find herself running a cooking school in Nice simply because of loving color. My journey to this small but feisty city really began in Paris, which is funny, since the two cities do not claim much in common. Situated as they are at opposite ends of the country, their people eye each other with a combination of envy and suspicion: I have met many Niçois who have never set foot in Paris, not because they can't, but because they don't see the need; and many Parisians who think of Nice as a giant retirement home. One basks in year-round sun, the other has weather so unpredictable that boots and scarves never get stored away. One remains fiercely proud of its country roots, earning its people the tongue-in-cheek nickname "chard poopers"; the other values sophistication in everything from wristwatches to pastries.

Visitors often think of Nice as part of Provence, a vast and ill-defined area that any Niçois will tell you stops abruptly at the Var River, west of Nice. Here begins the former County of Nice, which once stretched north toward the ski resort of Saint Etienne de Tinée, at nearly 4,000 feet elevation, and east toward the Italian border, although some coastal towns were attached to Monaco rather than Nice. From the fourteenth century to 1860, when the County of Nice joined France, this mostly mountainous region was under the rule of first the Kingdom of Savoy and later Piedmont-Sardinia. Italy was unified in 1861, meaning that Nice was never officially part of Italy, though Italian was spoken along with the local language, Nissart. My students often express surprise at finding so much Italian food in Nice (beyond the expected tourist-friendly pizza); I explain that this is Niçoise cuisine, which puts its own twist on the classic dishes of nearby Piedmont and Liguria.

Somehow, apart from salade Niçoise and ratatouille, Niçoise cooking has remained a bit of a secret, even in France. Maybe it's because, until recently, cafés all over France had no qualms about slapping the name *salade Niçoise* on random assortments of ingredients that might include such blasphemy as rice and canned corn. During my ten years as a food writer in Paris, I never came across socca (Nice's savory chickpea pancake) or even pissaladière, the popular caramelized onion tart, although nearly every other regional cuisine has representatives in the capital. Only in the past few years have a handful of restaurants serving Niçoise specialties opened.

Unlike the people of other French regions, such as Brittany, Alsace, the French Basque country, and the sparsely populated Auvergne in central France, southerners have not historically gone to the capital to seek their fortunes, and so remain poorly represented. Over the past three decades in France, butter-rich sauces have given way to lighter jus, vegetables have stepped into the spotlight, and pungent ingredients such as anchovies and capers have gone mainstream. Two major influences have been the *soeurs Scotto*, three prolific food-writing sisters with Algerian and Italian origins, and famed chef Alain Ducasse, who chose the French Riviera as his base for training a generation of chefs.

Nice's street food tradition sets it apart from other French cuisines; much of Niçoise cuisine is not food that you tackle with a knife and fork. The tradition of *la merenda*—the mid-morning or late-afternoon workers' snack—came to Nice from Genoa in the mid-nineteenth century, and it shaped the way people still eat today: there is nothing odd about snacking all day long, or eating outdoors standing up. This is a modest cuisine that does away with formalities, and while the Niçois take pride in their local dishes, perhaps they don't see them as easily exportable to other parts of France, let alone the rest of the world.

Besides the street food of Nice, there is a whole unexplored cuisine in the hills and mountains, where each village has its specialties, whose recipes are often closely guarded. With little access to the coast and its fish, people living inland relied for centuries on local ingredients, including wild game, mushrooms, and foraged greens. Large-scale farming remains impossible due to the steep, rocky landscape, and farmers labor on terraced slopes, producing only small crops. Shortly after I moved to Nice, an elderly vendor at the market told me about a dessert made in her village with dried fava beans (a winter staple) and anise, a cousin to the better-known tourte de blettes, which calls for Swiss chard; the next day, she handed me a hand-scrawled recipe, whispering, "Don't tell anyone I gave you this." Equally guarded are the locations where wild plants flourish, particularly those used for the prized genepi liqueur, which is made from a small white flower as elusive as the most precious wild mushrooms. Hunting is still an important source of meat in the *arrière-pays* (back country).

The most comprehensive collection of Niçoise recipes was put together by a former mayor, Jacques Médecin, best known for his openly racist views and for fleeing to Uruguay when facing corruption charges. Despite serving a prison sentence in France before living out his days in Latin America until his death in 1998, his authority when it comes to Niçoise cuisine has never been disputed. One chef told me that Médecin would regularly visit his kitchen to quiz him about the preparation of each dish. Still, the real keepers of Niçoise cuisine are the famously bossy *mamies*, or grandmothers, who will tolerate no insults to tradition (but who don't necessarily agree with each other on the best way to do things).

With its reliance on olive oil, fresh produce, oily fish, whole grains, and chickpeas, Niçoise cooking resembles the food of other Mediterranean countries more than what people usually think of as French cuisine. While this diet has now been recognized as one of the world's healthiest, people traditionally ate this way in Nice because they had to—meat and rich dairy products were not readily available. Desserts were based on fruit, because there was no chocolate; honey was used in place of sugar because farmers kept bees. Only recently have people grown proud of what was essentially a cuisine of scarcity, and the price of once-undervalued vegetables like cardoons, cauliflower, and Jerusalem artichokes has rapidly increased at the market. Even delicacies like the fragile zucchini blossom initially made their way to the table out of thrift.

As much as Nice has its humble roots in the land, it also has a glamorous image, and it's this double identity that I find captivating. After Nice became part of France in 1860, it began to attract Russian and British aristocracy, most notably Queen Victoria, known for her daily excursions by donkey cart, and her genuine interest in local culture. The luxurious 400-room Hotel Excelsior Regina (now private apartments) was built to house her extensive entourage and all the nobility who followed them, lured by the royal presence each winter from 1895 to 1899.

The Côte d'Azur's unique light also drew groundbreaking painters, writers, and musicians: Matisse, Chagall, Picasso, Berlioz, Paganini, Chekhov, and Nietzsche, to name only a few of those who spent time in and around Nice producing works that captured their vivid impressions. Louisa May Alcott, the author of *Little Women*, wrote about the nineteenth-century Promenade des Anglais: "The wide walk, bordered with palms, flowers, and tropical shrubs, is bounded on one side by the sea and on the other by the grand drive, lined with hotels and villas, while beyond lie orange orchards and the hills. Many nations are represented, many languages spoken, many costumes worn, and on a sunny day, the spectacle is as gay and brilliant as a carnival."

Today Nice is France's fifth-largest city, with a population of around 350,000 that doubles during tourist season. I love the contrast between the slanting buildings of the well-preserved Old Town and the rest of the city, which sprang up in the nineteenth and twentieth centuries, adding flamboyant Belle Epoque architecture and more discreet examples of art deco. Parts of the city could be mistaken for Paris (except for the dazzling sun), while others, lush with subtropical blossoms and citrus trees, could be in North Africa or Spain. The city has grown progressively greener over the past decade, creating two sleek tram lines, a maze of bike lanes, and a long stretch of park that separates the Old and New Towns. And the qualities that attracted Alcott–the color, the vibrancy, the surprisingly cosmopolitan atmosphere for such a small city– continue to make Nice a destination with its own bold character. As with my early days in Paris, though, what really attracts me to Nice is its less polished side, which is best exemplified by the rustic *cuisine niçoise*, made with products plucked fresh from the earth and the sea.

MY CULINARY
JOURNEY TO NICE

When I was five, my family left our home in Edmonton, whose greatest claim to fame was its hockey team, to live in Paris for a year. Romantic as this might sound, we did not lead a life of expat luxury. My parents, who had emigrated to Canada from England in the 1960s, had both grown up with scarcity and loss. Although my father would be working as a microbiologist at the prestigious Institut Pasteur, they were reluctant to invest too much in this sabbatical. Our family of five squeezed into a run-down rental in the 15th arrondissement, on the wrong side of the overground Métro line that separates regal Saint Germain from its less-blessed (at the time) stepsisters, the double-digit Left Bank neighborhoods.

As I quietly absorbed the French language at the local *maternelle*, or kindergarten, there was another aspect of our new life that made an even greater impression. Holding my father's hand, I began my first food explorations of the city. Each time we came across a pastry shop, he would study the window display with the intensity of one accustomed to looking down a microscope, and we would settle on the day's treat: perhaps a tart topped with a perfect spiral of raspberries, or a coffee éclair with a lick of gleaming frosting. After verifying the quality of the pastry, we would take some home to the rest of the family. My parents loved to shop at the open-air food markets, particularly the Marché Saxe-Breteuil on the chic side of the Métro tracks, with its view of the Eiffel Tower in the background and the elegant ladies of the 7th arrondissement picking out the best of the best.

Back in Canada, we resumed a life dictated by the extreme seasons instead of by food. My mother, who had left Prague as a child refugee to live in England, immediately seemed to erase Paris from her mind and reverted to plain postwar British cooking for our weekday meals. On weekends, though, my father still enjoyed concocting slow-cooked French stews, with several cookbooks open in front of him. I accompanied him to the supermarket, but it wasn't the same as in Paris; my treat was a Mint Aero or a Crunchie bar (either of which I would still happily eat) instead of an éclair.

When students ask me today what makes a good cook, I say that it's not any innate talent–just about anyone can acquire basic kitchen skills and follow instructions–but *gourmandise* (a much nicer word than *greediness*) and a willingness to accept failure and move on. I started with baking, which is far more difficult than cooking, because one mistake or misjudgment can ruin everything (believe me, it still happens to me today). But my occasional modest successes were enough to make the many flops and their accompanying tears worthwhile.

My learning curve was complicated by the fact that most French cookbooks of the day were sketchy and vague, assuming a wealth of knowledge. I began baking from Ginette Mathiot's classic *La Pâtisserie pour Tous* (*The Art of French Baking*), in the hope of one day re-creating the coffee éclair of my dreams. Mathiot could condense something as complex as the éclair down to a single paragraph, with cross-references to other pages that made my head spin. There was no Internet at that time, and therefore no YouTube videos to enlighten me. I was on my own.

When I turned twelve, my parents took another sabbatical year in Paris. This time I would attend French *collège*, the equivalent of middle school. At my *collège*, my French Canadian accent struck both the teachers and pupils as hilarious at first, but as a foreigner I found myself in the majority with the many recent immigrants there. I made friends with kids from countries I had barely heard of, and I developed a love for French literature, even if our teacher, M. Poulain (ironic, given my love for the chocolate of the same name), could be cruel.

Most of all, I looked forward to lunch in the school cafeteria. In those days, schools still had cooks on the premises, and we would line up with our trays for the day's hot *plat du jour*, which ranged from chicken cordon bleu (a cutlet stuffed with ham and cheese and fried) with mashed potatoes to rabbit stew, the one dish I refused to eat (this would change years later when I discovered lapin à la moutarde at the Cordon Bleu). It was no-frills, homemade French comfort food, and I loved it.

There were salads too–among them, a French take on tabbouleh with couscous, chopped raw vegetables, and herbs; carottes râpées, simple grated carrots in a zingy lemon dressing; and cooked beets with Belgian endives, their bitterness a revelation to me. Since my family still didn't frequent restaurants, most of what I knew about French food I learned at the school canteen.

At school, I made friends with a Texan girl, the only other English speaker in my year. With her family, I had my first bistro meal at a restaurant in rue Mazarine, then called La Cafetière. Written in curly handwriting, the menu spoke of solid French classics from which no animal part was exempt. When my main course arrived, I lifted the lid of the cast-iron pot to release the intoxicating scent of beef cheek cooked in inky red wine until it collapsed, its texture spoon-soft and slightly jellied. Next to it, a white porcelain dish of potatoes sautéed in goose fat until golden, then sprinkled with raw garlic and parsley, was the only accompaniment. For dessert, a gigantic cloud of frothy meringue floated on a sea of custard like something out of *Alice in Wonderland.*

I think now that in all my later years as a restaurant critic in Paris, I was always searching for a meal that lived up to this one. Of course it never could, because on that day, every detail of the experience was new, from the feel of the crisp napkin on my lap to the graceful dance of the waiters who made sure each glass was filled just so and each piece of heavy cutlery materialized and vanished at the right moment.

On Sundays, I often sat on a Formica stool next to my father as he prepared elaborate lunches at the small gas stove, using products he had found at the market. He made stews using pureed vegetables as a thickener instead of flour, like the innovative chefs of that period. Wearing boxer shorts and an apron, with his thinning white hair sticking out in all directions, he would stir and taste the contents of multiple pots, describing each step of the process in scientific detail.

Aromas of seafood and saffron also wafted up from Las Ramblas, the Spanish restaurant directly beneath us, but eating there was out of the question, and not just for financial reasons. On weekends, the restaurant would come alive with mournful flamenco guitar music, intense foot-stamping, and rhythmic clapping, and the lack of insulation gave us front-row seats even if we couldn't see the spectacle. This drove my mother crazy to the point that she would stomp her feet with as much passion and fury as the dancers.

Sometimes my father would descend the stairs to broach the subject in broken French with Madame Ropus, the restaurant's squat matron. Inevitably they would end up sipping sherry together and chuckling over something unrelated, so my mother would resort to calling the police when the noise became unbearable. Because the unseen party downstairs sounded like so much fun to me, I harbored dreams of running away to become a flamenco dancer.

As the days grew shorter and more drizzly, my parents decided we would spend the Christmas holidays in Nice. I remember my solitary explorations of the city—my parents never worried about me as a thirteen-year-old accustomed to navigating the streets of Paris. I wandered into the maze-like Old Town, which at that time was considered *infréquentable* (mugging territory), getting lost in the narrow streets shaded by colorful buildings. I had never before seen palm trees, which seemed impossibly exotic.

Ten years later, when I was working in my hometown of Edmonton as a food writer—a good job for a recent English graduate, but not yet a respected form of journalism—my mother sent me a Provençal almanac to use as a desk calendar. My parents had moved back to England while I was a student, and this was her way of reminding me not to get too complacent. She knew what she was doing: looking at the recipes for each month of the southern French seasons next to illustrations of lavender fields and olive groves, I began dreaming of returning to a now-distant France.

On New Year's Day 1994, I woke up and knew what I had to do.

"I'm going to Paris," I announced to my partner.

I was twenty-six, and I'd been with him for seven years, living a life of domesticity complete with a stucco house, a dog named Koko, and an actual white picket fence. Somehow I had skipped the dating and partying that for most people comes with student life, choosing instead to cook recipes from *Bon Appétit* and *Gourmet* at my vintage stove.

In March of that year, I flew to Paris, where I found an apartment share using FUSAC, a classified ad service that is still a lifesaver for English-speakers in Paris. My roommate, Catherine, was a staunch Catholic who turned out to be related to Antoine de Saint-Exupéry, the author of the children's classic *Le Petit Prince*. The real attraction of this sixth-floor apartment with worn furnishings, slanting ceilings, and a narrow L-shaped kitchen equipped only with a hot plate and toaster oven was its balcony, where I could watch the sun set over Paris rooftops and the Tour Montparnasse, an incongruous gray skyscraper that Parisians love to hate.

To complement my meager freelance income, I found a job at a nearby English-language bookshop and tearoom. There I met an American who told me about his job translating cooking classes at the Cordon Bleu. He was preparing to leave Paris and suggested I apply. Here was my opportunity to learn the secrets of classic French cooking without having to pay the exorbitant price of a diploma.

Soon I found myself standing in front of a class of fifty students, translating everything the chef said as assistants scurried around behind him, cleaning up and handing him the right tools. I would notice students dozing off at the back of the class, which amazed me, considering the price they had paid to be at this world-famous cooking school. Later I learned that the students fell into two categories: those who planned to launch their careers with the prestigious Cordon Bleu diploma, and those whose wealthy families thought they should acquire cooking skills before they got married. Watching these girls enjoy their freedom in Paris, I wondered if they would ever go back to Mexico, Brazil, or Japan.

For nine months, I translated the Cordon Bleu's cuisine and pastry courses, practically memorizing them by the end. During the morning demonstrations, I tried not to miss a word the chef said—one, who was half-American, would unnerve me with corrections like, "It's not poultry, it's fowl!" In the afternoons, I trailed a chef around the kitchen as he critiqued the dishes the quivering students produced. I also took a few shorter courses as a student, learning to stab a lobster between the eyes to minimize the pain of its death, and to knead bread dough using a "slamming and folding" technique that I still teach.

Although French cuisine has changed since then, moving away from butter and cream-rich sauces (my father knew what he was doing) to focus on intensifying the flavors of seasonal ingredients, I use the techniques I learned there every time I cook, and can still hear the chefs' voices in my head.

After my stint at the Cordon Bleu, I looked for steadier work so that I could afford my own apartment. Thanks to my background in journalism, I landed a job at the news agency Agence France-Presse, which involved translating news stories from French into English. During the three years I worked at AFP, I lived in a fifth-floor walk-up on rue Oberkampf, just before the 11th arrondissement became a fashionable place to live, and then put a deposit on a minuscule apartment overlooking Père Lachaise cemetery and the Jardin Naturel, a small garden designed to re-create all the vegetation of the Paris region (complete with a frog pond). I also met the Frenchman who would become my husband.

From a French point of view, leaving a job as steady and well-paid as the one at AFP would be sheer folly. But I felt as restless as a hamster in a cage, and I began writing freelance restaurant reviews for *Time Out Paris*, an English-language listings magazine with headquarters in London. As a recent addition to the team, I was assigned to review cheap eats in far-flung neighborhoods—and had a few bouts with food poisoning that I'm convinced gave me lifelong immunity.

Time Out provided my second culinary education, this time as a professional eater, although I continued shopping at the outdoor food markets and cooking at home. The late 1990s was a good time to be a food writer: I had a budget for reviewing several hundred restaurants a year, aided by a team of trusted freelancers, and my magazine assignments took me to places like Copenhagen, Milan, and Hong Kong. But even before the financial crisis hit in 2007, things were changing. *Time Out*'s English-language publications had a limited audience in Paris, and the London management shut the magazine down in 2004. I was sad to lose my dream job, but I was prepared.

By that time, I was married and had a baby son, Sam. Like many Parisians, my husband and I had a love-hate relationship with the city and often talked about starting a new life somewhere else. I had begun teaching occasional classes for my friend Paule Caillat, who ran a cooking school out of her Paris kitchen, and I dreamed of creating a similar business in the South of France.

We had spent some holidays in Cannes, where we had friends who occasionally lent us their apartment. I liked the sandy beaches, the port where colorful fishing boats bobbed next to superyachts, and the covered Provençal market, where I could stock up on herb-scented olives, fresh local goat cheese, and the most beautiful vegetables from small farmers in the nearby Var region. This is where I first saw bunches of golden zucchini blossoms and tasted sweet emerald-green fava beans straight from the pod. I also discovered local fish, like the delicate-fleshed rouget (red mullet), some so tiny that they were best used for friture (whole fried fish), and the fearsome-looking chapon, with its pockmarked orange skin and spiky dorsal fin.

Coming from Paris, though, we didn't see ourselves living in this sleepy town that comes alive for its annual film festival and for the summer holidays. Nice, on the other hand, felt big enough without being overwhelming, though I still saw the city with a tourist's eye.

To get to know the city better, we rented an Old Town apartment for a few days, bringing one-year-old Sam with us. A tiny door in the turquoise facade led to a steep flight of sixteenth-century stairs; inside, the windows onto the narrow street did not let in much natural light. Each morning at 5 a.m., the crashing and clanking of the garbage "train"—a small vehicle trailing several bins behind it—jolted us awake. Where others might have been put off, I was charmed.

One day, we stopped for lunch at the Restaurant du Gésu, across from the extravagant Baroque church known as the Eglise du Gésu and a couple of blocks from the Cours Saleya open-air food and flower market. We sat in plastic chairs on a makeshift terrace as the gravelly-voiced waiter called out the names of the dishes: pissaladière, merda de can, daube Niçoise. We were still in France, but it felt like another country.

I looked up and saw a "For Sale" sign in a window high above the narrow rue du Jésus, with laundry dangling from a clothesline. The building was painted ocher, with neat cream trim, its tall windows divided into small panes that reflected the light. It faced another similar building, whose deep cracks suggested that it might collapse at any moment. I ignored the graffiti at street level, imagining myself looking out that window at the top.

The phone number led us to a nearby real estate agency where the agent, looking me up and down, said, "I think it's your style."

We followed her as she pushed open the heavy metal door and began climbing a wide marble staircase—luxurious for the Old Town, though there was, of course, no elevator. The staircase got narrower and the ceiling became so low that we had to duck before we reached the door to the fifth-floor apartment. It opened into a hallway leading on the left to a bathroom with a sloping ceiling and a claw-footed iron bathtub—who knows how they had got it up the stairs. Straight ahead from the entrance were a kitchen and dining room, separated only by an archway, the rustic, hook-studded ceiling beams—logs, really—contrasting with modern custard-yellow cabinets. The deep red paint of the kitchen gave it warmth, and the dining room had a pale sand-colored lime wash that enhanced the irregular texture of the ancient walls.

This building had once been a monastery, the agent said; I tried to imagine the monks who had lived here centuries before, and all the changes that had led to this apartment looking like something out of *Elle Décor*. At 650 square feet, it was nearly twice the size of my tiny Paris pad, and priced at only slightly more because of the difference in property prices in the two cities. I was sold, and my enthusiasm was contagious. By the end of the day, my husband and I had signed a *compromis*, a commitment to buy the apartment.

At first, our plan was to remain in Paris and make frequent trips to Nice. But each time I spotted the glittering blue of the Mediterranean from the TGV train, which meandered along the coast after whizzing at high speed to Marseille, I felt like I was coming home.

As a food and travel writer, I had learned how to absorb cultures quickly, and I put my skills to use in Nice. I purchased every book I could find about Niçoise cuisine, and I quizzed the food producers, who—amused by this inquisitive foreigner—showed me how to select the best produce (which was not always obvious) and shared their recipes, some of them specific to small villages in the hills. I got to know chefs like Dominique Le Stanc at the local institution La Merenda, and Nadim Beyrouti at the olive oil shop and restaurant Oliviera, who generously wrote out recipes for me by hand. I began testing these recipes in my new kitchen, and I bought a dining table that could also serve as a workspace for my future students.

Two cooks from apparently opposite ends of the culinary spectrum helped me to understand Niçoise cuisine. Franck Cerutti ran the kitchen at the Louis XV restaurant in Monaco, where he was second-in-command to Alain Ducasse. He'd grown up in the mountains behind Nice, an entirely different world from show-offy Monte Carlo, and his humble childhood memories inspired the exquisite dishes that were served in a dining room dripping with crystal. Marie, my across-the-narrow-street neighbor who liked to toss candy from her window to ours for Sam, was the first *mamie niçoise* I met, a grandmother who had cooked the thrifty and often time-consuming local dishes all her life. From Franck I learned how to sniff out the best products and elevate the local cuisine through small flourishes, while Marie would quickly express her disapproval if I veered from tradition, keeping me on track.

LES
PETITS
FARCIS
Cooking Studio

12

LES
PETITS
FARCIS
• FOOD & WINE SCHOOL •

MARKET TOUR, COOKING
CLASS AND LUNCH

PASTRY WORKSHOPS

PROVENÇAL WINE TASTING

VEGETARIAN CLASS

STREET FOOD TOURS

COURS EN FRANÇAIS POUR
LES GROUPES

Location de Salle
Kitchen Rental

BOOKING/RESERVATION
WWW.PETITSFARCIS.COM

By the time I'd lost my job in Paris, I had already taught my first cooking class in Nice, to a couple from California who instantly felt like friends. It was just before Easter, and we cooked herb-and-garlic-infused leg of lamb, which we served with small artichokes and baby potatoes. I had intended to teach only during the French school holidays but was soon getting requests for other periods, making me realize there was interest in what I was offering. Once I no longer had a salary to tie me to Paris, we decided to make the leap to living full-time in Nice.

My freelance writing kept us going as tourists and travel agents gradually discovered my cooking classes. I was nervous about asking students to climb multiple flights of stairs to get to my kitchen, but they loved getting a peek at life in an Old Town building. Like me, they were enthralled by the wooden beams, the original windows—which were as pretty as they were ineffective at keeping out drafts—and the aromas of fougasse and my favorite almond-caramel tart wafting up from the bakery on the corner. For a few hours, they were not just visitors, but part of the family, with Sam popping in to say hello.

As I got to know the Old Town, I found there was rarely any reason to leave. Like a village, it was self-sufficient with its food market, small shops (many of them also dedicated to food), restaurants, and street food stalls. The layout encouraged me to walk in circles within its perimeter, which had once been surrounded by walls (work on the tram line unearthed the *porte fausse*, one of the original entrances). I would spot an intriguing-looking restaurant, then struggle to find the street again; even the rue Droite, which translates as "straight road," followed its own meandering path. The sixteenth-century architects had cleverly designed the area to remain shaded and cool, so it was always a shock to come out into the vivid sunshine of the Quai des Etats Unis and its pebbly beaches, a five-minute walk from my home.

Far from being just a sleepy place to retire, as Parisians often imagined, Nice had a mixed population, with plenty of students and tourists who roamed the pedestrian streets at night shouting, laughing, and arguing drunkenly. Any time I brought up the subject of the nighttime noise with a local, they would shrug and say, "It's the Old Town." This was a place where normal rules didn't apply, and accepting it was the only solution.

Things improved when our upstairs neighbor sold us her place, enabling us to add two bedrooms to our existing one-bedroom. If that sounds simple, it wasn't at all: the owner, Renée, was one of the Old Town's well-known eccentrics, an elderly woman with ice-blue eyes, a head of curly white hair, and mahogany-colored skin as thick as leather from her daily visits to the beach, where she would run though a series of exercises topless.

From each of these sunbathing sessions over the decades, Renée had brought back one or more pebbles, which she would paint and add to ever-growing piles around the apartment. By the time we saw it, the biggest of these—which happened to be directly above our bed—had grown to such proportions that it was a miracle it hadn't crashed through the ceiling as we slept. Two workers toiled for two weeks to empty the apartment of the rocks alone, and we spent six months renovating the dilapidated space.

I lived in the Old Town for ten years before I finally decided to leave this rambunctious village for what had once been the countryside but was now ten minutes away, thanks to a tram line completed in 2007.

The Borriglione area, built on farmland in the nineteenth century, sits next to a sprawling food market known as Libération, or *la Libé* to the locals. While the Cours Saleya caters to tourists with its cheerfully painted olive dishes, lavender sachets, and paintings by local artists next to the produce stands, Libération is a purist's food market, overflowing with farm-fresh local produce, gleaming Mediterranean fish, herb-scented goat cheeses from the mountains, and olives from Provence and beyond. The focal point of this market is the Gare du Sud, a train station built in 1892 that now houses a modern food hall.

Much as I love living in the Libération area, which reminds me of Paris with its broad boulevards planted with chestnut trees and its nineteenth-century architecture, I decided to keep my cooking school in the Old Town so that I—and my students—could have the best of both worlds (once a week, I take groups to Libération before returning to the Old Town to cook). In 2015, I sold the apartment on rue du Jésus and opened my cooking studio on rue Saint-Joseph, on a hill leading to the park known as Castle Hill, though there has not been a castle there since 1706. The site is blissfully quiet, and the big picture windows look out onto a small square whose palm trees with their fan-like fronds remind me daily that I am just where I want to be.

Once a soap-making workshop, the one-room space with solid wood flooring had been home to a wine shop, a plumbing business, and an artist's studio, to name a few incarnations. I turned it into a kitchen with a black granite island, cream-colored Shaker cabinets, and a long beech-and-steel table made by a local artisan, aiming to create a feeling of home. It was not an easy path to get here: in the years leading up to the move, the financial crisis hit, making the future of my classes uncertain; my marriage disintegrated, leaving me to raise then seven-year-old Sam on my own; and my parents both fell ill with cancer and passed away.

Dark as that period felt, it was also a time of discovery and laughter. Even on days when I felt overwhelmed as I headed to the market to meet my students, the instant I saw them, I would forget my troubles for at least the next few hours, enjoying their company and their delight at being in Nice. Hundreds of students turned into thousands, and many of these encounters have led to enduring friendships, especially with those who have come more than once. I chose assistants not just for their love of food but also for the fun I sensed we could have together, and for their interest in people. Sam pitched in from the age of fourteen, having grown up talking to strangers. Now that my school is no longer inside my home, I have brought in other teachers who understand intuitively that our classes are about much more than food.

If the classic French cooking I learned at the Cordon Bleu felt a little impersonal–there was never any talk of seasons, nor of who grew the vegetables–Niçoise cuisine remains dependent on nature's cycles and on products that often appear only briefly at the market stalls; herbs and wild plants play an essential role, and I know each farmer by name. Tourism has brought glamour to the French Riviera, but Nice keeps its feet firmly planted in the earth even as the city grows more cosmopolitan.

Living here has taught me to put aside my big-city impatience and take pleasure in slow processes, whether it's waiting in line for an oil-stained paper cone filled with pepper-dusted socca as the vendor chitchats with every customer, or letting a daube simmer all afternoon until the beef collapses in the herb-scented wine sauce at the touch of a spoon. What I hope to share in this book is an adaptable approach to cooking that celebrates the most modest finds–tender dandelion leaves, freshly dug potatoes, fruit that has fallen off the tree–and brings people together around hearty dishes that are made for sharing.

The food of Nice has helped me to stop wanting everything all the time, and to appreciate what is fleeting. I hope the recipes in this book–some of them famous but misunderstood, like ratatouille and salade Niçoise, others little known, like sweet chard pie and green tomato jam–will have the same effect on you.

HOW TO USE THIS BOOK

I have organized this book by season, because Niçoise cooking has never strayed from an approach that is dictated by the land. If you have the time and means to shop at a local farmers' market at least occasionally, you will experience the joy of spotting the first asparagus spears that herald spring, or biting into a strawberry that tastes as sweet as candy. That delight will carry over into your cooking, requiring less effort from you, since the ingredients will speak for themselves. All this is my way of saying, please follow the seasons where you live when making these recipes—and find yourself a good Swiss chard supplier, since you will need it for many of the recipes in this book!

Because I know that some of these local ingredients may be difficult to find or will taste different in other countries—and even in the rest of France—I have mainly chosen the more accessible recipes from the Niçoise repertoire. I could not resist including a few personal favorites, like Artichokes Stewed in Wine (page 50), Stuffed Sardines (page 153), and Stuffed Squid (page 221), which may be trickier to source but are worth the effort. For any mamies or other Niçoise natives who might be reading this, please know that this is not meant to be an encyclopedic book on the local cuisine, but rather a collection of recipes that I have gathered and perfected over my years here, some of them originating outside Nice. I also wanted this book to reflect Nice's historically multicultural population, which has grown ever more cosmopolitan since I moved here.

To ensure that the recipes work in home kitchens outside Nice, I sent each recipe to testers in the U.S. and Canada. Their observations were invaluable in ensuring that the recipes are easy to follow and to reproduce, making this book very much a team effort rather than a solo one.

For each recipe, I have included U.S. and metric measurements. Metric measurements are generally more accurate, and if you are willing to make the investment, you will not regret spending 20 dollars or even less on an electronic scale. Other tools that I often mention are a plastic pastry scraper (less than 5 dollars), an old-fashioned food mill (nice to have but not essential), and metal tart pans with removable bases.

Finally, I am aware that a number of the recipes in this book are time-consuming and would not be considered "weeknight cooking." Think of these rustic dishes as a meditation, which will take you back to a time when cooks rarely looked at the clock. If you can find a few extra pairs of hands to pitch in, so much the better—this is the spirit of *cuisine niçoise*, and of my cooking classes.

ABOUT THE PHOTOGRAPHY

The photographs in these pages are the result of a dream collaboration with Jan Hendrik van der Westhuizen, better known as chef of the Michelin-starred Restaurant Jan in the Port of Nice. A man of many talents, Jan is a celebrity in his native South Africa, where he runs two restaurants and the Jan Innovation Studio, hosts a cooking show, and publishes a luxury magazine, as well as his own cookbooks. His background in design and photography shines through in every project he undertakes.

Since Jan lives in Nice, we were able to schedule photo shoots throughout the year so that the visuals would truly reflect the seasons. He relied solely on natural light, and as you flip through these pages, you will see how that flattered the ingredients, from a burst of spring sunshine on a strawberry tart to the shadows cast by fading light on a plate of mushrooms. For the photo shoot, I followed the recipes to the letter, and we used no trickery beyond a spritz of water or olive oil. Our aim was to show that you too can produce dishes this simple and beautiful if you take a little time to seek out ingredients that inspire you.

THE NIÇOISE PANTRY

Niçoise cuisine grew out of scarcity, with cooks making use of ingredients that were readily available and inexpensive. Olive oil is the main cooking fat, and dried or fresh herbs play a more important role than spices. Depth of flavor, or umami, comes from ingredients like pissala, the local salted fish paste; dried mushrooms; salty olives; and small amounts of aged cheese.

Chickpea flour

Finely ground chickpea flour plays a more important role in Niçoise cooking than whole chickpeas. The flour may be cooked like polenta before being fried, as for Panisses (see page 239), or combined with water, olive oil, and salt to make La Socca, the classic street food (page 268). I look for chickpea flour from the mountain town of Annot, in the Alpes de Haute Provence, or Italy, where it's a common ingredient from Liguria to Sicily. Indian gram flour may be substituted, though its texture is a little more coarse. For optimum freshness and to keep it away from insects (moths are very drawn to it), I store chickpea flour in the freezer.

Wheat flour

All-purpose flour, called "type 55" in France, will be all you need for the recipes in this cookbook; if you are able to find organic stone-ground flour, however, you will taste the difference. I often substitute Italian 00 flour in bread dough and pastry, since it produces a particularly light result; if you do the same, you might find you need to use a little less liquid (or more flour) than the recipe calls for.

Herbes de Provence

Herbes de Provence seem to be everywhere when you visit a market in the South of France, yet often the real thing is nowhere. The heaps of dried herbs that are sold by weight or in neatly tied burlap bags often have unidentified origins, with none of the intensity of the wild herbs that spring up on the mountainsides, where the sun concentrates their flavor before they are even picked. The term *herbes de Provence* is not protected with an Appellation d'Origine Protégée (AOP) like wines and many French foods ranging from Brie to Niçoise olives, so if you want to find wild herbs, you will need to be resourceful.

I have found high-quality herbes de

Provence in local organic shops and at the herbalist Nice Organic (see page 370). The classic mix consists of thyme, oregano, rosemary, marjoram, and savory (a wild cousin of thyme), though some mixes may also (controversially) include lavender. If you are lucky enough to find true herbes de Provence, a pinch will be enough to transport you to the *garrigue*, or scrub-covered mountainside. Otherwise, follow the lead of most Niçoise cooks and use a bouquet garni instead (see below).

Bouquet garni

In classic French cooking, the term *bouquet garni* refers to a small bundle of herbs that usually includes bay leaf, thyme, celery leaf, and parsley, all of which may be tucked inside a leek leaf and tied with string. At the markets in Nice, it's a bouquet-like bunch of wild thyme, rosemary, and bay leaf, sold fresh or partially dried, since these herbs grow under such arid conditions that they dry within a week of being picked. Rather than using commercial herbes de Provence (see above), most Niçoise cooks keep a big bouquet garni in the kitchen and pick off sprigs and leaves as needed. Thyme and bay leaf go into almost everything, while rosemary is reserved for specific dishes, since its flavor is more intense.

If you don't have access to fresh herbs of this quality, the best solution is to grow your own from plants purchased at your local garden center, as all of these herbs are hardy. Should you decide to dry the herbs, keep them out of the sunlight when you do so, or they will discolor and lose their flavor. Once dried, they will keep for a few weeks in the open, or they can be transferred to sealed jars or bags for longer storage.

Pissala

Translated as "salted fish," pissala is a potent paste that fishermen traditionally prepare in the spring by layering fresh anchovies in a barrel with coarse salt, herbs, and spices. Over a period of forty-five days, they stir the mixture daily until the fish break down and ferment. The pinkish-gray mixture is then strained to remove the bones and create a paste that brings depth to salad dressings (it's particularly good in a vinaigrette for artichokes) and provides a salty contrast in Pissaladière, the popular caramelized onion flatbread (page 191).

In Nice Old Town, you might find pissala at the fish market in place Saint-François in late spring; I have also bought it from the fisherman who sells his catch at the market in Villefranche-sur-Mer. Otherwise, the best substitute is to finely chop anchovies preserved in oil or salt; commercial anchovy paste can have a bitter flavor.

Anchovies

Anchovies preserved in salt or oil are a key ingredient in Salade Niçoise (page 63) and Pan Bagnat (page 133), and they also enter into sauces and dips like Anchoïade (page 122) and Bagna Cauda (page 275). Since salted anchovies are not always easy to find outside the Mediterranean and are more fussy to prepare— they require a brief soaking before being filleted—look for good-quality jarred anchovies in oil, which will be identifiable by their pink color. Once the jar is open, the anchovies will keep for months in the refrigerator as long as they remain covered in oil.

Tuna in oil

Since fresh tuna is a seasonal ingredient that was not easily available to those who lived in the hills, preserved tuna became a staple of Niçoise cooking, albeit one that was considered relatively luxurious (the original salade Niçoise and pan bagnat contained only anchovies). I look for tuna preserved in olive oil; for salade Niçoise, I prefer the long strips of fillets that come in jars. Mediterranean tuna stocks are under threat, so, like the older Niçoise cooks, I treat preserved tuna as a rare ingredient to be savored rather than as an everyday food.

Strained tomatoes

At the peak of summer, in late July, local farmers sell crates of extra-ripe tomatoes for making coulis (see page 337), or strained tomatoes. If you can't find suitable tomatoes or don't have time to make your own coulis, it's perfectly acceptable to buy strained tomatoes, sometimes known as *passata*; look for Italian brands that contain only tomatoes and a little sugar and salt.

Niçoise olives

True Niçoise olives are tricky to find even in Nice, since they are produced in such small quantities that supplies often run out before the next harvest. When in Nice, look for the Appellation d'Origine Protégée (AOP) label, which guarantees that these small, purply-black olives are of the Caillette variety and grown in the region around Nice. The same olive is known as Taggiasca in Liguria, and though the locals might disapprove of my saying this, Niçoise and Ligurian olives (as well as their oil) may be used interchangeably.

Olive oil

Niçoise olive oil is a rare golden-colored nectar that is made by pressing ripe Caillette olives immediately after harvest. Delicate and almost buttery, with notes of almond and artichoke, it's especially good with fish; in a simple Vinaigrette (page 349); and in desserts such as my Lemon Tart (page 307) and Chocolate Mousse (page 314).

Provence has many other unique oils to explore, and in Nice there are several shops—including one with its own restaurant (see Eggplant Caviar, page 123)—where you can taste the oils before you buy. Besides my precious Nice olive oil, I like to keep a supply of oil from Les Baux de Provence, which is made with a blend of olives from the region. *Fruité vert* olive oils from Provence, made with green olives, taste like spring, with a fresh, grassy quality, while *fruité noir*, the product of very ripe olives, has hints of cocoa and truffle that make it particularly sensational with chocolate. Because the French production is so small, I treat these oils like a good perfume—to be used at the right moment, and not too sparingly.

For cooking, I usually choose extra-virgin olive oils from southern Spain or

Greece, since these are readily available in supermarkets, relatively inexpensive, and flavorful without being too bitter or strong. It's a myth that extra-virgin olive oil can't be heated; it will lose some of its flavor properties when cooked, but will not burn below a temperature of 375°F (190°C). This makes it safe to use for pan-frying meat, fish, and vegetables at anything but the highest heat.

Sea salt

For slow-cooked dishes and salt crusts, I use coarse gray sea salt from Brittany, known as *sel gris de Guérande*, which is rich in natural minerals, most notably magnesium. The same salt is available finely ground, and I use that for seasoning meat and fish, as well as for baking. Fleur de sel is a salt that comes from Brittany or the Camargue, a coastal area between Marseille and Montpellier that is known for its pink flamingos and wild bulls. Its purity and the irregular shape of its crystals, which are harvested from the surface of the water with wooden rakes, make fleur de sel a perfect finishing salt.

Unless you have managed to stock up on these salts in France, where they are inexpensive, I recommend using Diamond Crystal-brand kosher salt as a substitute for coarse gray salt. Maldon sea salt flakes (which have a flakier texture) and Trapani Sicilian sea salt can stand in for fleur de sel. If you use iodized salt, keep in mind that it has a stronger flavor than natural sea salt. Rather than slavishly following the salt quantity given in a recipe, I suggest doing as the chefs at the

Cordon Bleu taught me and adding a pinch of salt every time new ingredients go into the pot. This is why many of my recipes do not specify an exact quantity of salt.

Black pepper

Niçoise cooks like to sprinkle preground pepper on socca (the chickpea pancake) fresh from the oven—perhaps because it creates more of a fine dusting—but I still have a preference for freshly ground black pepper, whether as a finishing touch or an ingredient. Spice vendors along rue Pairolière in Nice Old Town and at the Cours Saleya market sell many different types of black peppercorns; I choose the well-rounded Malabar peppercorns from India for everyday cooking, and Kampot pepper from Cambodia for its more complex fruity and floral flavor, but there are many other varieties to explore. Crushing high-quality peppercorns in a mortar or grinding the pepper at the last moment will allow you to best appreciate their unique aromas.

Pink peppercorns

Pink peppercorns are the fruits of the Peruvian pepper tree, also known as the California pepper tree, whose dangly branches are reminiscent of a weeping willow's. Although it is not especially common in the South of France, it thrives in this climate, and I have seen it growing around Saint-Jean-Cap-Ferrat and at Pierre Magnani's farm in the hills above Nice. Growing in bunches that dry naturally once picked, pink peppercorns taste fruity and zingy rather than peppery. In Nice, they are often used in an olive oil marinade for goat cheese, and may also be crushed to sprinkle on fish fillets or duck breasts (page 227).

Dried chile peppers

Although Niçoise cuisine is rarely hot and spicy, chile peppers do play a selective role. Small dried peppers called *pili pili* (the *Capsicum frutescens* variety common in Africa, the Caribbean, and South America) may enter into ratatouille (page 163), the spiced-up aïoli called rouille (page 348), and a herb-and-spice mixture that produces a surprisingly fiery pizza oil. To prevent these chiles from overpowering a dish, they may be used whole in a sauce or stew and then removed at the end. The Espelette chile, which grows in the French Basque region near Spain, is sold in powdered form and, with its mild yet complex flavor, works well in many dishes.

Fennel, anise, and pastis

Southern French cooks have a penchant for all things licorice-flavored, whether in the form of the alcohol pastis (made with star anise and other plants), dried wild fennel, fennel seeds, or green aniseed. These flavors may enhance duck (as in Duck Breasts with Honey and Aniseed, page 227), chicken (see Chicken with Pastis, page 224), or most frequently fish, which is often stuffed with twigs of dried wild fennel before being roasted. Pastis (sold under brand names such as Ricard and Pernod), a popular apéritif when diluted with water, is used in cooking as well, its strong licorice flavor mellowing with the heat. Green anise seeds also go into crunchy biscuits that are served with coffee, tea, or dessert wine.

Saffron

Dating back to before 5000 BC, saffron has long been cultivated in the Mediterranean, as well as North Africa, the Middle East, Persia, and India. During the nineteenth century, France was an important saffron-producing country, with farms mainly concentrated in the Gâtinais region south of Paris. These days, this orange-gold spice—prized for its medicinal properties in treating the bubonic plague—is enjoying a mini-revival in Provence, with a number of small farms dedicated to its labor-intensive production.

In southern French cooking, saffron goes into bouillabaisse or fish soup, as well as the accompanying sauce called rouille (page 348). Because of its price, restaurants often use paprika and/or turmeric as a substitute, but there is no replacing the real thing. To avoid counterfeits, it's best to buy whole saffron threads with a label guaranteeing their origin. Store saffron in a sealed container in a cool, dark place, where it will keep for two to three years.

When I refer to a pinch of saffron in recipes, I mean about 20 threads, but some saffron is more potent than others, so use your judgment once you have tasted your saffron in a dish.

Vanilla

Vanilla is the spice most loved by French pastry chefs, partly because of France's historic ties to Madagascar, which produces much of the world's vanilla supply. Today, with the price of vanilla soaring due to supply-and-demand issues, fresh beans have become a luxury. In recipes that call for vanilla, you can substitute vanilla bean paste or, if in France, vanilla powder made from whole ground vanilla beans, which is available in supermarkets and organic shops.

Cinnamon

One of the the oldest known spices, cinnamon was beloved of the Romans and, thanks to the European spice trade, became a prized ingredient during the Middle Ages. While most French children do not grow up eating cinnamon–I remember a group of Sam's primary school classmates turning up their noses at my homemade cinnamon rolls–it can be found in old Niçoise recipes like Pears Poached in Red Wine with Spices (page 251), roasted figs, rice pudding, and Sweet Swiss Chard Pie (page 317).

Wine and vermouth

The dry, fruity whites and pale rosés from Provence can be used interchangeably in cooking; I always advise students to cook with a wine they would also drink. When just a splash of wine is required, I often reach for a dry white vermouth, such as Noilly Prat, which has a complex flavor thanks to the herbs, spices, and orange peel that go into this fortified wine. I consider it a a secret weapon in my cooking, since it's an easy way to give a sauce or jus more depth. Once open, white vermouth, which is also a staple for cocktail making, keeps for months in the refrigerator. In recipes that call for red wine, you can use a wine from Provence, a Côtes du Rhône, or any fruity red wine that is not too tannic.

Rum

Produced in the Caribbean islands since Christopher Columbus brought the first sugar canes to Cuba in 1493, rum is the preferred alcohol in classic French pastries such as baba au rhum, but also enters into the humble Tourte de Blettes Sucrée (page 317), a pie filled with a sweet mixture of Swiss chard, raisins soaked in rum, and pine nuts. You can add a splash of rum to crêpes or to clafoutis, a seasonal fruit dessert (see page 105), if you like. In Nice, I buy my rum from the wine and spirits shops Caves Caprioglio and Apéritiv, which both have extensive selections. Dark rum is best for pastries and desserts; I seek out the best I can afford since it really does make a difference to the flavor.

Pine nuts

Somewhat confusingly, pine nuts are conspicuously absent from Pistou (page 343), the Niçoise take on pesto, but they appear in other dishes such as Sweet Swiss Chard Pie (page 317) and Swiss Chard Omelet (page 208). When buying pine nuts, the more elongated their shape, the better the quality; I look for those from Italy and store them in the refrigerator or freezer to prevent them from going rancid.

Garlic

When I was twelve, my mother tried to smuggle southern French garlic into Canada by sneaking it into my suitcase, unbeknownst to me. On arrival, the airport dogs immediately sniffed it out; this experience forever reminds me that the pink-and-purple-skinned garlic favored in these parts rarely goes undetected. A single clove adds an unmistakable kick to Aïoli (page 347) or Pistou (page 343), and even chopped up and sizzled, a little goes a long way. Only when it is slowly roasted, preferably steeped in fat, does this garlic turn sweet, mellow, and buttery enough to slather on bread (though I also love crunchy garlic-rubbed croutons in a green salad).

Ail de Provence has a deeper purple color than the southwestern French ail rose de Lautrec, whose pink-skinned cloves remain firm and plump throughout the winter. In spring, heads of fresh Provençal garlic as big as a fist appear at the market stands; juicy and with no bitter aftertaste, their pungent cloves are delicious shaved paper-thin into a salad or cooked with spring vegetables in a stew (use them for aïoli if you dare!). I save the long stems and soft layers of skin that envelop the cloves to add to my vegetable stock. Before using winter garlic, always cut the clove lengthwise in half and remove the green sprout, which can be bitter and indigestible.

Spring onions

Tender, round-bulbed spring onions, known as cébettes, are a common ingredient in Niçoise cooking; if these are not available, you can substitute scallions or half a sweet onion, such as Vidalia.

Parmesan or Sbrinz

Although southern French cooking does not rely on dairy products (see Où Est le Fromage?, page 130), no household would be without a hunk of Parmesan or Sbrinz, a cheese made from the milk of the Swiss brown cow and aged for at least 18 months. So popular was Sbrinz in northern Italy from the sixteenth century onward that a "Sbrinz Route" was created for mules to lug giant wheels of the cheese across the mountains. Once a cheaper alternative to Parmesan, Sbrinz is now produced by only twenty-six farms in Switzerland. It remains popular with Niçoise cooks, who swear by its rich and nutty flavor, with a hint of butterscotch.

Dried porcini mushrooms

Known as cèpes in French, porcini are among the few mushrooms that are just as good dried as fresh, bringing a deep, earthy, almost meaty flavor to dishes. I always keep some in my pantry to add to beef daube (page 295) or to make a quick risotto.

Honey

I have loved honey since I was a child, eating it by the spoonful or slathering it on my buttered toast, but only when I moved to Nice did I begin to see it as an essential ingredient for cooking and baking. I always have two or three types on hand—at least one mild honey, such as lavender or acacia, and a stronger one like chestnut or thyme. Mixed-flower honey is a good compromise, since it usually falls somewhere in between these two, with a complex flavor. I try to buy honey directly from the beekeeper, since supermarket honeys are often adulterated. A friend who grew up on a farm in the Var region, west of Cannes, swears that the secret to good health is eating a spoonful of honey a day, so I follow his lead and add it to my Greek yogurt and berries in the morning.

Lavender

Tourists come from all over the world to see the Provençal lavender fields in bloom each summer, and with good reason–it's impossible not to feel thrilled at the spectacle of neat stripes of purple interspersed with vivid yellow fields of sunflowers, as if painted with an Impressionist's brush. I had been never inspired to cook with lavender until I stood among the purple-tipped bushes and inhaled their dizzying scent as the bees thrummed with excitement around the blossoms.

In Provence, the dominant type of lavender is lavandin, a hybrid of true lavender (*Lavandula angustifolia*) and spike lavender (*Lavandula latifolia*) that is rich in essential oils. Lavandin has a sharp, herb-like quality, and it can just as easily be rubbed into lamb as sprinkled on Madeleines (page 323) or infused in cream for Crème Brûlée (page 172). With shorter stems and more compact flowers than lavandin, true lavender often grows wild and can be found in the mountains around Nice. It has a sweeter scent and flavor that makes it particularly suited to desserts.

Use lavender judiciously, remembering that as with other potent Provençal ingredients like rosemary and garlic, a little goes a long way. Make sure it is organic, since lavender produced for cosmetic purposes may be treated with chemicals. If lavender is not easy to come by where you live, consider growing a variety that thrives in your local climate; my parents grew lush lavender bushes in rainy England. Stored in an airtight container, the blossoms will keep their aroma and flavor for years.

Orange flower water

The mysterious perfume-like scent of orange flower water (also known as orange blossom water) transports me to North Africa and the Middle East, but it's also an essential ingredient in Niçoise breads and biscuits, flavoring the sweet flatbreads known as Fougassettes (page 358), an Easter bread known as échaudé, and navettes, crunchy biscuits that accompany tea or coffee.

Orange flower water distilled from the blossoms of the bitter orange tree tastes more subtle than the more commonly found artificially flavored variety (not my first choice), so adjust the quantity if necessary depending on which type you are using. Another way to use orange flower water is as a topping for fresh cheese curds, known here as brousse, along with a sprinkling of sugar. A Lebanese friend also taught me to make the digestive drink "white coffee" by diluting a teaspoon of orange flower water in a cup of boiling water.

Butter

Once a rarely used ingredient in Niçoise cooking, butter now plays a supporting role, mainly in piecrusts and desserts (I have also seen mamies throw a chunk of butter into caramelized onions at the end of cooking). For baking and cooking, I usually choose unsalted beurre moulé de Bretagne, which is cultured (meaning the cream has been fermented) and churned rather than produced in a centrifuge. I buy the same butter with salt crystals added for making specific recipes such as salted butter caramel or shortbread, and for slathering on baguettes. Outside France, look for unsalted, preferably cultured, butter with 82 percent butterfat.

Eggs

For testing the recipes in this book, I used large free-range eggs, organic when possible. Since Niçoise cooking is rustic, though, small differences in size usually won't matter. When friends give me eggs from their own chickens, a rare treat, I save these for soft-boiling or poaching.

Cream

When cream is called for, it should be at least 30 percent fat (i.e., heavy cream or whipping cream). In France, this is sold under the name *crème entière liquide* if it is ultrapasteurized for longer storage, or *crème fleurette* if it is simply pasteurized. A few of these recipes call for crème fraîche, which is slightly fermented and has a tangy flavor, but if it is not available, you can substitute heavy cream.

SPRING

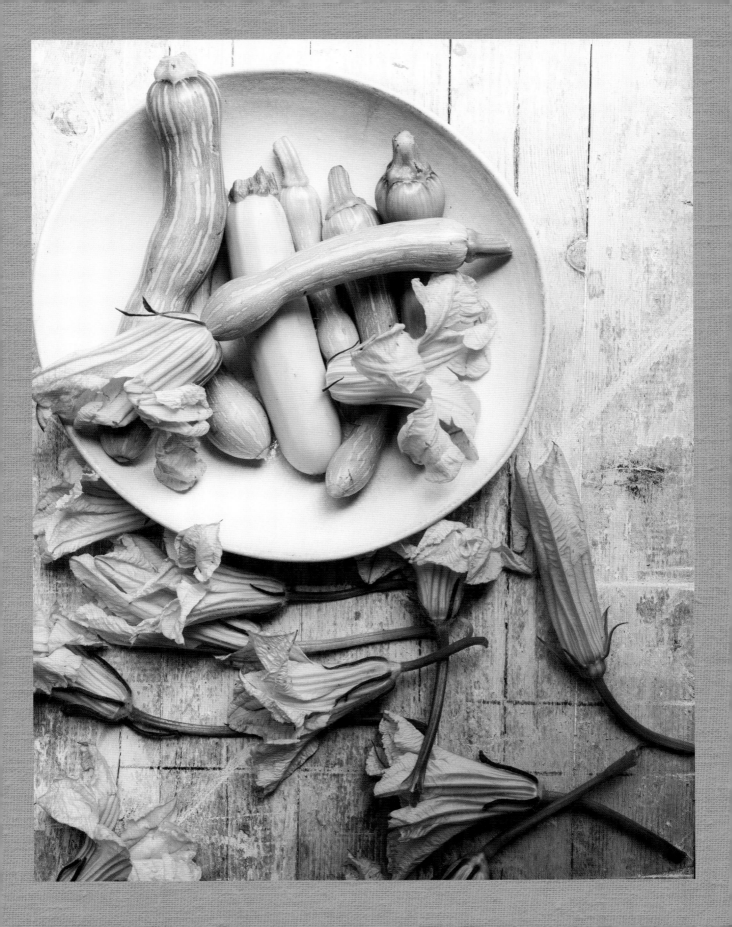

Although I wouldn't go so far as to name a favorite season in Nice, I find spring particularly inspiring. It seems there is no wrong way to treat spring vegetables, whether it's serving them raw with a simple dip like anchoïade or aïoli; gently stewing them in olive oil, with or without meat; or roasting them. I love the way sweet spring vegetables like peas, fava beans, fennel, and broccolini cut through starchy ingredients; this is my favorite time of year to make gnocchi and risotto.

Spring can be an unpredictable season weatherwise here, with sudden torrential rains that send nature into overdrive: flowers are everywhere, from cascading purple wisteria to roses in gentle shades of pink and yellow, and overabundant lemons, oranges, and kumquats pop out among their glossy, deep-green leaves. Possibly my favorite spring blossoms are those of the jasmine bushes that serve as hedges along my street; I often stop my bicycle to inhale the tiny white flowers' heady aroma, which transports me to a long-ago vacation in southern India.

Easter weekend brings the first influx of visitors to Nice, and by the end of May, the spring tourist season reaches a peak, with the Cannes Film Festival and the Monaco Grand Prix driving up the price of hotels and rental properties. Aside from this brief period, spring is an ideal time to discover the French Riviera before the sweltering heat of summer sets in and the beaches fill with sunbathers gingerly stretching out on the pebbles. Locals show up at the end of the day to share a bottle of rosé and snacks with friends; Niçoise cuisine is perfectly suited to this kind of casual eating.

I take advantage of breezy spring days to spend time in the kitchen, preparing dishes that are as pure a celebration of the products as possible. I make generous use of fresh herbs like mint, parsley, and tarragon; this is not a time for heavy spicing or slow cooking. Many of the dishes in this chapter come together quickly, while the desserts preserve the qualities of delicate fruits that have been selected with great care.

Pierre Magnani (see page 340) inspecting his fava bean crop at Le Potager de Saquier.

ARTICHAUTS À LA BARIGOULE

Artichokes stewed in wine

It's unclear exactly what the word *barigoule* refers to in this recipe—some say it evoked a now-rare type of mushroom that was once used to stuff the artichokes, while others claim that it comes from the term *farigoule*, another word for thyme. Even if its meaning has been lost, I like the sound of the word as much as this popular method for cooking small artichokes. If these are unavailable, you can substitute larger artichokes, trimming them down to the hearts, or even frozen artichoke hearts.

Artichauts à la barigoule can be served warm or at room temperature as a starter, or as an accompaniment to meat or fish (though I think it deserves to stand alone). At the restaurant Bistrot d'Antoine in Nice, I have eaten a delicious variation with diced smoked sausage replacing the bacon. Since I often have a bottle of rosé open, I use it interchangeably with white wine in this recipe. For a vegetarian version, you can leave out the bacon and add another smoky ingredient, such as a pinch of smoked salt or smoked paprika (be cautious, or it will dominate the flavor). Don't be tempted to reduce the amount of olive oil called for, since artichokes benefit from cooking with plenty of fat; they should be what the French call *confit*, or completely soft. Because artichokes lose their vivid color when cooked, I like to add a topping of arugula to both brighten the plate and add a peppery flavor contrast.

SERVES 4

Juice of 1 lemon

7 small artichokes, ideally weighing no more than 4 ounces/110 g each, or 7 artichoke hearts (fresh or frozen)

¼ cup (60 ml) extra-virgin olive oil

1 medium onion, diced

1 medium carrot, cut into ¼-inch (0.5 cm) dice

½ cup (100 g) thick-cut smoked bacon or pancetta cut into ¼-inch (0.5 cm) dice

½ cup (120 ml) dry white or rosé wine or dry white vermouth

1 sprig fresh or dried thyme

1 bay leaf

Sea salt and freshly ground black pepper

FOR THE ARUGULA SALAD

2 teaspoons sherry or red wine vinegar

2 tablespoons extra-virgin olive oil

3 cups (60 g) arugula leaves

Fleur de sel

Fresh Parmesan shavings for serving

1 Place the lemon juice in a large bowl and half-fill it with water.

2 If using small artichokes, trim them as described on page 55, cut lengthwise in half, and keep them in the lemon water. If using artichoke hearts, cut them in half and place in the lemon water.

3 Heat 2 tablespoons of the olive oil in a sauté pan or Dutch oven over medium heat. Add the onion, carrot, and bacon and cook, stirring, until the onion begins to turn golden and the bacon starts to brown, about 10 minutes.

4 Lift the artichokes (or artichoke hearts) out of the lemon water with your hands and add them to the pan; reserve the lemon water. Stir gently, then add the white wine or vermouth and let it boil and reduce for 1 minute.

5 Add 1 cup (240 ml) of the reserved lemon water, the thyme, bay leaf, a big pinch of sea salt, and the remaining 2 tablespoons olive oil to the pan. Bring to a boil, then cover and let the artichokes simmer gently over low heat for about 45 minutes, without stirring, which could break them up. At the end of the cooking time, they should be completely soft.

6 Lift the artichokes, vegetables, and bacon out of the liquid with a slotted spoon and place in a serving dish. Turn up the heat and let the liquid reduce until it is slightly syrupy, 5 to 10 minutes. Season to taste with salt and pepper. Pour the liquid over the artichokes.

7 Meanwhile, make the dressing by whisking together the sherry vinegar and olive oil. Toss the arugula with the dressing in a salad bowl and season with fleur de sel.

8 Serve the artichokes warm in shallow bowls, topped with the arugula. Finish each bowl with a few shavings of fresh Parmesan.

Edible thistles

I once watched in fascination at a Paris bistro as a girl no older than six deconstructed a giant artichoke with studied precision. I was twenty at the time and thought of artichokes as sophisticated fare. In France, I discovered that they were commonplace and accessible to everyone, even if I continue to be bowled over by their beauty today.

An unlikely vegetable—part of the thistle family, it has been domesticated for culinary use since antiquity—this relative of the sunflower, when left to its own devices, produces a vivid violet blossom consisting of hundreds of tiny flowers. The artichokes we eat are buds, which may be big or small, depending on the variety.

At least five different cultivars thrived in Louis XIV's vegetable garden at Versailles, and today the most popular French artichoke is the Camus de Bretagne, developed in 1810. Growing as big as a pomelo, it has tightly packed green leaves that give way when steamed or boiled, allowing patient gourmands access to its velvety heart once they have dipped each leaf in some form of fat (usually a vinaigrette, melted butter, or mayonnaise) and scraped off the fleshy base with their teeth. I wonder if the artichoke's reputed aphrodisiac properties—Catherine de Medici scandalized and fascinated French society with the amount she consumed—were as much about how it is eaten as any natural stimulants it might contain.

A smaller and slimmer artichoke with stunning purple-streaked leaves dominates the market stalls in Nice, reaching its peak in spring, although it also appears in the fall. It goes by the name *violet* because of its color; *bouquet*, as it is sold in bunches, like flowers; or *poivrade*, which originally referred to the tiny artichokes that sprout on the stems of larger ones. When picked at its prime, this dwarf variety is so tender and delicate that it is often served raw, either sliced thin and marinated with olive oil and lemon or as part of a Salade Niçoise (see page 63) or Pan Bagnat (page 133). A similarly small artichoke with a fierce spike at the end of each leaf grows across the border in Liguria—most famously around the town of Albenga—and occasionally finds its way to our markets, where it is prized for its almost buttery flesh, as long as you can get past its thorns unscathed.

In Venice and Sicily, two of the great artichoke-growing areas of Italy, I have seen market vendors selling small artichokes pretrimmed and soaking in lemon water to prevent discoloration, with a mountain of discarded leaves next to them. Here in France, this convenience has not caught on and we must do the work ourselves. The most skilled cooks "turn" artichokes with a knife, removing all but the tender parts in a few deft strokes, but since this creates more waste than is strictly necessary, I use a slower (and easier) method; see below.

We often cook artichauts à la barigoule—the classic southern French dish of small artichokes stewed in white wine (page 50)—in my classes as a way of introducing students to the small violet artichoke. Preparing them gets easier—and definitely faster—with practice, but it requires no special skill other than a bit of patience. →

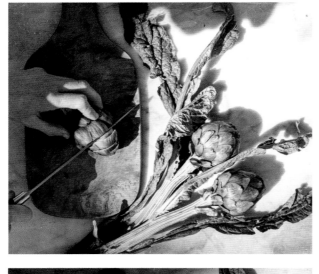

Tackling the small artichoke

1 Fill a large bowl with water and add the juice of a lemon (a few parsley sprigs or a splash of vinegar also works) to prevent the trimmed artichokes from oxidizing. Work with one artichoke at a time, dropping the trimmed pieces into the water as you go to prevent discoloration.

2 Cut off longer stems, leaving about 1 inch (2.5 cm) of stem attached to the artichoke.

3 Then cut about 1½ inches (4 cm) off the top of the artichoke and discard the trimmings. Dip the cut part in the lemon water before continuing.

4 Break off the tough outer leaves, starting near the stem and working your way up. I discard at least three layers, until the remaining leaves are pale yellow-green tinged with pink rather than dark green or purple.

5 Next, trim the stem using a small knife or a vegetable peeler, as the outer layer tastes bitter. Cut the artichoke lengthwise in half, and scoop out any choke (silky hairs) with a small sharp spoon, along with the pointy-tipped pale-pink inner leaves. (The youngest artichokes have no choke—these are perfect for slicing thin and eating raw.) Drop the trimmed artichoke into the lemon water.

6 After preparing artichokes, be sure to wash your hands and the cutting board well, as they leave a bitter, brownish residue. You can also rub your hands with the inside of the squeezed lemon to remove stains.

SOUPE DE FANES DE RADIS, RICOTTA, ET CIBOULETTE

Radish-top soup with ricotta and chives

Who decided we should keep only the pretty pink roots of radishes and throw away the peppery leaves? Certainly not the Niçois, who long ago learned to use every edible part of any vegetable. For this recipe, the radish leaves should be very fresh, not wilted or yellow; you can substitute young spinach or even nettle leaves, if you are lucky enough to find them.

SERVES 4

2 tablespoons extra-virgin olive oil

2 small or 1 medium leek, white and pale green parts only, sliced ½ inch (0.5 cm) thick (about 2 cups/180 g sliced)

1 sprig thyme

1 garlic clove, smashed with the flat side of a knife and peeled

1 medium potato (6 to 8 ounces/180 to 225 g), peeled and cut into ½-inch (1 cm) dice

2 cups (480 ml) vegetable stock, homemade (page 355) or store-bought

4 cups (80 g) loosely packed roughly chopped radish leaves, carefully washed

¼ cup (60 ml) Greek yogurt or sour cream, or a squeeze of lemon juice, to taste

Sea salt and freshly ground black pepper

FOR THE GARNISHES

4 radishes

A few fresh peas in their pods, if available

½ cup (120 ml) sheep's- or cow's-milk ricotta

1 tablespoon minced chives

1 tablespoon grated lemon zest (preferably from an organic lemon)

Sea salt and freshly ground black pepper

1 In a medium saucepan, heat the oil over medium heat. Add the leeks, thyme, garlic, and a pinch of sea salt and cook over low heat, stirring frequently, for 7 to 8 minutes, until the leeks are softened but not browned.

2 Add the diced potato and stir for 1 minute, then add the stock. Bring to a boil over medium heat, then lower the heat to a simmer and cook, partially covered, for 15 minutes, until the potato has completely softened. Add the radish leaves and cook for another 5 minutes at a simmer.

3 Meanwhile, for the garnishes, slice the radishes as thin as possible, using a mandoline if you have one. Shell the peas, if using. Mash together the ricotta, chives, half the lemon zest, and salt and pepper to taste in a small bowl. Adjust the flavorings to taste.

4 Remove the thyme sprig from the soup. Using an immersion or stand blender, blend the soup with the yogurt or sour cream, or lemon juice, until completely pureed, seasoning it with salt and pepper to taste. You can serve the soup immediately or chill it for at least 2 hours and serve it cold.

5 Place a heaped tablespoon of the ricotta mixture, a few radish slices, and a few raw peas, if using, in each bowl. Pour the soup around the garnishes, sprinkle with the remaining lemon zest, and serve.

Cook's notes

To wash leeks, first remove any tough outer leaves. Cut each leek lengthwise almost all the way through, leaving it attached at the root end. Open up the leeks and rinse them well under cold water, being sure to clean between the layers of outer leaves, where sand often collects. If you are not sure that the leeks are completely free of sand, you can wash them a second time after slicing them. Swish them around in a large bowl of cold water, lifting them out with your hands into a colander so that any sand stays at the bottom of the bowl.

When using an immersion blender, I find it safer (for myself and for the base of the saucepan!) to transfer the soup to a tall jug before blending. Use a ladle to do this rather than pouring the hot soup into the jug, so as not burn yourself if the soup splashes.

Does your soup taste bland? Add more salt! It's miraculous how the right amount of salt transforms any soup, bringing out all the flavors. You can also add an acidic ingredient like lemon juice, wine or cider vinegar, sour cream, or yogurt, as in this soup (keep in mind, though, that after a few minutes, these will dull the vivid color of green soups).

Whenever I am using citrus zest in a recipe, I look for organic fruit, since citrus is often sprayed with pesticides and fungicides, and may also be coated in shellac to lengthen its shelf life. Local citrus sold at the Nice markets may look less uniform and shiny than commercial fruits, but they have the advantage of being free of chemicals.

RAGOÛT DE LÉGUMES DU PRINTEMPS

Spring vegetable stew

This is my favorite way to cook spring vegetables—with as little liquid as possible, so that they retain all their color, flavor, and nutrients. Choose the smallest, sweetest vegetables you can find, using the recipe as a guideline rather than a formula: I might add small turnips, trimmed baby artichokes, young fennel, or broccolini. You can serve it with roast chicken or fish, but I love this stew on its own as a starter or light lunch.

SERVES 4

2 tablespoons extra-virgin olive oil

3 spring onions, white and pale green parts only, cut into ¼-inch (0.5 cm) rounds

Sea salt

8 skinny carrots, cut diagonally into 2-inch (5 cm) lengths (no need to peel them if they are young)

8 fingerling potatoes, cut lengthwise in half (no need to peel)

3 sprigs thyme

1 garlic clove, smashed with the flat side of a knife and peeled

Up to 1 cup (240 ml) vegetable stock, homemade (page 355) or store-bought, or water

8 asparagus spears about ½ inch (1 cm) thick, tough ends removed and discarded, cut diagonally into 2-inch (5 cm) lengths

1¼ cups shelled fresh peas (1 pound/450 g in the shell; you can also use frozen peas, or leave them out)

Freshly ground black pepper

FOR SERVING

Good-quality extra-virgin olive oil

Fleur de sel

Arugula leaves

Parmesan shavings

1 Heat the olive oil in a sauté pan or Dutch oven over medium heat. Add the spring onions and a pinch of salt and cook, stirring, until the onions soften, 2 to 3 minutes.

2 Add the carrots, potatoes, thyme, garlic, and ½ cup (120 ml) of the vegetable stock or water, cover, and cook over medium-low heat for about 10 minutes, until the vegetables start to soften.

3 Add the asparagus and another pinch of salt, then add more vegetable stock or water if needed to cover the bottom of the pan. Cover and cook for 3 to 5 minutes, until all the vegetables are almost tender.

4 Add the peas and cook for 2 to 3 minutes if fresh, 5 to 6 minutes if frozen, until just cooked. Season with pepper.

5 Serve the vegetables warm with a drizzle of olive oil and a sprinkling of fleur de sel. Top with arugula leaves and Parmesan shavings.

The skinny on asparagus

During peak asparagus season, the fattest spears fetch the highest price at French markets. This often surprises my students, who assume that skinny spears must be the most tender and flavorful.

Like artichokes, asparagus are one of those miraculous vegetables that pop spontaneously out of the ground every spring. Once planted in carefully prepared soil, all they require is patience: it takes two to three years for asparagus to produce a crop. Thérèse, the unofficial asparagus queen at the Cours Saleya market, explained to me that the fatter spears develop a deeper flavor, because they are more mature. Far from being woody, they are tender enough to shave raw into a salad, once you have broken off the hard ends.

Prized by the Greeks and Romans, asparagus came relatively late to the South of France: another favorite of Louis XV, they were cultivated in the Loire Valley before making their way to Provence in the nineteenth century. Though the local conditions don't lend themselves to growing uniform asparagus, the small quantity produced by Albert Luciano at his farm outside Nice is snapped up within minutes at the market–even if the spears are mismatched and curved, their grassy, nutty flavor is impossible to beat.

I confess a preference for green asparagus, whose chlorophyll-rich spears make a better match for olive oil and Mediterranean flavors, though I do have a soft spot for the violet-tipped white spears, which have only partially been exposed to sunlight. Asparagus that are completely ivory colored have been sheltered from the sun, like a nineteenth-century aristocrat; those from the Landes near the French Atlantic coast grow horizontally in sandy soil, searching fruitlessly for the light. Dramatic deep purple asparagus occasionally makes an appearance at the markets; this is a different variety, more fruity-tasting than its green cousin.

Not to be overlooked, although hard to spot, is the wild asparagus that shoots up in early spring next to scrubby plants like thyme and rosemary or bordering pine forests. Deep green and as skinny as a rose stem, the spears make a perfect match for eggs in an omelet or quiche, but I love to serve them on their own with the delicate local olive oil, to best appreciate their herbal quality and slight bitterness. They are an increasingly rare sight at the Cours Saleya market and I snap them up whenever I see them, knowing it might be my last chance until next year.

Whatever the variety, my favorite way to cook asparagus is in a covered sauté pan with olive oil, salt, a sprig of thyme, and very little water, so that it keeps all of its color and nutrients. White asparagus needs thorough peeling, while green asparagus is ready to cook once you have snapped off the tough ends. Rather than throwing away these ends, save them to make a stock for risotto or a pureed soup; this seasonal luxury is too precious to waste.

The mimosa trail

In February, mimosa trees burst into bloom on the Côte d'Azur, especially in the Var region, west of Cannes, signaling that spring is nearly here. Native to Australia, mimosa first made its way to England in the eighteenth century thanks to botanists who accompanied the explorer James Cook (known as Capitaine Cook in France), before being planted near Cannes in the mid-nineteenth century. The conditions there proved ideal for the mimosa species known as *Acacia dealbata*, which originated in Tasmania, and the plant quickly spread in the wild, becoming particularly dominant in the Esterel Mountains.

Each year, thousands of mimosa pilgrims make their way to the mountains by car, motorcycle, or bicycle—or on foot along the hiking paths—to take in the spectacle of the vivid yellow blossoms, which look like tiny pompoms. Even if this species is not universally loved (especially by those who are sensitive to its pollen), for me it's simply impossible to dislike something that looks so resolutely cheerful, especially when it comes with such a sweet scent.

Though it's not common to find mimosa in culinary preparations, the blossoms are edible. Cycling the mimosa trail to the village of Tanneron, I came across a stand selling crumbly shortbread biscuits with a dab of butter-yellow jelly in the center, its flavor recalling honey and the delicate taste of linden blossoms. The flowers can be infused in oil (to drizzle on fish, for instance) or sugar syrup (wonderful in a Champagne cocktail), or crystallized with egg white and sugar to decorate a cake. Before using mimosa in the kitchen, make sure that it has not been sprayed with chemicals, and prepare yourself for the meticulous task of picking the tiny blossoms off the stems—the effort is well worth it.

ASPERGES MIMOSA

Asparagus with yogurt dressing and egg

For the French, asparagus mimosa has kitsch connotations reminiscent of the 1970s–much like shrimp cocktail in America. But for me, this dish should never go out of fashion; it is one of those slightly unlikely combinations that is meant to be. The name comes from the sprinkling of grated or sieved hard-boiled egg, whose yolk recalls the bright yellow mimosas that bloom all along the French Riviera in early spring. The dressing may be a vinaigrette or a creamier sauce, like this one made with Greek yogurt and sherry vinegar. When it's not asparagus season, you can serve the same sauce and mimosa topping with steamed or braised small leeks.

SERVES 4

2 large free-range eggs, at room temperature

12 thick (½ inch/1 cm or larger) asparagus spears or 24 skinny ones, tough ends broken off

Sea salt

1 tablespoon extra-virgin olive oil

FOR THE SAUCE

2 tablespoons sherry vinegar or freshly squeezed lemon juice

1 tablespoon finely minced shallot

½ cup (120 ml) Greek yogurt

½ teaspoon Dijon mustard

3 tablespoons very thinly sliced herbs–any combination of flat-leaf parsley, chives, chervil, dill, and/or mint

Sea salt and freshly ground black pepper

Paprika or Espelette chile powder for sprinkling

1 Bring a small pot of water to a boil (there should be enough water to cover the eggs). Lower the eggs into the boiling water with a spoon and set a timer for 10 minutes. When the eggs are done, drain and place in a bowl of ice water to cool, then remove the shells.

2 In a sauté pan or a frying pan with a lid (you can use a circle of parchment paper in a pinch; see Cook's Note), heat the olive oil over medium heat. Add the asparagus and a pinch of salt, cover, and cook for about 3 minutes for thin asparagus, 5 to 7 minutes for thick asparagus, until tender when pierced with a knife but still bright green. (I like to squeeze the stem end of a spear with my fingers; it should give a little.) Transfer to a serving platter or individual plates.

3 In a bowl, whisk together the vinegar or lemon juice, shallot, yogurt, and mustard. Add 2 tablespoons of the herbs and stir. Season with salt and pepper to taste.

4 Grate the boiled eggs using a coarse grater (the trick is not to press them too hard against the grater).

5 Divide the sauce among four plates, or spoon it onto a serving platter, then arrange the asparagus spears on top. Sprinkle with the grated egg and the remaining 1 tablespoon herbs, finish with a hint of paprika or Espelette chile powder, and serve immediately. →

Cook's note

Using a circle of parchment paper instead of a lid is one of the most useful tricks I learned at the Cordon Bleu. This is called a *cartouche* in French and a "drop lid" in Japan, since the parchment paper rests directly on the surface of the pan's contents, keeping heat and steam in while still allowing for some evaporation. It's also particularly useful when you have several pans on the stove and want to keep an eye on each one. A cartouche is easy to remove and will not burn your fingers or drip water like a lid. As the chefs at the Cordon Bleu used to say, "It's cheaper than a lid."

To make a cartouche, fold a square of parchment paper diagonally in half to make a triangle. Fold it once more to make a smaller triangle. Then fold it two or three more times over itself so that it looks like a paper airplane, with a pointed tip. Bring it to your pot, hold the tip over the center, and cut off the excess paper just inside the edge of the pot. Unfold, and voilà! You will have a circle the size of your pot.

LA SALADE NIÇOISE

Niçoise salad

How did a thrown-together salad of tomatoes, crunchy raw vegetables, and preserved anchovies morph into a plate of potatoes and green beans topped with tuna? It seems that Auguste Escoffier, the chef credited with modernizing haute cuisine in the late nineteenth century, is to blame. Escoffier grew up in Villeneuve-Loubet–barely an hour from Nice, but far enough that he must have felt he could take liberties with the local traditions without suffering the wrath of the mamies. His career, which began at age twelve in the kitchen of his uncle's restaurant in Nice, eventually took him to Monaco's Grand Hotel and the Savoy in London, where he created many of his most famous dishes, including Pêche Melba (page 174).

Escoffier's version of salade Niçoise left out the fava beans, raw artichokes, and radishes that often made their way into the original, replacing them with easier-to-find potatoes and green beans. His admittedly well-conceived salad then took on a life of its own, supplanting the original everywhere except Nice, where local cooks remain horrified at the idea of letting a cooked vegetable anywhere near the dish. This is understandable considering that along with its sandwich variation, Pan Bagnat (page 133), salade Niçoise is one of the rare raw vegetable dishes in the local cuisine.

Long before Escoffier came along, salade Niçoise began as a simple salad of ripe tomatoes salted with preserved anchovy fillets and doused in local olive oil. As agriculture began to diversify during the nineteenth century, the salad grew more colorful and crunchier. The addition of boiled eggs and tuna–preserved in oil rather than fresh, since much of the population did not have easy access to the sea–turned it into a light meal in itself. Like many Niçoise dishes, it serves to stretch a small amount of protein.

The salad might have remained an obscure regional dish had tourism not flourished in the late nineteenth and early twentieth centuries, bringing English and Russian aristocrats and, later, the French, who were taking advantage of their first paid holidays. Charmed by the colorful dish, these visitors dubbed it salade Niçoise, a name that had never occurred to the farmers and fishermen who first assembled it using what they had on hand.

The best time to make salade Niçoise is in late spring, when the first ripe (but still slightly firm) tomatoes coincide with fava beans, small artichokes, and pert pink-and-white radishes that are not yet too peppery. Spring onions, long green peppers, and celery are standard ingredients, while the addition of cucumber remains controversial. Salad greens should be barely present, if at all; I like to add a few inner leaves of Little Gem lettuce.

My one concession here to modern times is to occasionally sear fresh Mediterranean tuna for an updated version. Since one of my favorite restaurants in Nice, Bistrot d'Antoine, does the same, I feel that this does not endanger my status as an honorary citizen of Nice.

SERVES 6

FOR THE SALAD

3 large free-range eggs, at room temperature

6 medium vine-ripened tomatoes, preferably an heirloom variety, cores removed

Fine sea salt

8 ounces (215 g) good-quality tuna in olive oil or 6 small chunks fresh tuna, about 1 inch (2.5 cm) thick and 3 ounces (80 g) each

Herbes de Provence, if using fresh tuna

Extra-virgin olive oil

3 spring onions, white and pale green parts only, thinly sliced

2 Anaheim or banana peppers, or 1 yellow pepper, cored, seeded, and thinly sliced

12 radishes, thinly sliced

1 celery stalk, strings removed, thinly sliced

3 small artichokes, trimmed as described on page 55, thinly sliced, and held in lemon water (optional)

½ cup (120 g) shelled fava beans (optional; see Cook's Note on page 66)

12 anchovy fillets

1 head Little Gem lettuce (optional)

Leaves from 2 sprigs basil for garnish

18 Niçoise olives

FOR THE DRESSING

2 tablespoons freshly squeezed lemon juice or red wine vinegar

Fine sea salt and freshly ground black pepper

½ cup (120 ml) mild-tasting extra-virgin olive oil

1 Bring a medium pot of water to a boil. Lower the eggs into the water using a spoon and set a timer for 8 minutes if you like your yolks slightly soft in the center (as I do), or 10 minutes for hard-boiled eggs. When the eggs are done, drain and transfer to ice water to cool, then peel and cut lengthwise into quarters.

2 Cut each tomato into 6 wedges, place on a plate lined with paper towels, and sprinkle with fine sea salt to draw out the excess juice and intensify the flavor. Set aside for at least 15 minutes.

3 Meanwhile, if using fresh tuna, season it on both sides with fine sea salt and a light sprinkling of herbes de Provence and set aside for at least 15 minutes. During this time, the salt will draw moisture to the surface of the fish, which will then be reabsorbed, so that the fish is evenly seasoned.

4 Pat the tuna dry. Heat a little olive oil in a frying pan over high heat, add the tuna, and sear for 1 to 2 minutes on each side, until golden brown. Transfer to a plate.

5 For the dressing, in a small bowl, whisk the lemon juice or wine vinegar with a large pinch of salt and a few grindings of pepper until the salt has dissolved. Whisk in the olive oil.

6 Assemble the salad on a large platter (or in individual shallow bowls): Arrange the tomatoes on the platter, and then 3 or 4 inner leaves of Little Gem lettuce, if using. Top with the other vegetables and sprinkle with fine sea salt and pepper. Arrange the hard-boiled egg quarters on top and drape the anchovy fillets over the egg wedges. Place the chunks of seared or preserved tuna on top and garnish with the basil leaves and olives. Drizzle with the dressing and serve. →

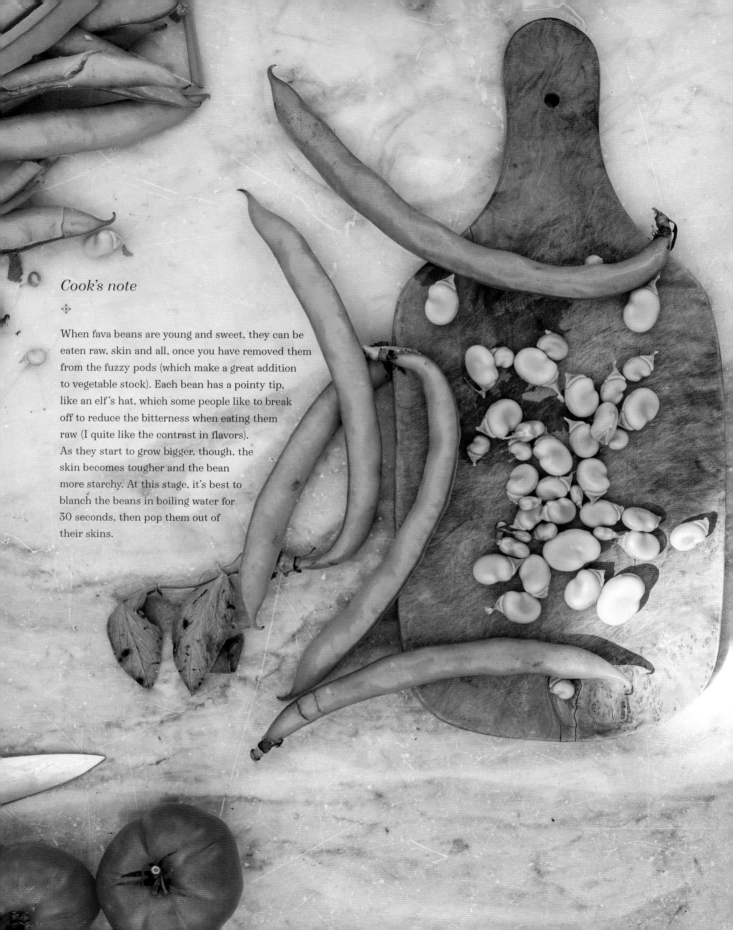

Cook's note

✽

When fava beans are young and sweet, they can be
eaten raw, skin and all, once you have removed them
from the fuzzy pods (which make a great addition
to vegetable stock). Each bean has a pointy tip,
like an elf's hat, which some people like to break
off to reduce the bitterness when eating them
raw (I quite like the contrast in flavors).
As they start to grow bigger, though, the
skin becomes tougher and the bean
more starchy. At this stage, it's best to
blanch the beans in boiling water for
30 seconds, then pop them out of
their skins.

MERDA DE CAN, SAUCE TOMATE ÉPICÉE

Green gnocchi with spicy tomato sauce

The Niçois are so famous for their love of Swiss chard that at one point in their history they became known as *caga blea*, or "chard poopers," in the local language. Just as irreverent is the name of these gnocchi, whose traditional pointy-ended shape apparently evoked *merda de can*, or "dog turd." The name has not stopped the Niçois from loving this variation, which is more richly flavored and colored than the original.

The trick to making cloud-like gnocchi is to add just enough flour to create a soft but not-too-sticky dough, so start with the minimum amount listed below, then add a little more as needed (there should be at least one quarter of the weight of the potatoes in flour, or the gnocchi may fall apart in the water). The choice of potato also matters: this is the time to embrace those that look old, knobbly and even a bit wrinkled, since their moisture content will be lower. I love gnocchi made with yellow-fleshed potatoes like Yukon Gold, but you can also use Russets.

If you want to make extra gnocchi to eat another time, you can freeze them on baking sheets (make sure they are not touching each other), then store them in a freezer bag—they can go straight into boiling water without defrosting.

SERVES 4

2 large baking potatoes, such as Russet, or large Yukon Gold potatoes (about 1 pound 2 ounces/ 500 g), scrubbed

Coarse sea salt

1 bay leaf

4 cups (about 4 ounces/110 g) Swiss chard leaves, stems removed, or the same amount of nettle leaves

1 large egg yolk

1 teaspoon fine sea salt

1¼ to 1½ cups (150 to 180 g) all-purpose flour, plus more for sprinkling and rolling

Extra-virgin olive oil for serving

Quick Tomato Sauce (page 339), made with chile flakes

½ cup (40 g) grated aged pecorino or Parmesan for serving

To make the gnocchi

1 Place the potatoes in a large saucepan and cover with water. Add a large pinch of coarse sea salt and the bay leaf, cover, bring to a boil, and cook at a slow but steady boil for 40 to 45 minutes, until the potatoes show no resistance when pierced with a knife. Drain in a colander and let cool for 5 to 10 minutes (no longer).

2 Meanwhile, bring a medium pot of water to a boil and salt it generously. Add the chard or nettle leaves (handle raw nettle with rubber gloves to avoid its sting) and blanch for 3 minutes. Drain in a colander, rinse under cold water, and, using your hands, squeeze out as much water as you can so that the leaves are very dry. Finely chop by hand or in a food processor; set aside. →

3   Using a small knife, peel the potatoes while they are still hot. Cut into large pieces, place on a wooden board or large platter, and mash with a potato masher. Or, if you have a food mill or ricer, pass the potatoes through it onto the platter or board. Let the potatoes cool for a few minutes, until they are no longer giving off steam (you can fan them to speed up this process).

4   Line two baking sheets with clean dish towels and lightly sprinkle with flour.

5   Make a well in the center of the potatoes, add the egg yolk, chopped chard or nettles, and fine salt, and mix into the potatoes using a pastry scraper or fork. Do not be tempted to do this in a food processor or with a mixer, or the potatoes will be transformed into glue.

6   Add 1¼ cups (150 g) of the flour to the potatoes about a third at a time, gently incorporating it with your hands, until you have obtained a dough that is soft but barely sticky, similar to pizza dough. Add up to ¼ cup (30 g) more flour if necessary; the amount you need will very much depend on your potatoes. Knead gently for up to 30 seconds, until the dough appears smooth and turns a nice green color; do not overwork the dough, which could make it elastic.

7   Divide the dough into 8 pieces. Sprinkle a work surface with flour. Roll one piece of dough into a rope about ½ inch (1 cm) thick, adding more flour to the work surface as needed. Cut the dough into pieces about ½ inch (1 cm) long, using a pastry scraper or small knife. Roll each piece between your hands, cupping it in your palms so it becomes pointy at each end, like a miniature baguette, and place on one of the floured dish towels; the gnocchi should be not be touching each other.

8   Repeat the rolling and shaping with the remaining pieces of dough. Lightly sprinkle the gnocchi with flour. At this stage, you can wait up to 2 hours to cook the gnocchi, leaving them at cool room temperature, or freeze them on trays and then store in freezer bags for up to 2 months. Cook them directly from the freezer, removing them from the boiling water when they float to the surface (1 to 2 minutes).

To cook the gnocchi

1   Bring the tomato sauce to a simmer in a sauté pan or large frying pan.

2   Meanwhile, bring a large pot of water to a boil and add a handful of sea salt. Cook the gnocchi in two or three batches so as not to crowd the pot. To transfer the gnocchi to the boiling water, fold over the corners of each towel at both ends so that they are touching, pick up the towel by the corners, and tilt it to shake the gnocchi into the pot. As soon as the gnocchi rise to the surface of the boiling water–after about 1 minute–lift them out with a slotted spoon and transfer to the pan of tomato sauce, adding a little of the gnocchi cooking water as needed to thin the sauce.

3   Serve the gnocchi drizzled with olive oil and sprinkled with the pecorino or Parmesan.

Variations

Although they are most commonly colored with Swiss chard, these gnocchi may also be made with spinach, fresh herbs, or nettles, a wild green with many health benefits that proliferates in the spring. If you use nettles, wear gloves to handle them before they are blanched. To make white gnocchi, which I love to serve with spring vegetables like peas, asparagus, and broccoletti, simply omit the greens from the dough.

Armand Crespo's magic touch

As a former restaurant critic, I am constantly on the lookout for new places to try. But somehow, I always find myself back at Bistrot d'Antoine, the flagship restaurant of Portuguese-born Armand Crespo. Not long after I moved to Nice, Armand transformed what had been a beloved local café into a modern bistro, serving a brief chalkboard menu of signature dishes plus frequently changing specials, inspired by his finds at the nearby Cours Saleya market. It was an instant success, and Armand went on to open several other establishments in the Old Town, each with its own character—some of these are now owned by his protégés.

Le Bar des Oiseaux, which he runs in partnership with the owners of the pasta shop Maison Barale (see page 300), is remarkable for its superb-value lunch menu, while Le Comptoir du Marché shares the same spirit as Bistrot d'Antoine, with a different chef and menu. Peixes serves tapas-style seafood with a creative flourish, and Type 55 (from the French name for all-purpose flour) boldly reinvents the pizza. One of the better-kept secrets in the Old Town is his wine bar La Cave du Cours, which is open only on Thursday to Saturday evening, attracting locals rather than tourists thanks to its discreet location in a back street. Customers choose their wines from the shelves, and small plates appear as if by magic to accompany the drinks.

Armand seems to constantly have a new project in the works, yet his restaurants never feel like part of a chain—when taking over a landmark spot, like the Bar de la Dégustation, facing the courthouse, he often keeps the original name and the features that made it so popular (in this case, great-value drinks and simple food). Like me, he came to Nice later in life but has thoroughly adopted its culture, bringing an always-curious outsider's eye to its history and cuisine. When I see him on his bicycle at the market, he shares my excitement at spotting the first zucchini blossoms of the season or grabbing a few bunches of wild asparagus from the hills around Nice. These go into the simple but refined dishes that, along with the unfailingly professional service, keep his restaurants packed with happy crowds of food lovers.

TOURTE DE BLETTES SALÉE

Savory Swiss chard pie

At bakeries in Nice, the popular Sweet Swiss Chard Pie (see page 317) is so eye-catching with its layer of powdered sugar that it's easy to overlook the savory version, which often sits next to it. Traditionally made with olive oil pastry, this sturdy pie makes great picnic food and can also be served for lunch with mesclun (see page 350), or as part of a brunch. Across the border in Liguria, home cooks produce many such pies (known as *torte verde*) with vegetables ranging from zucchini to artichokes, but in Nice, unsurprisingly, the chard version dominates. If you'd like to use a vegetable other than chard, the principle is exactly the same. You can leave out the pancetta or replace it with toasted pine nuts for a vegetarian version.

If you want to save time by using premade pastry, puff pastry works best, also making this tart more indulgent than the original.

SERVES 6 TO 8

FOR THE FILLING

¼ cup (50 g) short-grain white rice, such as Arborio

1 large bunch thin-stemmed Swiss chard (about 1 pound/450 g)

2 tablespoons extra-virgin olive oil

1 red onion, finely minced

½ cup (100 g) smoked pancetta cut into ¼-inch (0.5 cm) dice (or ¼ cup/35 g pine nuts; see headnote)

2 large eggs

⅔ cup (50 g) freshly grated Parmesan

2 tablespoons chopped flat-leaf parsley

A pinch of dried thyme or 1 teaspoon fresh thyme leaves

Sea salt and freshly ground black pepper

A double recipe of Olive Oil Pastry (page 360)

Flour for rolling the dough

1 egg, beaten, for egg wash

1 Bring a small pot of water to a boil. Add the rice and cook for 10 minutes, or until al dente. Drain in a sieve and set aside.

2 Separate the chard leaves from the stems. Roll up the leaves in handfuls, slice crosswise into ⅛-inch- (3 mm) wide strips, and place in a bowl. Slice the tender parts of the stems ⅛ inch (3 mm) thick and place in a separate bowl (use only stems that are less than ½ inch (1 cm) thick; large ribs are not suitable for this dish).

3 In a medium frying pan, heat the olive oil over medium heat. Add the onion, chard stems, and pancetta (or pine nuts) and cook, stirring, over medium-low heat until the pancetta (or pine nuts) starts to turn golden and the stems have softened, 7 to 8 minutes. Add the chard leaves and cook until the leaves have completely wilted, 3 to 4 minutes.

4 Transfer the mixture to a large bowl, add the eggs, cooked rice, Parmesan, parsley, and thyme, and stir to mix well. Season generously with salt and pepper. →

5 Preheat the oven to 375°F (190°C).

6 Divide the dough into 2 pieces, one about twice as large as the other, and shape into disks about 1 inch (2.5 cm) thick. Set the smaller piece aside for the top crust. On a lightly floured surface, roll the larger piece out into an 11-inch (28 cm) round about ⅛ inch (3 mm) thick. Line a 9-inch (23 cm) pie plate with the pastry, letting it hang over the edges of the pan, and fill with the vegetable mixture. Then roll out the second ball of dough as thin as the first. Drape it over the top of the filling, press the edges of the pastry together, and, using scissors, trim the pastry to about a ½-inch (1 cm) overhang.

7 Roll the pastry overhang up from underneath so that you have a thick edge resting on the edges of the pie plate. Using the thumb of one hand and the thumb and index finger of the other, crimp the edges of the pastry (you can also crimp it by simply pressing down on it with the tines of a fork). Brush the surface of the pastry with the beaten egg. Prick the pastry all over with a fork.

8 Bake the pie for 35 to 40 minutes, until golden. Serve warm or at room temperature.

Cook's note

❉

This recipe will leave you with leftover pastry, which you can use to make an individual fruit galette, such as the Rustic Plum Tart (page 177), or quiche. The dough will keep, well wrapped, for 1 day in the refrigerator or up to 3 months in the freezer.

RISOTTO OLIVE ET ARTICHAUT, PANCETTA GRILLÉE

Olive and artichoke risotto with crisp pancetta

Thomas Hubert is one of those chefs who is happiest cooking in a small open kitchen, where he can watch his diners' reactions. With his partner, Aurélie Marion, tending to the always-packed dining room, he turns out homestyle dishes with haute cuisine flair, like a variation on Pissaladière (see page 191) with crisp puff pastry and marinated vegetables, or grilled sea bass alongside local artichokes. Though Thomas and Aurélie are both from Brittany, the name of their restaurant, Olive et Artichaut, gives away their love of Mediterranean produce.

Throughout the year, Thomas serves seasonal variations on risotto. A classic in the spring is this olive and artichoke version, prepared with the restaurant's namesake ingredients. Though it might seem at first glance to be an Italian recipe, the use of thyme, bay leaf, and Niçoise olives places it on the southern French side of the border. Since the artichokes are barely cooked, only the fist-sized variety known as bouquets or violets is suited to this recipe. If these are impossible to find, you can substitute raw asparagus, thinly sliced on the diagonal, or tender greens, such as baby spinach.

**SERVES 4 AS A MAIN COURSE,
6 AS A STARTER**

5 cups (1.2 l) chicken stock, homemade (page 355) or store-bought

3 baby artichokes (or 4 asparagus spears, about ½ inch/1 cm thick, tough ends removed)

2 tablespoons freshly squeezed lemon juice

5 tablespoons (75 ml) extra-virgin olive oil

Sea salt

1 onion, diced

1⅔ cups (350 g) risotto rice, such as Arborio or Carnaroli

2 sprigs thyme

2 fresh or dried bay leaves

1 garlic clove, smashed with the flat side of a knife and peeled

⅔ cup (160 ml) dry white wine

6 slices pancetta, about ⅛ inch (3 mm) thick

⅓ cup (60 g) Niçoise olives, pitted and roughly chopped

3 tablespoons (45 g) unsalted butter

⅔ cup (50 g) freshly grated Parmesan

Freshly ground black pepper

1 Bring the chicken stock to a simmer in a saucepan.

2 Meanwhile, trim the artichokes, if using, as described on page 55, cut them in half, and slice lengthwise very thin. In a small bowl, toss the artichokes with the lemon juice, 1 tablespoon of the olive oil, and a pinch of sea salt. (If using asparagus, cut them ⅛ inch (3 mm) thick on the diagonal and toss with the lemon juice and olive oil; set aside.) →

3 In a large saucepan or a Dutch oven, warm 2 tablespoons of the olive oil over medium-low heat. Add the onion with a generous pinch of salt and cook, stirring, until translucent but not browned, 7 to 8 minutes.

4 Add the rice, thyme, bay leaves, and garlic and cook, stirring frequently, for 2 to 3 minutes, until the grains of rice look translucent. Deglaze the pan with the white wine and cook, stirring, until the liquid has almost evaporated.

5 Add a ladleful of the chicken stock to the pan and cook, stirring frequently, until the rice has almost absorbed the stock, then add another ladleful and continue cooking and adding the stock in the same manner. The liquid should bubble gently the during the entire process, which may take up to 30 minutes; the rice is done when the grains have softened but retain a pleasant bite (you might not use all the chicken stock). If in doubt, err on the al dente side, as the rice will soften further off the heat. Remove the bay leaves and thyme, and the garlic, if you prefer not to bite into it.

6 Meanwhile, cook the pancetta in a frying pan over medium heat (no need to add oil) until crisp. Remove from the pan and drain on paper towels.

7 Remove the artichokes (or asparagus) from the marinade and gently squeeze to remove any excess liquid without damaging them. Remove the risotto from the heat and stir in the olives and artichokes (or asparagus), then stir in the remaining 2 tablespoons olive oil, the butter, and Parmesan. Season with salt and pepper to taste. The risotto should be creamy; if it seems too dry, add a little more chicken stock.

8 Serve the risotto in warmed shallow bowls, topped with the crisp pancetta.

CABILLAUD DEMI-SEL, AIL CONFIT, SAUCE AUX CÂPRES, CITRON, ET PIMENT

Semi-salted cod with garlic confit and caper, lemon, and chile sauce

I first tasted this dish at the wine bar and bistro Les Papilles in Paris; the flavors reminded me so much of Nice that, as soon as I returned home, I re-created it using local lemons and chile peppers from organic farmer Pierre Magnani (see Pickled Chile Peppers, page 340). It's a deconstructed—and lighter—take on brandade de morue, a puree of salt cod, garlic, cream, and potato. In this modernized version, fresh cod is salted, fried, and served on a bed of potatoes and celery root mashed with butter, olive oil, and fresh herbs. Garlic cloves cooked slowly in olive oil grow mellow and sweet; the leftover oil will keep in a sealed jar in the refrigerator for up to a month and can be used anytime you want to add a subtle garlic flavor to a dish.

You can substitute another mild white fish for the cod, but try to choose thick fillets (I like the more sustainable pollack or scorpion fish, a red-skinned fish that also goes by the name of redfish or red drum). Coating the fish with coarse salt firms up the fillets, allowing them to hold their shape better and develop a golden crust in the frying pan; the flavor is comparable to that of salt cod that has been rehydrated. Add a green vegetable such as broccoli or green beans on the side, if you like, for more color on the plate. Don't be put off by the fact that this recipe has several different components; these can be prepared in advance and then the dish assembled at the last moment, after you have fried the fish.

SERVES 4

FOR THE GARLIC CONFIT

6 garlic cloves, cut lengthwise in half, any green sprouts removed

¼ cup (60 ml) extra-virgin olive oil

FOR THE FISH

1½ cups (8 ounces/225 g) coarse gray sea salt or kosher salt

4 pieces skinless fresh cod, 1 to 1½ inches (2.5 to 4 cm) thick and about 5 ounces/135 grams each

1 tablespoon vegetable oil

FOR THE POTATO AND CELERY ROOT PUREE

1 pound (450 g) small yellow potatoes, peeled (8 to 10 potatoes)

1 celery root (about 11 ounces/300 g), peeled and cut into chunks about the size of the potatoes

Sea salt

3 tablespoons unsalted butter

¼ cup (60 ml) mild-tasting extra-virgin olive oil

Freshly ground black pepper

2 tablespoons chopped flat-leaf parsley

FOR THE CAPER, LEMON, AND CHILE SAUCE

1 to 2 small mild to medium-hot red chile peppers, fresh or preserved (page 342)

1 lemon

2 tablespoons small capers preserved in brine or salt, rinsed

¼ cup (60 ml) mild-tasting extra-virgin olive oil

For the garlic confit

1 Preheat the oven to 300°F (150°C).

2 Place the garlic cloves in a small ovenproof dish, such as a ramekin, and cover with the olive oil. Bake for 40 minutes, or until the garlic is very soft and golden. (You can also cook the garlic in a small saucepan on the stove, but the heat should be so low that you see only small bubbles.) Remove from the oven and set aside.

To salt the fish

1 Spread out half the coarse salt in a shallow dish or plate that will hold the cod in one layer. Place the cod on the bed of salt and cover with the remaining salt. Set aside in the refrigerator for 20 minutes if the fillets are 1½ inches (4 cm) thick, 15 minutes if they are 1 inch (2.5 cm) thick. The fish will feel firmer to the touch and the salt will look wet.

2 Rinse the fillets well under cold water, squeeze them gently between your hands to remove any excess water, and dry thoroughly with paper towels. (Discard the salt.) Place the cod on a plate lined with paper towels and refrigerate, uncovered, until needed. (You can do this step up to several hours in advance, as the fish will hold its shape better if it has thoroughly dried.)

For the potato and celery root puree

1 Place the potatoes and celery root in a large sauté pan or saucepan. Barely cover with cold water, then add a large pinch of sea salt and the butter. Cover with a circle of parchment paper (see Cook's Note, page 62) to keep in some of the steam. Bring to a boil over high heat and cook until most of the water has evaporated and the potatoes and celery root are soft, about 30 minutes. You should have about ½ cup (120 ml) of syrupy liquid remaining. (If the liquid has reduced but the vegetables are not yet soft, add a little more water and continue cooking, covered with the parchment, until they have softened.) Remove from the heat.

2 Pass the potatoes and celery root, with their liquid, through a food mill or ricer into a bowl, or mash them in the pan with a potato masher or fork. Stir in the olive oil. Season with salt and pepper to taste. Set aside, covered, in a warm place (or in a low oven) until needed; at the last moment, stir in the chopped parsley (if you do this too soon, the parsley will lose its vivid color).

For the caper, lemon, and chile sauce

1 Taste a bit of a chile to judge its strength; if it is hot, you may need only 1 chile. Cut the chile pepper(s) lengthwise in half and remove the white pith and seeds. Cut into tiny dice and transfer to a small bowl.

2 Cut off the top and bottom of the lemon, so that the flesh is exposed and the fruit can sit flat on one end. Using a small sharp knife, cut off the peel from top to bottom, following the curve →

of the lemon and removing as much of the white pith as you can. Slice each segment away from the membranes on each side, then cut the segments crosswise into ¼-inch (0.5 cm) slices. Place the lemon pieces in the bowl with the chile pepper.

3 Add the capers and olive oil to the chile-lemon mixture, stir, and set aside.

To finish the dish

1 Heat the vegetable oil in a large nonstick frying pan over high heat. Add the cod, whitest side down, and cook for 3 to 4 minutes, until golden and crusty on the first side. Carefully flip the fish using a spatula, and cook on the other side until golden, about 3 minutes. The fish should be flaky and no longer translucent.

2 Serve the cod on the potato-celery root mash, topped with the caper-lemon-chile sauce and garnished with the drained garlic confit (save the garlicky oil for another use).

Cook's note

Since fresh chile peppers are not a common ingredient in Nice, I often use preserved chile peppers (page 342) in this dish. Their texture works well in the sauce, but be sure to choose mild chiles, as too much heat would overwhelm the other ingredients. The small round peppers sold in jars and labeled *piquanté* are perfect for this dish. In summer, I find these round chiles fresh at the market; they freeze well and are easy to dice while still frozen.

BOURRIDE SÉTOISE

Fisherman's stew from Sète

Originating in the port of Sète, near Montpellier, bourride is a lesser-known (and simpler to make) cousin of bouillabaisse. Monkfish was at one time both plentiful and underappreciated along this stretch of coast, so the catch went into a fisherman's stew thickened with aïoli. Now prized for its meaty, lobster-like flesh, monkfish has become pricey and scarce, and I often substitute more readily available white fish such as scorpion fish (also known as redfish or red drum), haddock, or sea bream. It's important to choose a fish that is not too delicate, or it could fall apart when braised.

Shellfish is not a traditional addition to bourride, but mussels dress it up beautifully, and their juices deepen the flavor of the sauce. You can make it soupy if you like by adding more water or some stock, but I like a more concentrated sauce. Serve this with steamed or boiled new potatoes (or the Pan-Roasted Potatoes on page 94) and the extra aïoli.

SERVES 4

12 ounces (325 g) mussels

4 pieces skinless monkfish or other white fish fillet, about 6 ounces (160 g) each

Sea salt and freshly ground black pepper

2 tablespoons extra-virgin olive oil

1 medium carrot, cut lengthwise in half and thinly sliced

1 medium or 2 small leeks, white and pale green parts only, cut lengthwise in half and thinly sliced

8 thin-ribbed Swiss chard leaves, thinly sliced, leaves and stems kept separate

½ cup (10 g) celery leaves, thinly sliced (or substitute ¼ cup/5 g flat-leaf parsley, thinly sliced)

½ cup (70 g) fresh or frozen peas

Up to 1 cup (240 ml) warm water or fish or vegetable stock if needed

Aïoli (page 347)

Chervil, fennel, flat-leaf parsley, or dill sprigs for garnish

1 To clean the mussels, swish them around in a large bowl of water and lift out with your hands into a colander set in the sink, leaving the grit at the bottom of the bowl. Remove the beards by pulling on them with your fingers, and discard any mussels that remain open when pressed shut or that have broken shells. Rinse a second time in a large bowl of water and drain in the colander.

2 Place the mussels in a medium saucepan set over medium-high heat, cover, and cook for 3 to 5 minutes, shaking the pan once or twice, until all the shells are open. Remove the mussels with a slotted spoon and set aside in a warm place, covered. Strain the liquid through a fine strainer into a bowl.

3 Season the fish with salt and a little pepper and set aside while you prepare the other ingredients.

4 Heat the olive oil in a medium sauté pan or Dutch oven over medium-low heat. Add the carrot, leeks, and chard stems, along with a good pinch of sea salt, and cook, stirring frequently, for 5 to 7 minutes, until softened but not browned.

5 Add the chard and celery leaves and cook for 2 to 3 minutes, until the leaves are wilted. (You can prepare the dish up to this step ahead of time and then braise the fish just before serving.)

6 Add the fish, mussel juice, and peas, if using, to the pan. Cover and cook over medium-low heat for 5 to 7 minutes, until the fish is just cooked through, basting it once or twice with the pan juices. If the liquid evaporates too quickly, add enough water to cover the bottom of the pan (monkfish will give off more juice than other white fish).

7 Remove the fish from the pan and set aside, covered, in a warm place. Transfer about ½ cup (120 ml) of the liquid from the pan to a medium bowl, add half the aïoli, and whisk until smooth, then pour this back into the pan. Heat over medium-low heat, stirring constantly, until the sauce has thickened, 2 to 3 minutes—do not let it boil. Add a little more water if the sauce is thicker than heavy cream.

8 Adjust the seasoning with salt and pepper if needed (taste first, as the mussel juices will be salty). Serve in shallow bowls, starting with the sauce, then topping it with the fish, mussels, and herb sprigs. Dollop the remaining aïoli on the fish and potatoes (see headnote) at the table, if you wish.

Flavien Falchetto (see page 88)

LE GRAND AÏOLI DU PRINTEMPS

Fish fillets with aïoli and spring vegetables

The term *grand aïoli*—or sometimes simply *aïoli*—refers not just to the garlicky sauce but also to a generous spread that traditionally includes salt cod, seasonal vegetables, and perhaps boiled eggs and bulots, sea snails. Though it is often served in winter, with steamed carrots, potatoes, and leeks, I think grand aïoli comes into its own in spring when asparagus, baby carrots, and radishes are in season, bringing fresh flavors and vivid colors to the dish; in summer, you can replace the asparagus with green beans. I love that you can prepare the vegetables ahead of time and serve them at room temperature.

Instead of salt cod, which is difficult to find and time-consuming to prepare, I like to use local fish such as sea bream, sea bass, or rascasse (redfish or red drum), which I cook in a frying pan rather than poaching, in order to crisp the skin. Feel free to vary the fish and vegetables according to what you can find, but small potatoes are a must because they pair so perfectly with the aïoli. Restaurants often serve grand aïoli on Fridays, traditionally a no-meat day for Catholics, and it is also synonymous with the first day of Lent. It's well known that aïoli causes sleepiness, so if you are having it for lunch, allow plenty of time for an afternoon *sieste*.

SERVES 4

4 pieces white fish fillet with skin, about 6 ounces (160 g) each, preferably about ½ inch (1 cm) thick

Sea salt and freshly ground black pepper

12 to 20 small new potatoes or fingerlings, depending on size (about 1½ pounds/675 g)

1 bay leaf

1 teaspoon coarse sea salt

12 fat asparagus spears (about ½ inch/1 cm thick), tough ends broken off

3 tablespoons extra-virgin olive oil

12 skinny spring carrots, no thicker than a finger, green tops trimmed to ¼ inch (0.5 cm) (or 6 medium carrots, cut lengthwise in half)

12 radishes, green tops trimmed to ¼ inch (0.5 cm) and cut lengthwise in half

12 cherry tomatoes, cut in half

Aïoli (page 347)

Fennel or dill sprigs for garnish

1 Season the fish fillets with salt and pepper (going light on the pepper) and set aside for at least 15 minutes.

2 Place the new potatoes in a medium saucepan and cover with water. Add the bay leaf and coarse salt, bring to a boil, and cook the potatoes until they fall off the tip of a knife when pierced and lifted up, 15 to 20 minutes, depending on size. Drain and set aside.

3 Meanwhile, place the asparagus in a sauté pan with 1 tablespoon of the olive oil, ¼ cup (60 ml) water, and a pinch of salt. Bring to a boil, cover, and cook over medium heat, shaking the pan occasionally, until the asparagus are tender, about 5 minutes. Remove the lid and continue cooking over high heat until the water evaporates, about 2 minutes. Transfer the asparagus to a large plate. →

4   Place the carrots in the same sauté pan (no need to rinse it) with 1 tablespoon olive oil and a
    pinch of salt (no water, the carrots will cook in their own steam). Cover the pan and cook over
medium heat, shaking the pan occasionally, until the carrots are tender when pierced with a knife,
10 to 12 minutes. (Be sure to check occasionally that they are not sticking, as they can burn easily if
forgotten.) Transfer to the plate with the asparagus.

5   Heat a large nonstick frying pan over medium-high heat and add the remaining 1 tablespoon
    olive oil. Place the fish skin side down in the pan and cook until the fillets look white almost
all the way through, 5 to 7 minutes, depending on thickness. Turn off the heat and let the fish rest
in the pan, uncovered, until it has fully cooked in the residual heat. (If the fillets are thicker than
½ inch/1 cm, cover the pan when you turn off the heat so that they finish cooking in the steam.) The
fish can be served hot or warm.

6   Transfer the fish to a serving platter or to four plates and arrange the vegetables, including the
    radishes and cherry tomatoes, around it. Top the fish and vegetables with dabs of the aïoli and
garnish with fennel or dill sprigs.

La poutine

During my first spring in Nice, I was surprised to see an elderly woman in place Saint-François scooping a mass of translucent, worm-like creatures from a bucket and selling them by the name *poutine*, which I knew as a Quebecois dish of French fries coated in thick gravy and topped with cheese curds. A specialty of Nice and Liguria for centuries, these fish larvae, called *alevins* in English and *shirasu* in Japan, have traditionally been caught using fine nets near the shore at times when they are abundant. Most often baby gobies, which are ivory colored, they can also be undeveloped anchovies and sardines, with more of a silvery tinge.

With the fish population threatened, only a handful of fishermen between Nice and Menton have received special permission to fish for poutine during a forty-five-day period starting in early March, with strict restrictions on the amount they can catch. As early as the eighteenth century, nets were created that allowed some of the alevins to escape, reducing the impact of this practice on the fish population. Increasingly rare in the fish markets, poutine has come to be known as "Mediterranean caviar," prized by the few chefs who can get their hands on it.

Like caviar, poutine (also known as *nonats*, which translates as "not born," in Nice) is best treated simply. At Dominique Le Stanc's bistro La Merenda, I learned there is no better way to appreciate its almost oyster-like qualities than raw on toasted pain au levain (sourdough) with a drizzling of olive oil and a squirt of fresh lemon. You can also poach poutine in water, fry it in fritters, or stir it into eggs for an omelet, but to me these recipes are best suited to the larger, fishier alevins sold toward the end of the season.

Flavien Falchetto, one of the last remaining poutine fishermen in the port of Cros de Cagnes, told me that last season he caught no more than 1 kilogram (about 2 pounds) a day, selling it all at his family's fish shop in Cagnes-sur-Mer. Poutine's days are almost certainly numbered, and likely for the better, but it's hard not to feel a little wistful at seeing this ancestral tradition die out.

NAVARIN D'AGNEAU

Lamb stew with spring vegetables

Some say that the famed nineteenth-century French chef Antonin Carême named this dish as a tribute to France's role in the 1827 Battle of Navarino during the Greek War of Independence, while others claim that *navarin* refers to a derogatory variation of the word *turnip*, or *navet*. Whatever the true story, this lamb stew remains a quintessential spring dish, drawing on tender, vividly colored vegetables and meat that has not yet developed a strong flavor. Fresh peas in their pods will make a difference, if you can find them.

I first came across navarin d'agneau at the Cordon Bleu, whose recipe called for each vegetable to be cooked separately before it entered the pot. In Nice, I discovered a lazier and just as effective way of making it thanks to my friend Franck Cerutti, who, despite having earned three Michelin stars at the Louis XV restaurant in Monaco, thoroughly approves of no-fuss home cooking. He recommended cooking only the turnips separately, as they are delicate and could otherwise fall apart in the sauce; this also removes some of their bitterness, though spring turnips should be more sweet than bitter. You could make a stock using lamb bones, but I prefer to use chicken or vegetable stock, which gives the stew a milder flavor.

Some versions of this recipe call for the sauce to be thickened with flour, but a thick sauce masks the freshness of the vegetables, so I prefer to leave it broth-like or simply reduce it at the end of the cooking time.

SERVES 6 TO 8

1 small boneless lamb shoulder roast (about 2¼ pounds/1 kg), cut into 2-inch (5 cm) cubes, or the equivalent amount of lamb stew meat

Sea salt and freshly ground black pepper

2 tablespoons extra-virgin olive oil

4 sprigs thyme

2 bay leaves

2 sprigs rosemary

2 sprigs flat-leaf parsley

1 onion, cut into ¼-inch (0.5 cm) dice

2 garlic cloves, cut lengthwise in half and thinly sliced

½ cup (120 ml) dry white wine or dry white vermouth

2 tablespoons tomato paste

3 to 4 cups (720 to 960 ml) chicken or vegetable stock, homemade (page 355) or store-bought

Coarse sea salt

4 small (golf-ball-sized) turnips, peeled and cut into quarters

12 fingerling potatoes, cut lengthwise in half (no need to peel)

12 skinny spring carrots, cut on the diagonal into 2-inch (5 cm) lengths

1¼ cups fresh or frozen peas (1 pound/450 g peas in the pod)

1 Season the meat all over with salt and pepper and set aside for at least 15 minutes to let it absorb the seasonings.

2 Heat the olive oil in a Dutch oven or a large heavy saucepan over medium heat. Add the lamb, in two batches if necessary, and brown on all sides. Drain the meat in a colander and spoon most of the fat from the pot, leaving about 2 tablespoons.

3 While the meat is browning, make a bouquet garni by tying the herbs together in a small bundle with kitchen string.

4 Add the onion to the fat remaining in the pot, along with a pinch of coarse salt, and let it color very lightly over medium-low heat, about 5 minutes. Add the garlic and bouquet garni and cook, stirring, for 2 minutes.

5 Deglaze the pot with the wine or vermouth, scraping the bottom with a wooden spatula—all the delicious caramelized juices, known as *sucs*, should dissolve in the liquid. Let the wine bubble for a minute, then add the tomato paste and cook for 1 to 2 minutes, stirring. Add the lamb and stir to coat with the tomato mixture, then add 3 cups (720 ml) stock and bring to a boil. Cover the pot and cook for 40 minutes over low heat; the liquid should bubble very gently.

6 Meanwhile, half-fill a medium saucepan with water and bring to a boil. Add a large pinch of coarse salt and the turnips and boil for 8 to 10 minutes, until almost tender. Drain and set aside.

7 After the lamb has cooked for 40 minutes, add the potatoes and carrots to the pot, along with the extra 1 cup (240 ml) of stock (or water) if needed to cover the vegetables, and coarse salt to taste (depending on the saltiness of your broth). Cover and cook at a gentle boil over medium heat for another 30 to 40 minutes, checking the carrots and potatoes for tenderness toward the end of the cooking time with the tip of a small knife. The lamb should be tender and the potatoes and carrots cooked through—if this is not the case, cook for a few minutes longer. Remove from the heat. (The stew can be prepared up to several hours ahead to this point and reheated before serving.)

8 A few minutes before serving the stew, add the cooked turnips and the peas to the pot and cook at a simmer until the peas are tender but still bright green, about 5 minutes. If you like, you can transfer the meat and vegetables to a serving dish, covered to keep warm, and boil the cooking liquid for another 10 to 15 minutes to reduce and thicken it before pouring it over them—or simply serve it in its more soupy form in shallow bowls.

BOULETTES ÉPICÉES, POIS CHICHES, ET YAOURT

Spiced meatballs with chickpeas and yogurt

Sébastien Perinetti and Elmahdi (Mehdi) Mobarik make a winning duo at their bistro Le Canon. Sébastien hunts down organic ingredients and natural wines that have a story behind them, often driving far up into the mountains or across the border to Italy to visit markets and producers. Mehdi transforms his finds into a brief blackboard menu that changes every day at lunch and dinner, with the origin of each product proudly listed next to his creations.

A veteran of the natural wine bar scene in Nice, Sébastien named his restaurant after Nice's noon cannon and for the expression *boire un canon*, which refers to an ancient measuring unit and now simply means "to drink a glass of wine." Instead of imposing his own taste, Sébastien invites diners into the cellar to choose a bottle with his guidance.

Originally from Morocco, the haute-cuisine–trained Mehdi draws on the culinary traditions of North Africa and the Middle East as well as of Italy and southern France. Chickpeas are a staple in Niçoise cooking, and here he features them in a Moroccan-inspired dish that is vibrant with herbs and spices. I love it for a casual outdoor meal, since the chickpeas are served at room temperature and the meatballs can be cooked on a barbecue grill or plancha. Make the chickpea salad at least an hour ahead so that the chickpeas will soak up the lemon and spices.

SERVES 4 TO 6 (MAKES 25 TO 30 SMALL MEATBALLS)

FOR THE CHICKPEA SALAD

1 cup (200 g) dried chickpeas or two 14-ounce (400 g) cans chickpeas, drained

½ cup (10 g) thinly sliced cilantro leaves

¼ cup (5 g) thinly sliced flat-leaf parsley leaves

2 spring onions, white and pale green parts only, thinly sliced

¼ to ⅓ cup (60 to 80 ml) freshly squeezed lemon juice (from 1 to 2 lemons)

3 tablespoons extra-virgin olive oil

2 teaspoons ground cumin

Sea salt and freshly ground black pepper

FOR THE MEATBALLS

2 small slices day-old sourdough bread or 4 slices day-old baguette (about 2 ounces/50 g)

½ cup (120 ml) whole milk

1 pound 2 ounces (500 g) ground lamb or beef (not too lean)

½ red onion, finely minced

2 garlic cloves, finely minced

¼ cup (5 g) mint leaves, finely chopped

½ cup (10 g) cilantro leaves, finely chopped

¼ cup flat-leaf parsley leaves, finely chopped (5 g)

1 teaspoon ground cumin

¼ teaspoon grated fresh ginger or ½ teaspoon ground ginger

1 large egg

Sea salt and freshly ground black pepper

¼ cup (60 ml) vegetable oil for frying (optional)

FOR THE SAUCE

½ cup (120 ml) plain yogurt

½ teaspoon smoked paprika or mild to medium-hot chile powder

For the chickpea salad

1 If using dried chickpeas, soak them overnight at room temperature in plenty of water. (If you have a pressure cooker, there is no need to soak the chickpeas overnight. Place them in the pot, cover generously with water, seal, and bring up to pressure before cooking for 1 hour on high.)

2 The next day, if you soaked the chickpeas, drain them, place in a medium saucepan, and cover generously with water. Bring to a boil and cook for 1 to 1½ hours at a simmer, until you can crush the chickpeas with the back of a spoon. Drain the chickpeas and let cool to room temperature.

3 In a bowl, combine the drained chickpeas, cilantro, parsley, spring onions, ¼ cup (60 ml) lemon juice, the olive oil, and cumin. Season to taste with salt and pepper, then taste and adjust the seasonings, adding a little more lemon juice if you like. Set aside in the refrigerator for at least 1 hour, and up to 3 hours.

For the meatballs

1 Break the bread into 1-inch (2.5 cm) chunks, place in a small bowl, and cover with the milk. Set aside for at least 15 minutes.

2 Place the meat in a large bowl. Add the onion, garlic, mint, cilantro, parsley, cumin, ginger, and egg and season generously with salt and pepper. Squeeze the milk out of the bread and add the bread to the mixture, discarding any crusts that have not completely softened. Using your hands, knead the mixture for up to 1 minute so that everything is well mixed.

3 Shape the meatball mixture into 1-inch (2.5 cm) balls, flattening them slightly, or make them a little bigger if you are grilling them.

4 If you are cooking the meatballs in a frying pan, heat the oil in a large pan over medium-low (or cook them in two batches in a medium pan, using half the oil each time and cleaning the pan after the first batch). Add the meatballs and cook, turning once, for 6 to 7 minutes on each side, until browned and cooked through. Be careful not to turn the heat up higher, or the meat will cook before the onion and garlic have a chance to soften.

5 If you are cooking the meatballs on a grill or plancha, no fat is needed. Prepare a medium fire in a gas or charcoal grill, or heat a plancha over medium heat. Cook, turning once, for 5 to 6 minutes on each side, until browned and cooked through.

To serve

1 While the meatballs cook, make the sauce: Stir together the yogurt and smoked paprika or chile powder in a small bowl.

2 Serve the chickpeas in a bowl and the meatballs on a platter, with the sauce on the side. Drizzle the sauce over the meatballs on the platter, or dip the meatballs in the sauce.

Time for lunch: The noon cannon

You can spot the tourists in Nice by watching their reaction to the loud bang that sends the seagulls flapping every day at noon. Newcomers will jump in alarm, looking around for reassurance, while locals might glance at their watches or slightly speed up their step. For residents of Nice, the daily bang—which grows louder the closer you are to Castle Hill—is simply a friendly reminder that it will soon be time for lunch. Since the markets and many small food shops close at 1 p.m., this is the time to grab any last ingredients you might need.

Not surprisingly, the legend behind the cannon involves food. Niçoise lore credits the tradition to a wealthy Scottish couple who lived in Nice during the nineteenth century. The story goes that the wife loved to spend mornings strolling on the Promenade des Anglais or chatting with friends in the Old Town, and so often came home late for lunch. Growing frustrated with waiting, the husband offered to finance a noon cannon, inspired by the 1 p.m. Scottish gun (which itself was based on a smaller cannon that once signaled noon in the Palais Royal gardens in Paris). The population became so dependent on the cannon that it has sounded ever since.

If you dig a little deeper, though, it seems that this story contains a healthy dose of Niçoise exaggeration. The couple in question, Sir Thomas Coventry and his wife, Elizabeth, were English rather than Scottish, and her supposed tardiness was an embellishment. Sir Thomas was a hobbyist astronomer and meteorologist, and during their winter stays at the Hotel Chauvin (which is now the Aston Hotel), he liked to set up his instruments on the rooftop terrace. In conducting his tests, he realized that the city's church bells were not synchronized, so he met with the city council to propose his solution: a noon cannon. While teaching my cooking classes, I know that the bang is coming when I hear a nearby church bell ring three times, and I try to warn my students before they duck under the counter!

Since 1862, a fireworks professional has been responsible for climbing Castle Hill each day to ensure that the cannon goes off at the right moment. Only on July 14 (Bastille Day) does the cannon fall silent, paying tribute to the eighty-six victims of the 2016 terrorist attack in Nice. And in a twist that Thomas Coventry would have appreciated—it seems he was known for his sense of humor, which might explain the legend about his wife—on April Fool's Day, the cannon sounds at 11 a.m., throwing off the lunch plans of those who do not check their watches.

GRENAILLES RÔTIES À LA POÊLE

Pan-roasted potatoes with herbs

The small potatoes known as *grenailles* or fingerlings are a staple of my diet, and this is the way I most often cook them both in my classes and at home, because in 20 minutes or so, you can mimic roasted potatoes without having to turn on the oven. I picked up this surprising technique from Elizabeth David's classic cookbook *French Provincial Cooking*, though she used butter instead of olive oil. For this recipe, it's important to use a pot with a lid, because the potatoes cook only in the steam they create. They are delicious with Bourride (page 82), Le Grand Aïoli (page 85), Chicken with Pastis (page 224), and just about anything else!

SERVES 4 TO 6

12 to 16 fingerling potatoes
¼ cup (60 ml) extra-virgin olive oil

2 large sprigs rosemary, thyme, or tarragon
Fleur de sel

1 Scrub the potatoes (don't peel them) and dry them well.

2 Heat the oil in a medium-large heavy saucepan or sauté pan over medium heat. Add the potatoes, which should fit in one layer, arrange the herb sprigs atop the potatoes, and cover with a lid.

3 When you hear a strong sizzling sound, turn the heat down to low and cook the potatoes for 20 to 25 minutes, shaking the pan every 2 to 3 minutes, until they are browned. Test a potato or two with a knife to make sure they are completely cooked. (Be careful when you remove the lid, since the condensation might cause the fat to splatter.) You can make these up to an hour ahead of time; remove the lid once the potatoes are cooked so they retain their crispy skins, and rewarm them over medium heat before serving.

TARTE AUX FRAISES À LA CRÈME PÂTISSIÈRE

Strawberry and cream tart

Made with a sweet short crust, vanilla cream, and scarlet berries artfully arranged on top, tarte aux fraises may be one of the most eye-catching pastries in the French repertoire. Despite this, I rarely buy it from pastry shops, as I often find it too robust, designed more for carrying in a box than for savoring. I had even given up making it until I came across an ethereal version by Michelin-starred chef Bruno Cirino at his homey bistro Café de la Fontaine in the hilltop town of La Turbie, above Monaco. He was willing to share the recipe, which I have since adapted.

Because of its fragile texture, this tart demands to be eaten with a fork, not long after it has been assembled. An hour or two in the refrigerator helps the pastry cream set nicely, but if you leave it too long, the chill will mask the sweetness of the berries. Neither the crust nor the pastry cream is too sweet; their role is to highlight the star ingredient.

For his tart, Cirino prefers Gariguette strawberries, an elongated, orange-red variety that is one of the first to appear at the market stalls in the spring. Its delicate texture and balance of natural sugars and acidity make it perfect for the tart, but since the Gariguette is unique to France, you can choose any small, sweet berries in season for a similar result.

You can make the pastry dough and pastry cream up to 24 hours in advance; bake the tart shell on the day you are serving the tart. If you are taking this tart to a party, it's best to assemble it on the spot–this is not picnic food, as it is quite fragile and messy to eat, but in the best possible way. An alternative that I often choose is to make tartlets, which are easier to serve, though still fragile to carry. In the unlikely event that you have leftovers, you can keep the tart in the refrigerator overnight, but remove it 30 minutes before serving to fully enjoy it.

SERVES 6 TO 8

Quick Basic Pastry (page 361), chilled for at least 15 minutes

FOR THE VANILLA PASTRY CREAM
1 vanilla bean
1½ cups (360 ml) whole milk
4 large egg yolks

½ cup (100 g) granulated sugar
¼ cup (30 g) cornstarch
½ cup (120 ml) heavy cream

6 cups small sweet strawberries (about 1½ pounds/675 to 700 g)
1 tablespoon confectioners' sugar

For the pastry

1   Preheat the oven to 375°F (190°C). →

2 Roll out the pastry to a circle about ⅛ inch (3 mm) thick and at least 11 inches (28 cm) in diameter. Fit it into a 9-inch (23 cm) tart pan, preferably one with a removable bottom. Cut off the edges with a swipe of the rolling pin, then press the pastry all the way around the sides so that it comes slightly above the rim of the pan. (You can refrigerate the tart shell at this point, covered, for up to 24 hours.)

3 Cut a circle of parchment paper large enough to line the pastry with a 1-inch (2.5cm) overhang. Weigh it down with rice, dried beans or lentils, or pastry weights.

4 Place the pan on a baking sheet and bake for 15 to 20 minutes, until the edges have turned golden. Remove the paper and weights (save the rice or lentils in a jar for the next time) and bake for 10 more minutes, or until golden all over. Set the pan on a rack to cool completely.

For the pastry cream

1 Cut the vanilla bean lengthwise in half and use the blunt edge of a knife to scrape out the seeds. Place the milk, vanilla seeds, and pod in a saucepan and bring the milk just to a boil. Remove from the heat.

2 While the milk is heating, beat the egg yolks and sugar in a mixing bowl for 1 minute. Add the cornstarch, whisking until smooth.

3 Add the hot milk bit by bit to the egg yolk mixture, whisking gently to combine. Pour back into the saucepan and cook over medium-low heat, whisking vigorously to prevent lumps from forming, until thickened; the mixture should just come to a boil. Transfer the pastry cream to a shallow bowl, place a piece of plastic wrap directly against its surface to prevent a skin from forming, and transfer to the refrigerator to cool for at least 2 hours.

4 With a handheld electric mixer, beat the cream in a large bowl until it holds stiff peaks. Using a rubber spatula, fold it into the pastry cream.

Assemble the tart

1 Hull the strawberries (or not, for a more rustic look) and cut them lengthwise in half.

2 If your pan has a removable base, set the pan on a small bowl so that the rim falls away and place the tart shell, still on the metal base, on a serving plate. If not, leave the tart shell in the pan.

3 Spread the pastry cream in the tart shell (I like to use a pastry bag for this). Arrange the strawberries on top in an orderly or disorderly way, depending on your mood. Refrigerate for at least 1 hour before serving, but try to serve it the same day.

4 Just before serving, using a small sieve, sprinkle the top of the tart lightly with the confectioners' sugar.

Strawberry fields forever

Of all the stalls at the Cours Saleya market, the one run by Thérèse is the most colorful, with its array of gleaming berries that reaches its peak of abundance in late spring. Extolling the wonders of her fruits to passersby and lavishing each customer with terms of endearment, Thérèse is impossible to miss. She married into a family of market vendors at eighteen and has sold fruit for fifty years alongside her husband, children, and now grandchildren, who share the same pride in the quality of their wares. Since all her berries look equally tempting, I always ask her which are the sweetest that day: perhaps local strawberries from the fields around Carros, just outside Nice, or those from Carpentras in Provence, a village famed for its berries.

When imported strawberries appear at the market in February and March—as shoppers begin to tire of citrus—I resolutely ignore them, knowing their flavor will never live up to the burst of brightness they offer. Popping up a few weeks later, the first local berries might look less eye-catching, with a color that is more orange than red, but early varieties such as the slender Gariguette and the heart-shaped Ciflorette give off an unmistakable perfume that tells you this is the real thing. Pastry chefs love these varieties for their balance of sweetness and acidity, arranging the delicate berries on tarts and producing the first fraisiers (see page 101) of the season.

In May, before summer fruits begin to jostle with them for space, strawberries create a sea of scarlet at the market stalls. The ruby-red Cléry and Charlotte varieties take over then, both of them sweet and versatile berries to be savored *nature* (with no adornment) or added to simple desserts such as a berry gratin. Rather than whipped cream, I prefer to dip strawberries in crème fraîche lightly sweetened with vanilla sugar.

Strawberry season continues throughout the summer and into early fall, though the hot weather makes the delicate berries so fragile that they are best eaten the same day you buy them. The ultimate summer berry is the exquisite fraise des bois, a tiny, floral-scented strawberry that originated in the wild and is now cultivated to be sold to high-end restaurants and others who can afford this treasure. Mimicking the flavor of wild strawberries is the Mara des bois, the result of a hybrid developed in the 1990s. Now one of the most popular strawberries in France, it makes exceptional jam, as well as being suited to any berry dessert.

When buying strawberries, remember that pesticide use is common and be sure to wash them before indulging. Besides the berries that Thérèse recommends to me, I look for those grown by the Valerioti family near La Gaude, using predatory insects instead of pesticides. At a time when manure was the standard fertilizer for strawberries, many people soaked the berries in wine to disinfect them; this led to a dessert (see Strawberries in Rosé Wine, page 181) so delicious that its hygienic origins have been forgotten!

FRAISIER DANS UN BOCAL

Spring strawberry cake in a jar

Sophie Lim, who taught pastry classes at Les Petits Farcis, is a master at simplifying complex French pastries to make them accessible to the home cook. Looking at this recipe, you might think it has a lot of steps and ingredients, but it comes together much more quickly and easily than a classic fraisier, which is an all-day affair to make. Mascarpone cream replaces the traditional pastry cream, giving the dessert a lighter Italian touch. I love the idea of presenting it in individual jars, since the sight of the first spring strawberries lining the outside of the cake is what makes this seasonal dessert so irresistible in pastry shop windows.

You will need six 6-ounce (200 ml) wide-mouth jars measuring about 3 inches (8 cm) across to make this dessert, or you can use straight-sided 6-ounce (200 ml) glass ramekins. Because the dessert is a celebration of strawberries, do not be tempted to make it with flavorless imports out of season.

You can prepare the lime syrup, mascarpone cream, and sponge cake up to 24 hours ahead of time, making this easy to put together. Once in the jars, the cake will keep for another 24 hours in the refrigerator.

SERVES 6

FOR THE LIME SYRUP
⅓ cup (70 g) sugar
⅔ cup (150 ml) water
2 tablespoons freshly squeezed lime juice

FOR THE MASCARPONE CREAM
½ vanilla bean, split lengthwise, or ¼ teaspoon
   vanilla bean paste
¾ cup (200 ml) very cold heavy cream
½ cup (120 g) very cold mascarpone
⅓ cup (40 g) confectioners' sugar

FOR THE SPONGE CAKE (GÉNOISE)
4 large eggs
½ cup (100 g) sugar
¾ cup plus 1 tablespoon (100 g) all-purpose flour

FOR THE STRAWBERRIES
4 cups strawberries (about 1 pound/450 g)
2 tablespoons confectioners' sugar
1 tablespoon freshly squeezed lime juice

For the lime syrup

Combine the sugar and water in a small saucepan and bring to a simmer, stirring just until the sugar is dissolved. Remove from the heat and let cool, then add the lime juice.

For the mascarpone cream

1 If using a vanilla bean, scrape the vanilla seeds from the pod with the blunt side of a small knife; reserve the pod for another use, if desired.

2 In the bowl of a stand mixer fitted with the whisk attachment, or using a handheld electric mixer in a large bowl, beat the cream, mascarpone, confectioners' sugar, and vanilla seeds or vanilla bean paste together on medium speed for 2 to 3 minutes, until the cream thickens. Increase the speed to high and beat until the cream is fluffy and holds stiff peaks, 30 seconds to 1 minute.

3 Transfer to a bowl, cover with plastic wrap, and refrigerate until ready to use.

For the sponge cake

1 Preheat the oven to 400°F (200°C).

2 Line a 12-by-16-inch (30 by 40 cm) rimmed baking sheet with parchment paper, leaving a 1-inch (2.5 cm) overhang on the short ends.

3 In the bowl of a stand mixer fitted with the whisk attachment, or using a handheld electric mixer in a large bowl, whisk the eggs and sugar at medium-high speed until the mixture falls slowly from a spatula like a ribbon, 3 to 4 minutes. The mixture should be light in color and about triple the initial volume.

4 Remove the bowl from the mixer stand. Sift the flour into egg-sugar mixture and, using a rubber spatula, gently fold in the flour by lifting the batter from the outer edges of the bowl into the center, turning the bowl as you go.

5 Spread the batter evenly in the lined baking sheet; it should be about ½ inch (0.5 cm) thick. Bake for 5 to 7 minutes, until golden brown. Remove from the oven, cover with a clean dish towel, and let cool completely.

6 Flip the génoise out onto the towel and carefully peel off the parchment paper. Using a cookie cutter or the rim of one of your jars, cut out twelve 3-inch (8 cm) circles from the génoise. Set aside.

For the strawberries

1 Cut 1 cup (110 g) of the strawberries into ½-inch (1 cm) dice and place in a bowl. Add the sugar and lime juice and stir gently.

2 Slice the tops off the remaining strawberries so that they will sit flat, then cut them lengthwise in half.

Assemble the dessert

1 Place a disk of sponge cake in the bottom of each jar.

2 With a pastry brush, dab some of the syrup on top of each disk. Arrange the strawberry halves, cut side facing outward and tips pointing up, around the sides of the jars; reserve 6 strawberry halves for garnish. Using a pastry bag or small spoon, cover the cake with a ½-inch (1 cm) layer of the mascarpone cream. Spoon the diced strawberries onto the middle of the cream in each jar. Cover with a second layer of mascarpone cream. Place a second disk of cake on top of the cream in each jar and dab some syrup onto the cake. Press down on each round of cake so that the cream fills in the spaces between the strawberries. Finish each jar with a layer of the remaining mascarpone cream and place the strawberry halves on top, cut sides up.

3 Chill the cakes for at least 30 minutes before serving. If you are keeping them longer (for up to 24 hours), seal the jars with the lids or cover with plastic wrap.

CLAFOUTIS LIMOUSIN

Cherry clafoutis

Although it originated in the Limousin region, in central France, clafoutis is equally popular in the Nice area, which produces an abundance of cherries for a few glorious weeks in May and June. One of the simplest desserts to make, it consists of a rich crêpe batter poured over fruit and baked. For purists, only cherries will do, but peaches and apricots (on their own or mixed with cherries), plums (particularly the golden, honey-sweet Mirabelle), figs, pears, and berries—alone or in combination—all work beautifully as well.

I go against tradition in pitting the cherries for clafoutis: many French cooks leave them in for the almond flavor they are said to impart, but pitting them releases some juice into the batter, making the flavor more intriguing to me, as well as reducing the risk of someone losing a tooth—watch out for the inevitable stray pits! Baking the clafoutis in individual dishes makes an attractive alternative to the classic deep-dish version, which can be difficult to cut neatly. I add pastis, an anise-flavored alcohol, to give the clafoutis a southern French kick; you can use any alcohol you have on hand, from the traditional kirsch to brandy, rum, or Grand Marnier. If you happen to have spelt flour, it makes the batter even more delicate.

My students often express surprise at how simply I present clafoutis: at the most, I might add a small mint leaf or a sprinkling of powdered sugar. For me, as for many Niçoise cooks, the appeal of a rustic fruit dessert lies in the quality of the ingredients. Try this "less is more" approach and see what you think!

MAKES 1 LARGE CLAFOUTIS, SERVING 6 TO 8, OR 8 INDIVIDUAL CLAFOUTIS

1 teaspoon unsalted butter for the pie plate, 2 teaspoons for individual dishes

2 tablespoons sugar, preferably light brown cane sugar

1 pound (450 g) cherries

FOR THE BATTER

3 large eggs

½ cup (60 g) spelt, cake, or all-purpose flour

½ cup (100 g) sugar

Pinch of fine sea salt

¾ cup (200 ml) crème fraîche or heavy cream

2 tablespoons pastis (you can also use brandy, rum, Grand Marnier, or kirsch)

Confectioners' sugar for sprinkling

1   Butter a 9-inch (23 cm) deep-dish pie plate or round cake pan with the 1 teaspoon butter and sprinkle it with the sugar, tilting the pan so that the bottom and sides are coated. Alternatively, coat eight shallow crème brûlée dishes with the 2 teaspoons butter and the sugar and place them on one or two baking sheets.

2   In a large bowl, whisk the eggs for about 30 seconds, until slightly fluffy. Add the flour, sugar, and salt and whisk gently until smooth. Gradually whisk in the crème fraîche or heavy cream and pastis (or other alcohol). Set aside at room temperature, covered with a dish towel, for 30 minutes; this will relax the gluten in the flour and produce a more tender result.

3   Meanwhile, pit the cherries using a cherry pitter. (Or leave them intact, as in the traditional version.) Place them in the prepared baking dish(es), where they should fit snugly in one layer.

4   Preheat the oven to 350°F (180°C).

5   Pour the batter over the cherries and transfer the dish(es) to the oven. If making one large clafoutis, bake for 35 to 40 minutes. In individual dishes, the clafoutis will take 20 to 25 minutes to cook. The clafoutis should be browned around the edges, with a few brown spots in the middle, and a toothpick inserted in the center should come out clean. Do not be surprised if the clafoutis puffs up beautifully in the oven and falls as it cools; this is normal, and any wonkiness is part of its charm.

6   Serve warm, preferably, or at room temperature, sprinkled with a little confectioners' sugar.

Cook's note

Bakers from the Limousin prefer to use griottes, or sour cherries, for this dessert; their tartness cuts through the richness of the batter. But since these are difficult to find even in France, I look for small scarlet cherries, which have more acidity and create a better ratio of fruit to batter than the bigger ruby-red varieties.

Variation

For an equally delicious gluten-free clafoutis, replace the flour with ¼ cup (30 g) each almond flour and cornstarch.

Jean-François Torre

CHOUX AU CAFÉ

Coffee cream puffs

One of the things I loved about living on rue du Jésus was waking up to the invigorating scent of roasting coffee beans, which drifted from the end of my narrow street up to my fourth-floor window. Cafés Indien has been in the coffee roasting business since 1925, and the Torre family took over its two Old Town locations in 1975 (it seems no coincidence that the French word for coffee roasting is *torrefaction*).

The current owner, Jean-François, is a third-generation coffee roaster and part of the Third Wave coffee movement, which originated in the English-speaking world. "Instead of relying on the knowledge I had gained working alongside my father and grandfather, I chose to think that I was starting from scratch," he told me. Since his father retired in 2010, Jean-François has twice upgraded the roasting machine, and he changed the house style to a lighter, more aromatic roast that preserves the complexity of his hand-selected beans.

Even if Jean-François and his wife have subtly modernized the family business, it has none of the bare hipster vibe of most urban coffee shops—he describes the decor as a mixture of elbow grease and bargain vintage finds. The rue Pairolière location combines straight-backed wooden church pews with bistro chairs and tables; on the walls are advertising posters, some of them from Jean-François's travels in Tanzania. He is proud of the well-kept Formica shelves, which date from the 1970s and now carry a curated selection of goods, from the latest hand-cranked coffee grinder to locally produced honey and chocolate.

Jean-François's obsession with coffee does not extend to baking with it—"My wife despairs at my baking efforts," he laughs—but his barista and right-hand taster, Hansley Rose, applies his coffee-making precision to classic French pastries. Hansley supplied me with this recipe for choux pastries filled with coffee pastry cream, which I have slightly simplified for home cooks. Taking me back to my childhood love of coffee éclairs, these choux are perfect for spring, an in-between season for local fruit.

Though choux pastry might seem intimidating at first glance, it is surprisingly easy to master. Plan on making the pastry cream ahead of time, so that it can thicken up in the refrigerator before you pipe it. Equip yourself with a pastry bag and ⅓-inch (8 mm) plain tip before making this recipe.

MAKES ABOUT 24 CREAM PUFFS

FOR THE COFFEE PASTRY CREAM
½ cup (120 ml) whole milk
½ cup (120 ml) heavy cream
2 large egg yolks

¼ cup (50 g) sugar
¼ cup (30 g) cornstarch
2 tablespoons unsalted butter
⅓ cup (80 ml) strong coffee, at room temperature

→

FOR THE CHOUX PUFFS

⅓ cup (80 ml) water

⅓ cup (80 ml) whole milk

5 tablespoons (75 g) unsalted butter, cut into ½-inch
   (1 cm) dice

1 teaspoon sugar

1 teaspoon fine sea salt

¾ cup (90 g) all-purpose flour

3 large eggs

FOR THE COFFEE ICING

½ cup (50 g) confectioners' sugar

1 tablespoon strong espresso, or as needed

Coffee beans for decoration (optional)

For the pastry cream

1   In a medium saucepan, bring the milk and cream to a simmer over medium heat.

2   Meanwhile, in a medium bowl, whisk together the egg yolks, sugar, and cornstarch until smooth. Slowly pour in the hot milk and cream mixture, stirring constantly. Return the mixture to the saucepan and bring to a boil over medium heat, whisking constantly, until the pastry cream thickens like pudding. Remove from the heat.

3   Add the butter and coffee to the pastry cream and whisk to combine. Transfer to a shallow pan, press plastic wrap directly against the surface to prevent a skin from forming, and let cool to room temperature. Refrigerate for at least 2 hours, or up to 24 hours, until thoroughly chilled.

For the choux puffs

1   Combine the water, milk, butter, sugar, and salt in a medium saucepan and bring to a boil over medium-high heat, stirring until the butter has completely melted. Remove the saucepan from the heat.

2   Add the flour to the pan all at once and, using a wooden spoon, stir the mixture vigorously until it forms a smooth, shiny ball. Return the saucepan to medium heat and stir for about 30 seconds to dry out the dough a little; a thin skin should form on the bottom of the pan.

3   Transfer the dough to the bowl of a stand mixer fitted with the paddle attachment or to a large bowl. If using the stand mixer, turn it on low and beat for about 1 minute, until most of the steam has dissipated. If mixing by hand, press the dough bit by bit against the sides of the bowl for 1 minute to cool it off.

4   Whisk the first egg in a small bowl and add it to the dough, mixing on medium-low speed or whisking it in by hand. Once it is fully incorporated, do the same with the second egg, and then the third egg. The mixture will look lumpy before becoming smooth again each time, so don't be alarmed.

5   Preheat the oven to 375°F (190°C), with a rack in the bottom third of the oven.

6 Transfer the dough to a pastry bag fitted with a ⅓-inch (8 mm) tip.

7 Line two baking sheets with parchment paper, using a little choux mixture to hold the corners in place. Pipe 12 choux puffs measuring 1½ inches (4 cm) across onto one of the baking sheets, leaving at least 1½ inches (4 cm) between them and staggering the rows. Each chou will have a small peak; using a finger that has been dipped into a small bowl of water, gently flatten these peaks.

8 Bake the choux for 20 to 25 minutes, until puffed and golden. Do not open the oven door during the first 15 minutes; if the choux are not cooking evenly, turn the baking sheet around once the choux have puffed and partially browned.

9 While the first sheet of choux is baking, pipe the second sheet. After you remove the first sheet from the oven, bake the second sheet.

10 When they are cooked, remove the choux from the baking sheets and place on racks to cool for at least 1 hour, and up to overnight; the longer the shells cool, the more crisp they will be.

For the icing

Place the confectioners' sugar in a small bowl and stir in just enough coffee so that the mixture becomes slightly runny but not too thin.

Assemble the puffs

1 Remove the pastry cream from the refrigerator, transfer to a bowl, and whisk well to remove any lumps. Transfer to the cleaned pastry bag, fitted with the cleaned tip.

2 Poke a hole in the bottom of each chou using a skewer or the tip of a small knife, insert the pastry tip into the choux, and fill generously with the pastry cream.

3 Dip the top of each filled chou in the coffee icing and run a clean finger around the edges of the icing so that you have a neat circle. Top each one with a coffee bean, if you like.

4 Transfer the puffs to a plate and refrigerate until the icing sets, about 15 minutes. Serve immediately, or store in a loosely covered container in the refrigerator for up to 2 days.

Cook's note

※

The unfilled baked choux freeze well for up to 2 months. To refresh them, place the still-frozen choux on a baking sheet and heat in a 350°F (180°C) oven for 5 minutes, then cool and fill.

KUMQUATS CONFITS ET LEUR SIROP

Quick-candied kumquats and kumquat syrup

Just the right size to pop into your mouth, this zingy, grape-sized citrus fruit inspires strong feelings in its lovers or haters. I fall into the former camp, relishing the slight bitterness of its edible skin and the burst of acidity from its juicy flesh, which feels to me like a shot of vitamin C.

Even for me, though, there can be such a thing as too many kumquats, and when my kumquat-hating friend Ruby hands over a haul from her prolific tree each year, I find myself looking for ways to use them all up. Making kumquat jam is a labor-intensive process that I don't find rewarding, but when my son Sam used some of the fruits to make a syrup for cocktails, we discovered that the by-product, lightly candied kumquats, is delicious in itself. Cooking the fruits in syrup tempers their bitterness and transforms them into a not-too-sweet candy that even kumquat-skeptics can appreciate.

Round kumquats are generally sweeter than oval ones, but the deeper the orange color, the sweeter the fruit, so try to choose those that are completely ripe.

MAKES 20 TO 25 CANDIED KUMQUATS AND 2 CUPS (500 ML) SYRUP

20 to 25 kumquats (about 7 ounces/200 g)
1 cup (240 ml) water
1 cup (200 g) sugar
A ½-inch (1 cm) piece of fresh ginger, peeled
1 tablespoon mild-tasting honey

1   Cut the kumquats crosswise in half and use the tip of a small knife to remove the seeds (don't squeeze them too much, or you will lose their juice).

2   Place the water and sugar in a medium saucepan and bring to a boil. Add the kumquats, ginger, and honey, and heat until the syrup begins to bubble again, pressing the fruits lightly against the sides of the pan with a wooden spoon to release their juice.

3   Turn off the heat and leave the kumquats in the syrup for at least 1 hour. Then drain the fruits in a sieve set over a bowl; reserve the syrup.

4   Preheat the oven to 125°F (50°C). Line a baking sheet with parchment paper.

5   Spread the kumquats out on the lined baking sheet. Place in the oven for 30 minutes to dry slightly; this will make them a little chewy. (If you prefer, you can let the kumquats dry at room temperature overnight.) Remove from the oven.

6   Both the kumquats and the syrup will keep for several weeks in separate sealed jars in the refrigerator.

SIROP D'ESTRAGON

Tarragon syrup

Because tarragon is a rare find at the markets in Nice, I don't like to waste any of it, yet a little goes a long way in cooking. When I find myself with a large bunch of tarragon, I make this syrup inspired by a vivid green tarragon soda called Tarkhun that I discovered in the Republic of Georgia. My syrup is subtle in color but potent in taste—I like it best mixed with fresh lemon juice and sparkling water to create a slightly licoricey lemonade, but it also makes a creative addition to cocktails (try it with tequila or gin).

MAKES 1¾ CUPS (375 ML)

1 cup (240 ml) water

1 cup (200 g) sugar

About 10 sprigs (40 g) tarragon

1 Place the water and sugar in a medium saucepan and bring to a boil. Add the tarragon, lower the heat to medium, cover, and cook at a gentle boil for 5 minutes. Turn off the heat and let the tarragon infuse for 1 hour.

2 Strain the syrup and transfer to a bottle. It will keep in the refrigerator for 1 month.

SUMMER

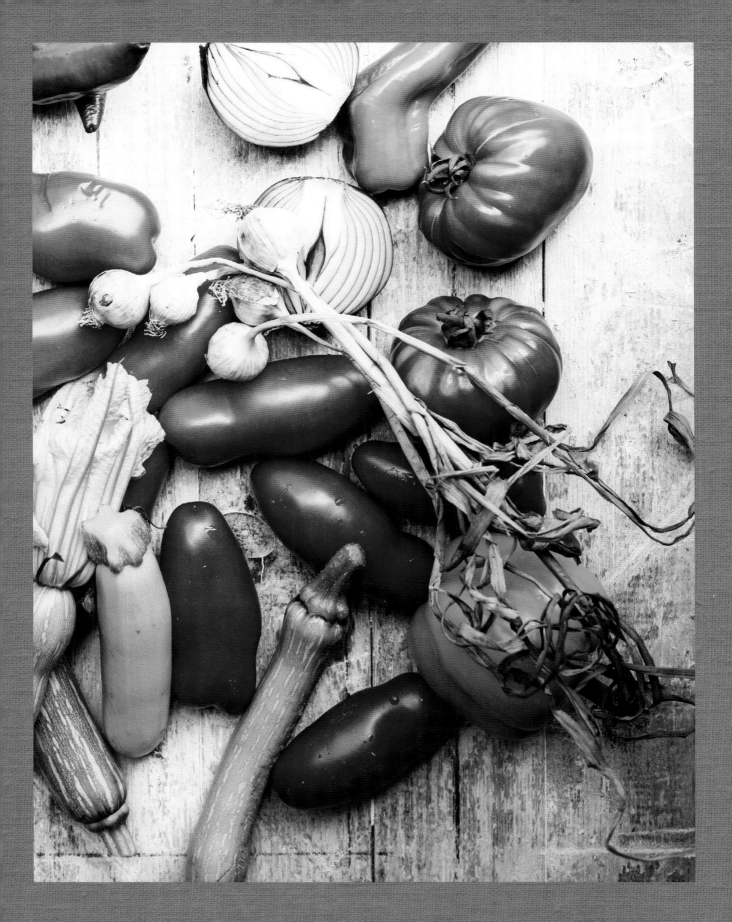

Like most people who live in Nice, I have a love-hate relationship with summer. We wait for it all year, complaining about the slightest cool breeze or drop of rain, and yet when the hot days come, we can't wait for them to be over. With roots in the *arrière-pays* (backcountry), many Niçois take the opportunity to vanish into the mountains for July and August, avoiding the summer crowds and the intense heat. For the rest of us, this season presents a strange dilemma: do we make the most of being in this holiday hotspot, or try to escape it?

My solution has been to embrace the festive atmosphere, but to move away from my narrow Old Town street where I could easily have collided with a somersaulting capoeira dancer when I stepped outside my front door. I love picnicking on the beach until late, eating gelato every day, lingering in the street to watch a jazz quartet, and seeing the joy on the faces of sun-starved (and often sunburned) visitors, but I also love cycling home to my quiet tree-shaded courtyard, a safe distance from the Old Town's raucous nightlife and early-morning street cleaning.

Given Nice's popularity as a summer destination, it's hard to believe that a hundred years ago, it attracted foreigners only in the winter. In the years after World War I, a wealthy American couple, Gerald and Sarah Murphy, arrived in Antibes to find a flourishing artistic scene, and they soon drew the likes of Scott and Zelda Fitzgerald, Ernest Hemingway, and Picasso into their charmed circle. Unlike the British and European aristocracy, who avoided the sun for fear of tanning and looking like peasants, these exuberant Americans took up sunbathing, swimming, and waterskiing during the hottest days of summer. Their love of the sea was infectious, and soon towns along the coast, including Nice, made their beaches accessible to all. The wild *années folles* lasted only a few years, ending in 1929 with the Great Depression, but they changed the French Riviera for good, creating a fantasy to which everyone could aspire.

With the extension of *congés payés*, or paid holidays, to all workers in 1936, the Riviera became popular with French tourists who had heard stories of its endless sunshine and glamorous residents. These visitors discovered a way of eating entirely different from what they knew, and they kept coming back for the salade Niçoise, socca, pissaladière, and pan bagnat, all of them doused with golden olive oil. Even today, northern French tourists come to Nice as if they are visiting another country, which in a way they are.

In my kitchen, the arrival of the long-awaited local tomatoes in mid-June transforms the way I eat for the next three months. The French food writer

Edouard de Pomiane once advised, "When you don't know what to cook, start by boiling a pot of water." In summer, I replace that with, "When in doubt, slice a ripe tomato." With tomatoes come all the vegetables that make up ratatouille, the colorful vegetable stew that the movie of the same name didn't get quite right (see page 163). This is a season for chilled soups, vegetable tians (like a casserole, only sexier), fish with light sauces, and the beloved *merenda* (now more commonly known as the *apéro*), a substantial snack that usually stretches into a meal.

Although some dishes come together quickly, it would be wrong to assume that speediness defines hot-weather cooking in Nice: one of its most emblematic dishes, Petits Farcis (see page 159), requires the stovetop, the oven, and considerable patience to put together. Fortunately, since summer is a time for gatherings of friends and family, you will usually find plenty of extra hands ready to pitch in.

Clockwise from top left: Rustic plum tart (page 177); Cherry clafoutis (page 105); Zucchini baked with eggs and goat cheese (page 142); Ratatouille (page 163); Summer vegetable sandwich (page 133); Little stuffed vegetables (page 159)

ANCHOÏADE
Anchovy dip

In the same family of bold dips as Aïoli (see page 347), anchoïade is an unapologetic ode to the anchovy in all its salty, fishy glory. If the sound of this scares you, keep in mind that a little goes a long way—a dollop of anchoïade has a way of enlivening almost anything, from a classic Vinaigrette (page 349) to steamed artichokes. Provençal cooks once grilled bread over grapevine trimmings to create the perfect, smoky accompaniment; if you don't have these handy, toasted sourdough or baguette will do fine.

Like Pistou (page 343), this sauce would traditionally have been pounded by hand in a mortar; these days, the food processor is your friend. In this version, inspired by one from chef Edouard Loubet in the Luberon, parsley and spring onion add freshness, and a pinch of sugar balances the salty, tangy flavors. It's traditional to use salted anchovies to make anchoïade, desalting the fillets in water for 10 minutes first, but good-quality anchovies in oil work just as well. If you are able to find them in a jar, look for those with rosy flesh rather than the uninspiring gray ones.

Serve the anchoïade with crudités (such as carrot, fennel, cucumber, radishes, radicchio, and mushrooms), crackers, toasted baguette, and/or hard-boiled eggs.

MAKES ABOUT 1 CUP (240 ML)

1 spring onion, white part only (or the white parts of 2 scallions), cut lengthwise in half and sliced into ½-inch (0.5 cm) pieces

1 small garlic clove, cut lengthwise in half

¼ cup (5 g) flat-leaf parsley leaves

A pinch of sugar

15 anchovy fillets, drained of their oil (about 2½ ounces/65 g), roughly chopped

1 teaspoon red wine vinegar

½ cup (120 ml) extra-virgin olive oil

2 to 4 tablespoons (30 to 60 ml) ice water

1   In a food processor, preferably a small one, finely chop the spring onion or scallions, garlic, and parsley with the sugar. Add the anchovy fillets and vinegar and blend thoroughly.

2   With the processor running, pour in the olive oil in a very thin stream. By the time you have added all the oil, the mixture should be very thick and smooth.

3   Add 2 tablespoons ice water 1 tablespoon at a time, processing until the mixture has turned pale in color and thinned to the texture of mayonnaise. If desired, you can add up to 2 tablespoons more ice water, depending on how thick and bold-tasting you would like your anchoïade to be.

4   Serve immediately, or cover and refrigerate for up to 3 days.

CAVIAR D'AUBERGINES AU FROMAGE DE CHÈVRE ET YAOURT

Eggplant caviar with goat cheese and yogurt

With his striped suspenders and electric Mercedes bike, Nadim Beyrouti is one of the most familiar characters at the Cours Saleya market, where he can be found most mornings sniffing out the best produce at the small farmers' stands. At his Old Town restaurant and shop Oliviera, he transforms these treasures into Niçoise dishes with an unmistakable hint of the Middle East.

Born in Palestine and raised in Lebanon, Nadim practically has olive oil running through his veins, so it's easy to see why he has dedicated the past several decades to the lifeblood of the Mediterranean. Southern French olive oil production is small but surprisingly diverse, favoring quality over quantity, and Nadim visits each farm in person during the olive harvest to select the oils that best represent this terroir. For the past several years, he has also produced his own oil at a farm in Castagniers, thirty minutes north of Nice.

In his restaurant, the simple but colorful dishes coming out of the open kitchen serve as a foil for these finds, with Nadim brandishing his bottles like a magician with a wand as he visits each table. Drizzling Bouteillan olive oil over a dish of smoky roasted eggplant mashed with yogurt, goat cheese, lemon, and garlic, he asks playfully, "Does this remind you of a fruit?" Dipping warm baguette into the oil, the guests take a stab: Apple? Citrus?

"It's an exotic fruit," he hints.

Guava? Mango?

"Green banana!" he exclaims.

A spherical olive that's usually picked green and pressed for oil, the Bouteillan is native to Aups, a town in Provence best known for its truffles. Its herbal quality and characteristic notes of fresh hay make it a great match for fish and vegetables as well as Nadim's local take on baba ghanoush, in which fresh goat cheese replaces the traditional tahini. If you don't have access to Bouteillan olive oil, use what you have on hand, tasting the dip with and without the oil. The chile pepper is my addition; I like it for the color and extra bite that it brings to this dish.

Nadim grills his eggplants under the broiler, which gives them a smoky taste, but you can roast them in a very hot oven if you don't want to supervise them so closely. Although this dish is very easy to prepare, allow some time for the eggplants to cool and drain. The dip tastes quite tangy and garlicky at first but mellows after a few hours, so I usually make it ahead of time and store it in the refrigerator until I'm ready to serve it. Nadim likes to serve this dip with bell peppers roasted as for Marinated Bell Peppers with Garlic and Thyme (page 342); you can roast the peppers along with the eggplants. You can also serve it with fresh or toasted baguette, crackers, or crudités.

3 medium eggplants (about 3 pounds/1.3 kg)

1 large garlic clove

A pinch of coarse sea salt

3 ounces (80 g) fresh goat cheese

½ cup (120 ml) Greek yogurt

3 to 4 tablespoons (45 to 60 ml) freshly squeezed lemon juice

Fleur de sel

Bouteillan olive oil or your favorite extra-virgin olive oil for drizzling

Hot or smoked paprika or Espelette chile powder for sprinkling

1 Preheat the broiler to its highest setting.

2 Pierce the eggplants with the tip of a sharp knife, to prevent them from exploding in the oven. Place them on a foil-lined baking sheet.

3 Grill the eggplants about 2 inches (5 cm) from the broiler element, turning once or twice, until their skin is blackened and they feel completely soft when pierced with a knife (check the stem end, as it is usually the last to soften); this should take about 20 minutes. Alternatively, roast the eggplants on a parchment-lined baking sheet in a 400°F (200°C) oven until they have softened completely and their skin is black in patches, about 45 minutes. Remove the eggplants from the heat and set aside on a plate, uncovered, until cool enough to handle, about 15 minutes.

4 Set a sieve over a bowl. Cut the eggplants lengthwise in half, scoop out the flesh with a large spoon, and transfer to the sieve; discard the skins. Let the eggplant flesh stand for at least 30 minutes to drain off any excess liquid and cool completely.

5 Crush the garlic clove to a puree with a pinch of coarse salt in a mortar, or use the flat side of a large knife to crush the garlic on a cutting board, adding a little coarse salt to help reduce it to a paste.

6 Discard the liquid from the eggplant and place the flesh in the bowl of a food processor. Crumble in the goat cheese and pulse a few times—you want to keep some texture. Add the yogurt, garlic, 3 tablespoons lemon juice, and fleur de sel to taste and pulse a few times, until everything is combined but not completely smooth. Taste and adjust the flavor to your liking with more lemon juice and/or salt, if you like. (You can also do this step by hand, as Nadim does, chopping the mixture in a bowl with two round-tipped table knives.)

7 For each serving, spread a couple of heaped tablespoons of the eggplant mixture on a plate or in a shallow bowl and sprinkle with paprika or chile powder. Drizzle generously with olive oil.

COCA FRITA

Turnovers filled with tomato, pepper, and onion

Nothing to do with *le Coca*, the French way of referring to Coca-Cola, la coca frita (plural: cocas) is a vegetable-filled turnover, sold in most bakeries in Nice. The recipe was brought to Nice by the *pieds noirs*, Europeans who lived in Algeria during French rule, and recalls the coca (plural *coques*) found in Catalonia, though the Catalan version may be sweet or savory, with many possible fillings. Empanadas, thought to have originated in Galicia, are another close cousin.

The word *coca* refers to the pastry shell, and *frita* is the name for the filling, which is also delicious on its own as a starter or side dish, or shakshuka-style, with eggs poached in it. Although the frita is not usually spiced, I like to add just enough chile pepper to bring out the other flavors, as I do in ratatouille. I also add a little paprika to the olive oil dough, to give it an intriguing flavor. Goya (goya.com/en/empanada-dough) produces frozen empanada disks that can be found in the freezer section of major grocery stores in the U.S.

If you want to try coca frita in Nice, one of my favorite bakeries, Boulangerie Jean-Marc Bordonnat, sells a superior version, as well as a similar-looking turnover encasing soubressade, a spicy pork and beef sausage that also originated in North Africa.

MAKES 6 TURNOVERS

FOR THE FILLING

4 plum tomatoes (about 1 pound/450 g)

2 tablespoons extra-virgin olive oil

1 red onion, cut lengthwise in half and thinly sliced

Sea salt

3 bell peppers, roasted and peeled as for Marinated Red Peppers with Garlic and Thyme (page 340)

¼ teaspoon chile flakes or Espelette chile powder

FOR THE PASTRY

Olive Oil Pastry (page 360), made with the addition of ½ teaspoon smoked or sweet paprika and chilled for 30 minutes, or 6 ready-made empanada disks (see headnote)

Flour for rolling out the pastry

1 egg

1 Half-fill a medium saucepan with water and bring to a boil. Cut a small cross in the base of each tomato, and remove the cores with a small knife. Lower the tomatoes into the boiling water using a slotted spoon and leave them in the water for 15 to 30 seconds, turning them once or twice with the spoon, until the skin starts to split at the cross. Transfer to a bowl of ice water to cool for a few seconds, then drain and peel off the skins. Dice the tomatoes.

2 Heat the olive oil in a medium frying pan over medium heat. Add the onion with a pinch of salt and cook, stirring occasionally, until pale golden, 8 to 10 minutes.

3 Meanwhile, cut the roasted peppers into strips about 2 inches (5 cm) long and ½ inch (1 cm) wide, saving any juices. →

4 Add the diced tomatoes and any pepper juices to the onions, along with another pinch of salt, and simmer for about 10 minutes, stirring occasionally, until the mixture has thickened.

5 Add the pepper strips and chile flakes or Espelette powder and simmer, stirring occasionally, for another 10 minutes, or until the mixture thickens and starts to stick to the bottom of the pan. Taste and adjust the seasonings. Remove from the heat and set aside to cool to room temperature.

6 Preheat the oven to 350°F (180°C). Line a baking sheet with parchment paper.

7 If using the olive oil pastry, divide it into 6 pieces, shape into balls, and flatten them with the palm of your hand. On a lightly floured surface, roll each piece into a circle about 6 inches (15 cm) in diameter, turning the dough frequently as you roll. Trim the edges using a small bowl as a guide if your circles are too uneven.

8 Place about 2 tablespoons of the filling in the center of each round of dough or empanada disk. Be careful not to overfill the pastries, or the edges will not seal. Fold one half of each round of dough over the filling and press the edges firmly together with your fingers to seal them.

9 Starting at one end, fold and twist the edges of the dough onto itself, ½ inch (1 cm) at a time, so that the border looks like a rope. (You can also simply press the edges down with the tines of a fork to seal them.) Seal each end tightly with your fingers. Place the finished cocas on the baking sheet.

10 Whisk the egg in a small bowl. Brush the pastry with the beaten egg, being careful not to miss any spots.

11 Bake the pastries for 30 to 35 minutes, or until golden brown. Serve warm or at room temperature.

Cook's note

✳

Cocas taste best the day they are made, but they reheat well in the oven the next day—allow about 5 minutes at 350°F (180°C). Any extra filling will keep for up to 3 days in the refrigerator and can be eaten warmed or at room temperature.

TARTE À LA TOMATE, PERSILLADE

Tomato flatbread with garlic and parsley

At La Socca du Cours, always my first stop at the Cours Saleya market, big trays of tarte à la tomate–really more of a flatbread than a tart–glisten with olive oil and give off an intoxicating scent of garlic and herbs. Displayed side by side with Pissaladière (page 191)–made with the same olive-oil-enriched dough and topped with caramelized onions, anchovies, and olives–this tart is a reminder of the lesser role that dairy products play in Niçoise cuisine. Sure, you could add a crumbling of fresh goat or sheep cheese, but the tart is complete without it–for the locals, a few olives would be a more likely addition.

It's fine to use store-bought strained tomatoes, or passata, but be sure to choose beautiful ripe tomatoes to layer on top of this base, which is there to intensify the tomato flavor and to prevent the dough from becoming soggy. Many heirloom varieties, such as the Coeur de Boeuf (beefsteak) sold in France, are meatier than standard tomatoes, which makes them ideal for this tart.

You can serve tarte à la tomate as part of a meal, or cut it into bite-sized pieces to snack on with a glass of rosé. Like so much Niçoise food, it also makes great picnic fare.

SERVES 6 TO 8

2 large or 3 medium tomatoes, preferably heirloom and different colors (about 1 pound/450 g)

Fine sea salt

FOR THE PERSILLADE

½ cup (10 g) lightly packed flat-leaf parsley leaves

1 to 2 garlic cloves, depending on their strength

2 to 3 tablespoons extra-virgin olive oil, plus more for the pan and for drizzling

Fleur de sel or other sea salt

Olive Oil Bread Dough (page 357), allowed to rise until doubled in size

½ cup (120 ml) Coulis de Tomates (page 337) or store-bought passata (Italian strained tomatoes)

1 Cut the tomatoes into slices about ⅛ inch (3mm) thick and place on a rack, without overlapping the slices, set on a large plate or tray. Sprinkle the tomatoes on both sides with fine sea salt and leave to drain for at least 20 minutes. Doing this removes some of the excess liquid that might otherwise make the crust soggy.

2 Meanwhile, make the persillade: Place the parsley leaves and garlic cloves on a cutting board and chop together until finely minced but not pureed (a mezzaluna works well for this). Transfer to a small bowl and stir in enough of the olive oil to make the mixture slightly runny, then add a good pinch of fleur de sel or other sea salt.

3 Preheat the oven to 400°F (200°C). Oil a 12-inch (30 cm) pizza pan or a 12-by-16-inch (30 by 40 cm) baking sheet.

4 Turn the dough out onto the pan and gently press out the air with your hands. Cover with a dish towel and let it rest for 5 minutes, which will make it easier to stretch.

5 Using the palms of your hands, gently stretch the dough until it covers the surface of the pizza pan, or stretch it into an oval about 10 by 13 inches (25 by 35 cm) on the baking sheet.

6 Spread the tomato coulis over the dough, leaving a ½-inch (0.5 cm) border all around, and top with the fresh tomatoes, overlapping them by about ½ inch (1 cm). Do not be tempted to pile up the tomatoes, or they will give off too much juice and make the dough soggy.

7 Bake for 20 minutes. Remove the tart from the oven and top with dabs of persillade, using all of it. Then return it to the oven for 5 minutes, or until the dough has browned on the bottom as well as around the edges. Serve warm or at room temperature, drizzled with a little more olive oil.

Où est le fromage?

Cheese does not play a prominent role in Niçoise cooking, even on flatbreads that vaguely resemble pizza, like Tarte à la Tomate (see page 128) and Pissaladière (page 191). The steep, rocky slopes of the Alpes Maritimes are best suited to agile goats and sheep, though higher up in the mountain plains, especially around Mercantour National Park, some farmers also raise cows to produce fresh milk, yogurt, and wheel-like tommes (aged mountain cheeses).

When I moved to Nice, it was not unusual to see producers selling a few handmade cheeses alongside their vegetables (if you asked nicely, a bottle of homemade wine or beer might also materialize from under the table). But when the European Union tightened its hygiene regulations in the 2000s, requiring all cheesemakers to invest in dedicated stainless steel kitchens, this tradition died out. Now only a handful of committed dairy producers sell their wares at the city's food markets.

Everything has a season in Nice, and cheese is no exception. Goat cheese tastes best in spring and summer, when the animals have been feasting on fresh grass and wildflowers. Jorge Monteiro, who produces exceptional goat cheeses in Peymeinade, near Grasse, explained to me that any shortcuts, even something as seemingly innocuous as picking fresh grass and wildflowers to feed to the goats, have an impact on flavor. "The animals need to choose what they eat."

With his wife, Isabelle, Jorge has been making cheese since the 1970s, when he came to France from Portugal to work on a goat farm. His first employer had a mishap with a beehive that landed him in the hospital, and sixteen-year-old Jorge took over. To thank him, the farmer gave him two goats, which was enough to convince him to stay in France at a time when Portuguese immigrants were not especially welcome. "I couldn't leave my goats," he told me.

Working with his son and daughter-in-law, he now sells his cheeses to a handful of *fromageries* in the region, and to top restaurants like the Louis XV in Monaco. Instead of becoming dry and chalky as they age, his cheeses grow creamy just beneath the rind, without ever developing the "barnyard" flavor that often characterizes goat cheese.

When goat cheese season ends in late fall, sheep's-milk cheese season begins: Jean-Luc Trannoy, who sells his fromages de brebis at the Cours Saleya market, comes only during the winter and early spring. Jean-Luc is the only farmer I know who also sells brousse de brebis, fresh cheese curds, that have the texture of soft tofu. Their mild, milky flavor makes them especially good with jam or honey, but they are also delicious with olive oil and herbs.

Compared to more cheese-centric cities like Paris or Lyon, Nice does not have many cheese shops, so I was delighted when my friend Thomas Métin opened his fromagerie on rue Pairolière, alongside many of the Old Town's historic food shops. I first met this native Niçois in Paris, where he lived after perfecting his craft in New Zealand and at Harrod's in London, and he opened a shop in the town of Vence before branching out into Nice. Each shop has a cellar where he ages the cheeses that he hand-selects directly at the farms, putting his own stamp on the finished product.

Thomas sells cheeses from all over France, bringing out oozy vacherins and crackly aged Comté at Christmas, but I love his display of fresh goat's- and sheep's-milk cheeses, some of them coated with flowers or herbs at the shop. To find these, he often ventures beyond the Alpes Maritimes to Provence, where the animals graze on aromatic plants that give the cheeses an especially complex flavor. My son worked at Fromagerie Métin for a summer, and although we sampled many cheeses during that time (and Sam developed a bit of an obsession with the fluffy cheesecake), it would be impossible to taste the hundreds Thomas has on offer.

Because local cheeses are not available in large quantities, the Niçois have historically served them as a separate course. That is the best way to appreciate cheeses that have been aged for a few days to bring out their subtle floral and herbal flavors. These call for nothing more than a slice of Quince Paste (page 253) or a handful of seasonal fruits like grapes or cherries for contrast—in summer, Thomas especially loves the burst of acidity that comes from red currants. I also like to sprinkle the milder-tasting fresh cheeses with crushed peppercorns or herbes de Provence and drizzle them with fruité noir olive oil, which tastes distinctly of olives. For breakfast, I eat Jorge's cheese on toasted baguette with fresh figs and chestnut honey—being a purist, he thoroughly disapproves of this adulteration!

Thomas Métin

PAN BAGNAT

Summer vegetable sandwich with tuna

Pan bagnat, which translates as "bathed bread," originally made use of stale bread, which was broken into rough chunks and tossed with tomatoes and olive oil. The recipe has evolved over the years, and today it's a kind of salade Niçoise in a bun that has been doused in olive oil and red wine vinegar. You will find pan bagnat in every bakery in Nice and at roadside kiosks, the best of which have legions of loyal customers. At the Cours Saleya market, you can still see the vendors assembling this sandwich with the ingredients they have on hand to calm midmorning hunger pangs, just as workers have done since the nineteenth century.

Though some bakeries prepare mini pan bagnats using soft brioche dough, pan bagnat normally comes in a crusty bun so gargantuan that it looks unfinishable (though that is, in fact, rarely the case). Some places—including one of my favorites, the bistro La Vieille Maison in Eze Plage—replace the bun with baguette, which, although not traditional, creates a pleasing balance of bread to filling. Another trick for achieving this balance is to scoop out some of the bun's crumb, making more space for the other ingredients.

This sandwich inspires such strong feelings that since 1991, a local association known as the "Free Commune of Pan Bagnat" has defended it by awarding a label of authenticity to establishments that follow their official recipe. Permitted ingredients include ripe tomatoes, radishes, spring onions, long green peppers, tuna and/or anchovies in oil, hard-boiled eggs, basil, and black olives (no celery or cucumber!). You may remove elements but not add ingredients beyond what is on the list, or the ban bagnat risks becoming "a vulgar vegetable sandwich."

My complaint with some pan bagnats is that they are heavier on the tuna and egg than on the vegetables; I love this sandwich when it is fresh, crunchy, and colorful. I often leave out the egg, which to me has its place in salade Niçoise but can make the sandwich a little pasty (if you do include it, try cutting the egg into thin wedges, as the locals do). If you can make the sandwiches an hour or two in advance, so much the better.

FOR THE ROLLS

A double recipe of Olive Oil Bread Dough (page 357), allowed to rise until doubled in size, or 4 or 6 store-bought crusty buns (6 buns measuring about 5 inches/12 cm across or 4 measuring about 6 inches/15 cm across)

Flour for the work surface

FOR THE FILLING

3 large eggs, at room temperature (optional)

1 garlic clove, cut in half (optional)

6 tablespoons (90 ml) extra-virgin olive oil

Red wine vinegar for sprinkling

Three 4.5-ounce (120 g) cans tuna in olive oil, drained (or tuna in jars, weighing about 14 ounces/360 g total)

2 beefsteak tomatoes (about 1 pound (450 g) total), sliced ¼ inch (0.5 cm) thick

6 to 8 radishes, thinly sliced

2 spring onions, white and pale green parts only, thinly sliced

1 celery stalk, thinly sliced (optional)

2 mild-tasting long green peppers, such as Anaheim, thinly sliced

One 2-ounce (50 g) can anchovies in oil

¼ cup (45 g) pitted Niçoise olives

12 large basil leaves

Sea salt and freshly ground black pepper

For the rolls

1 Turn the dough out on a lightly floured board, gently press out the air, and divide it into 4 or 6 pieces, depending on the size of sandwich that you would like. Shape each one into a ball and place on a baking sheet lined with parchment paper. Flatten the balls to about 1 inch (2.5 cm) thick, using the palm of your hand. Set aside to rise for about 30 minutes.

2 Preheat the oven to 400°F (200°C).

3 Make three shallow slashes around the sides of each bun, using a sharp or serrated knife, and bake for about 20 minutes until golden brown. Transfer the buns to a rack to cool completely.

For the eggs, if using

Bring a small pot of water to a boil. Add the eggs to the boiling water and cook for 8 minutes if you like the yolks slightly creamy, or 10 minutes for hard-boiled eggs. Transfer the eggs to a bowl of ice water to cool, then drain, peel, and cut each one into 6 wedges.

Assemble the sandwiches

1 Split the rolls in half and remove some of the crumb from the top halves, if you like. Gently rub the bottom halves with the cut garlic clove, if using. Drizzle with the olive oil and sprinkle with red wine vinegar to taste.

2 Place 2 slices of tomato on the bottom half of each bun. Flake the tuna onto them and top with the sliced vegetables. Finish with the eggs, if using, anchovies, olives, and basil and season with salt and pepper. Press the top half of each bun down so that the bread absorbs some of the juices. Let stand for at least 10 minutes, and up to 2 hours, before serving.

Blossoms, blossoms everywhere

Zucchini blossoms are so plentiful and cheap at the markets in Nice that it's easy to take the big bunches of vivid yellow blossoms for granted. Yet there is something miraculous about these flowers, whose petals are sturdy enough to hold a cheese filling, but so delicate that they turn translucent when cooked.

I didn't really understand why zucchini blossoms played such a big role in Niçoise cooking until I planted a single trompette zucchini plant in my *jardinet*, or mini-garden. Niçoise cooks take little interest in the common dark green zucchini, which I now dub "last resort zucchini," since—following their lead—I only ever buy it when the local trompette variety or the pale green Italienne are not in season.

The trompette is a zucchini that morphs into a winter squash if allowed to fully mature. In its zucchini phase, it has a lime-green color with beautiful emerald stripes, and a slightly bulbous end (hence the name *trumpet*); as you slice it, you'll find a curled pattern inside that recalls musical notes, and no seeds. The taste is delicate and slightly nutty, and it takes equally well to being lightly sautéed, grilled, or slow-cooked (or even served raw, carpaccio-style), always holding its shape.

If you let it grow—that is, if you turn your back on it for a few seconds—the skin turns dark green and the flesh takes on an orange tinge, with seeds beginning to form in the rounded end. At this point, the zucchini can still be sliced and sautéed, but the flavor is stronger; I prefer it grated into fritters or American-style zucchini bread. Finally, around September, it reaches full size—which can be as long as a limb—with musky orange-gray skin and deep orange flesh. The fully developed squash is known as *courge de Nice*, and it makes beautiful soup (see page 204) and gratins. At the market, it's sold in chunks, since lugging a whole one home would be more like carrying a trombone than a trumpet.

By the time I planted my single seed, I had long since figured out that the courgette trompette and courge de Nice came from the same plant. What I didn't know then was just how many blossoms each plant produces. Seeing the abundance of male flowers (the ones that grow on stems and never develop fruit) compared to the handful of female flowers (which cling to the end of each zucchini), I realized that the local love of zucchini blossoms simply grew out of a desire to use up this surplus. Male flowers are the ones most often used for cooking because their stems make them easy to handle, and the petals are less likely to tear.

When you see a bunch of wide-open zucchini blossoms at the market, you can be sure that they were picked the same morning; within a day of being parted from their vine, they start to close up, making them impossible to stuff. The sight of bees buzzing around them is a good sign, since it means that they are organic; bees feel the same way about chemically treated produce as Niçoise cooks do about dark-green zucchini. I rush the flowers back to the kitchen, lay them on a plate (after gently releasing any bugs), and cover them with a damp paper towel or cloth; they will keep like this in the refrigerator for several hours if you can't use them right away.

In Nice, zucchini blossoms may be dipped in batter and fried, or stuffed and baked, but they are never stuffed and fried, as you see in Italy. I have come to embrace this restrained approach, which highlights the blossoms' delicate squash flavor. When I find myself with extra blossoms, like the ones that come on the ends of very fresh zucchini, I often tear them up and throw them into a salad; lay them on top of a tian, like rays of sunshine, before baking (see page 138); or sauté them with other vegetables. I do not bother to remove the three-pronged stigma from the female flowers or the smaller, pollen-coated anther from the male blossoms, though some cooks pick them out assiduously, claiming they can taste bitter.

If you would like to grow a similar squash, look for trombetta di Albenga or trombocino squash seeds, which are sold by some specialty companies in North America. Although not identical to the trompette de Nice, with longer, skinnier necks, they are just as flavorful and generous with their blossoms.

FLEURS DE COURGETTE FARCIES, SALSA NIÇOISE

Stuffed zucchini blossoms with Niçoise "salsa"

In Nice, there are two possible ways to stuff zucchini blossoms. One is rice-based, with diced zucchini, onion, ham, and egg; the other a mixture of brousse, Parmesan, herbs, and just enough egg to bind it all together. The latter version is my favorite, and it also happens to be the quickest to make.

Like ricotta, brousse is made from the whey of cow's, sheep's, or goat's milk; the word means "to beat," because the liquid is beaten to separate the curds from the whey. Depending on the richness of the milk and how thoroughly the cheese has been drained, it may be quite dry, very soft, or somewhere in between. If the brousse (or ricotta) has excess liquid when you buy it, place it in a strainer set over a bowl to drain for at least 30 minutes before mixing it with the other ingredients; alternatively, if it seems dry, you can enrich it with a little cream or milk. Sheep's-milk ricotta is the creamiest, with a slightly more distinctive flavor, but the cow's-milk version also works well here, providing a neutral foil for the herbs, Parmesan, and lemon zest.

I like to serve these stuffed blossoms with a cherry tomato salad that I have dubbed Niçoise salsa; I add a shallot rather than onion or garlic so as not to overwhelm the subtle flavor of the cheese filling. A spoonful of Coulis de Tomates (page 337) also makes a good match, along with a handful of arugula or other lively greens. The blossoms look prettiest when served fresh from the oven, as they deflate a little as they cool, but they do reheat well in a frying pan with a little olive oil.

SERVES 4 TO 6

1¾ cups (450 g) cow's- or sheep's-milk ricotta

1 large egg

¼ cup (20 g) freshly grated Parmesan

1 tablespoon grated lemon zest (preferably from an organic lemon)

½ cup (10 g) basil leaves, thinly sliced

¼ cup (5 g) mint leaves, thinly sliced

Sea salt and freshly ground black pepper

12 "male" zucchini blossoms (see box, page 136), with ½ inch (1 cm) of stem

A little olive oil for the baking dish

2 tablespoons unsalted butter

2 tablespoons water

2 tablespoons breadcrumbs

FOR THE NIÇOISE SALSA

2 cups (8 ounces/225 g) cherry tomatoes

1 shallot, finely minced

2 tablespoons thinly sliced basil leaves

1 tablespoon thinly sliced mint leaves

3 tablespoons extra-virgin olive oil

1 tablespoon sherry vinegar (or substitute wine vinegar)

Fleur de sel

1 Preheat the oven to 350°F (175°C).

2 Mash the ricotta with a fork in a medium bowl. Add the egg, Parmesan, lemon zest, herbs, and salt and pepper to taste and mash together well. Taste and adjust the seasoning if necessary.

3 Using a pastry bag fitted with a tip at least ½ inch (1 cm) wide, or using a small spoon, fill the zucchini flowers generously with the ricotta mixture (they should bulge appetizingly), twisting the ends of the petals to close them. Place the flowers in an oiled baking dish with the twisted ends against the sides to keep them closed.

4 Melt the butter and whisk in the water. Using a pastry brush, paint the zucchini blossoms with this mixture; this will help them retain moisture as they bake while also making them glossy. Sprinkle lightly with the breadcrumbs. Pour any excess butter-water mixture over the blossoms.

5 Bake the zucchini blossoms for about 20 minutes, until they are pale golden.

6 Meanwhile, make the salsa: Cut the cherry tomatoes into quarters and place them in the bowl. Stir in the shallot, slivered herbs, olive oil, vinegar, and fleur de sel to taste (season the salsa at the last minute so as not to draw too much juice out of the tomatoes).

7 To serve, spoon the salsa into a shallow bowl and top with the zucchini blossoms.

Variation

If you can't find zucchini blossoms, you can use this filling to stuff 12 small round zucchini or 4 medium-sized long zucchini. For round zucchini, cut off the caps and hollow out the zucchini. For long zucchini, cut them lengthwise in half and then into 2-inch (5 cm) chunks. Hollow out each chunk to make a little boat. Parcook the zucchini in boiling salted water for 4 to 5 minutes, until tender when pierced with a knife; drain upside down on paper towels. Stuff the zucchini with the ricotta mixture, top with the breadcrumbs, drizzle with olive oil, and bake as for the flowers.

FLEURS DE COURGETTE, FAÇON TEMPURA

Tempura zucchini blossoms

The traditional batter for frying zucchini blossoms can be heavy, but many chefs are switching to this lighter Japanese version, which allows you to appreciate the flowers' vivid yellow color and subtle squash flavor.

These blossoms are often eaten as street food, but you can also serve them as a starter.

SERVES 6

1 cup (240 ml) ice water

1 large egg

1¼ cups (150 g) tempura flour or 1 cup (120 g) all-purpose or cake flour mixed with ¼ cup (30 g) cornstarch

2 to 3 cups (500 to 750 ml) peanut or sunflower oil, depending on the size of your pan

12 "male" zucchini blossoms (see box, page 136), with ½ inch (1 cm) of stem

Fleur de sel

1   In a medium bowl, combine the water and egg with chopsticks or a fork. Add the tempura flour (or flour and cornstarch) all at once and stir briefly. The batter will be a bit lumpy.

2   Heat the oil in a wok, sauté pan, or medium saucepan to 350°F (180°C); the oil should be at least 1½ inches (4 cm) deep. Test the temperature using a thermometer, or drop a little batter into the hot oil; if it sinks to the bottom and then immediately floats to the top, the oil is at the correct temperature.

3   Working in batches, dip the flowers into the batter, turning them so that they are completely coated, then add to the oil and fry, turning once, until crisp and pale golden, about 1 minute on each side. Be careful not to overfill the pan; fry no more than 3 blossoms at a time.

4   Drain the fried blossoms on paper towels and serve immediately, sprinkled with fleur de sel.

TIAN DE COURGETTES ET DE CHÈVRE

Zucchini baked with eggs and goat cheese

This eggy variation on a tian (oven-cooked Provençal vegetables) is like a baked frittata or crustless quiche. Zucchini blossoms make for a stunning presentation when you arrange them on top like the rays of the sun. But even without them, this is a perfect dish to take to a summer barbecue or to serve as part of a brunch or lunch.

SERVES 4 TO 6

8 small or 4 medium zucchini (a mixture of green and yellow if possible; about 1 pound 6 ounces/600 g)

2 spring onions, white and pale green parts only

1 tablespoon extra-virgin olive oil, plus a little more for the baking dish and (optional) zucchini blossoms

Sea salt

Half a garlic clove, with its skin

1 teaspoon unsalted butter

2 tablespoons freshly grated Parmesan

6 large eggs

⅓ cup (80 ml) heavy cream

Freshly ground black pepper

¼ cup (5 g) basil leaves, thinly sliced

3 ounces (80 g) soft goat cheese

4 zucchini blossoms (optional)

1 Preheat the oven to 350°F (180°C).

2 Cut the zucchini into matchstick pieces about 2 inches (5 cm) long and ¼ inch (0.5 cm) thick. Thinly slice the spring onions.

3 In a large frying pan, heat the olive oil over medium-high heat. Add the zucchini and spring onions, spread them out, and cook for 1 minute undisturbed. Then continue to cook, tossing occasionally (which damages the vegetables less than stirring), until the zucchini has some pale gold spots, 3 to 4 minutes. Season with salt and remove from the heat.

4 Rub a 9-inch (23-cm) deep-dish pie plate (preferably ceramic) with the half garlic clove, then coat with the butter. Sprinkle the bottom and sides of the dish with the Parmesan.

5 In a medium bowl, beat the eggs with the cream and season with salt and pepper to taste. Stir in the basil.

6 Place half the zucchini in the dish, crumble half the goat cheese over top, and top with the remaining zucchini and the rest of the goat cheese. Pour the egg-cream mixture over the top.

7 Cut the zucchini blossoms, if using, lengthwise in half, and brush the outsides with olive oil. Place them on top of the egg mixture, oiled side up, and press down lightly, so that they partially sink in.

8 Bake for 30 minutes, or until the tian is lightly puffed and set in the center. Serve warm or at room temperature.

AUBERGINES ROULÉES AUX SARDINES ET AU PAMPLEMOUSSE

Eggplant rolls with sardines and grapefruit

Nazih Borghol and I met through Instagram when he was living in his native Beirut, and we became friends when he moved to this region and attended one of my classes. When I invited him to a beach picnic, he showed up with these light and deceptively simple eggplant rolls, whose unexpected combination of flavors is typical of his Mediterranean-Japanese cooking style. You could grill fresh sardines, but these rolls are equally delicious with sardine fillets packed in olive oil, which are easier to find. Look for Japanese green chile-yuzu paste in Asian supermarkets, or use grated lemon zest and chile powder instead.

SERVES 4 TO 6

⅓ cup (30 g) walnut halves

2 medium eggplants (about 1 pound/450 g each), sliced lengthwise ½ inch (1 cm) thick

Sea salt

¼ cup (60 ml) extra-virgin olive oil

1 pink or yellow grapefruit

Two 4-ounce (110 g) cans sardine fillets, drained and oil reserved

Freshly ground black pepper

Green yuzu kosho (Japanese green chile-yuzu paste) to taste, or 1 tablespoon finely grated lemon zest (preferably from an organic lemon) and your favorite chile powder to taste

¼ cup (60 ml) freshly squeezed lemon juice (from 1 large lemon)

¼ cup (5 g) mint leaves, thinly sliced

Freshly ground black pepper

1 Preheat the oven to 325°F (160°C).

2 Spread the walnuts on a baking sheet and toast in the oven for 10 minutes, or until fragrant. Remove from the oven and let the walnuts cool, then break into smaller pieces. Turn the oven temperature up to 450°F (230°C).

3 Line two baking sheets with parchment paper. Lay the eggplant slices on the baking sheets, sprinkle lightly on both sides with salt, and brush on both sides with the olive oil.

4 Roast the eggplant slices for 15 minutes, then flip over with a spatula and roast for 5 more minutes, or until golden but not dry. Remove from the oven.

5   While the eggplant is roasting, cut off the top and bottom from the grapefruit, so that the flesh is exposed and the fruit can sit flat on one end. Using a small sharp knife, cut off the peel from top to bottom, following the curve of the grapefruit and removing as much of the bitter white pith as you can. Trim off any remaining pith. Slice each segment away from the membranes on each side, then cut crosswise into ½-inch (1 cm) slices.

6   Brush the warm eggplant on both sides with some of the oil from the sardines and the lemon juice. Sprinkle with salt and pepper and let cool.

7   Dab the eggplant with a little green yuzu kosho, if using (keep in mind that it is quite spicy). Or sprinkle with the lemon zest and chile powder to taste. Lay one sardine fillet across the bottom end of each slice of eggplant and roll up in the eggplant.

8   Arrange the rolls in a serving dish and scatter the toasted walnuts, grapefruit chunks, and mint over them. Serve at room temperature.

SALADE DE COUSCOUS

Summer couscous salad

I first tasted couscous salad in my school cafeteria when I spent a year in Paris at age thirteen, and instantly fell in love with it. You will see it sold in any French *charcuterie*, which sells pork products alongside an assortment of salads. Some versions of this salad are more inspired than others–my son swears by the prepackaged one sold in the supermarket chain Monoprix for around 2 euros. For me, salade de couscous must always have raisins, plenty of parsley and mint, olive oil, and lemon juice, but all the other ingredients are variable, depending on your mood (or your leftovers!) and the season.

Here is a colorful ratatouille-inspired version that you can make in summer, dressing it up with feta or goat cheese or leftover slices of lamb or chicken to make a complete meal. This salad makes great picnic or barbecue fare, and you can easily double the recipe, though it would be best in that case to cook the vegetables in two batches so that they are not piled up in the pan. Be sure to choose North African couscous, which has fine grains, rather than the small pasta known as Israeli couscous (although that would make a nice variation, cooked according to the package directions). You can replace the couscous with another grain, such as cooked quinoa, bulgur, wheat, or rice, if you like.

SERVES 4 TO 6

¾ cup (125 g) medium-grain couscous

¼ cup (60 ml) extra-virgin olive oil

1 teaspoon ground cumin

A pinch of ground cinnamon

¼ teaspoon chile powder or hot paprika (optional)

¼ cup (40 g) golden raisins

Sea salt

¾ cup (180 ml) water or vegetable stock, homemade (page 355) or store-bought

1 red or yellow bell pepper, cored, seeded, and cut into ¼-inch (0.5 cm) dice

1 small red onion, cut into ¼-inch (0.5 cm) dice

1 medium zucchini (about 6 ounces/150 g), cut into ¼-inch (0.5 cm) dice

½ cup (10 g) packed flat-leaf parsley leaves, thinly sliced

¼ cup (5 g) packed mint leaves, thinly sliced

¼ cup (60 ml) freshly squeezed lemon juice (from 1 large lemon), or more to taste

Very good extra-virgin olive oil for drizzling

1 Place the couscous in a heatproof serving bowl that can later hold all the vegetables, and add 1 tablespoon of the olive oil, the cumin, cinnamon, chile powder or paprika, if using, raisins, and a big pinch of sea salt. Stir with a metal spoon to coat all the grains with oil.

2 Bring the water or stock to a boil and pour it over the couscous, making sure all the grains are immersed. Cover with a plate and set aside for 5 minutes, then remove the plate and fluff the couscous with a fork.

3   Heat 2 tablespoons of the olive oil in a large frying pan over high heat. Add the vegetables, with a sprinkling of salt, and cook, tossing or stirring occasionally, until they are light golden in patches but still retain some bite, 7 to 8 minutes. Remove from the heat.

4   Add the vegetables to the couscous and stir well. Set aside to cool for about 10 minutes.

5   Add the parsley and mint, the remaining tablespoon of olive oil, and the lemon juice to the couscous-vegetable mixture and stir to combine well. Adjust the seasonings to taste.

6   Serve at room temperature or cold, with a drizzle of very good olive oil.

SOUPE DE POISSONS DE ROCHE

Rockfish soup

What bouillabaisse is to Marseille, soupe de poissons is to Nice. Here cooks make a pureed orange-red soup with an assortment of the small fish found in the rocky coves along the coast from Cannes to Menton. These might include lesser-known Mediterranean fish like scorpion fish, bogue, goby, and wrasse, as well as the small crabs called *favouilles*. The fish are simply cooked with onion, ripe tomatoes, plenty of garlic, and spices, then pureed and strained to make a powerfully flavored soup that is served with the equally potent rouille, a garlic, saffron, and chile mayonnaise.

Fortunately, soupe de poissons is more flexible than bouillabaisse, and you can make it with any combination of small white fish; I have provided a few examples, but use what you can find, as long as the fish are whole. Avoid oily fish, though, such as mackerel or sardines, which taste too strong for this soup. Do not be surprised at the generous amount of olive oil, nor the seemingly reckless quantity of salt; fishermen once cooked this soup using seawater, and the result truly tastes of the Mediterranean. You will need a blender or food mill and a conical stainless steel strainer, known as a chinois, or other strainer, to obtain the right texture.

I like to serve soupe de poissons followed by a selection of local cheese and some mesclun. If you want to make the meal more substantial, add a vegetable tian (pages 142, 166, and 201) as a separate course.

SERVES 6

A pinch of saffron threads

Fine sea salt

4 cups (1 l) water, plus 1 tablespoon

Sea salt

2½ pounds (1.2 kg) mixed whole white fish such as sea bream, sea bass (branzino), red gurnard, and redfish (ideally no longer than 10 inches/25 cm, but you may need to adapt according to what you can find), cleaned and scaled

2 onions, cut lengthwise in half and thinly sliced

½ cup (120 ml) extra-virgin olive oil

1 head garlic, washed and cut horizontally in half

2 tablespoons tomato paste, diluted in ¼ cup (60 ml) water

4 large ripe tomatoes (about 2 pounds/900 g), cut into rough chunks (without peeling), or one 28-ounce (800 g) can plum tomatoes

A 3-inch (7 cm) strip of orange zest, removed with a vegetable peeler

1 teaspoon fennel seeds

1½ tablespoons coarse sea salt

Freshly ground black pepper

½ teaspoon chile flakes

1 baguette, cut into ½-inch (1 cm) slices

FOR SERVING

Rouille (page 348)

1 cup (70 g) freshly grated Parmesan or Emmental

1 Crush the saffron in a mortar with a pinch of salt (or rub the threads and salt between your fingers to crush them and put in a small bowl) and add the 1 tablespoon water. Set aside. (If you have not yet made the rouille, double the quantity of the saffron-water mix so that you have some for the rouille.)

2 Cut any fish larger than 4 inches (10 cm) long into pieces about 3 to 4 inches (7 to 10 cm) long, without discarding the head(s).

3 In a large heavy saucepan, cook the onions in the olive oil with a generous pinch of salt over low heat for about 15 minutes, stirring frequently, until translucent but still pale.

4 Add the fish, raise the heat to medium, and cook, stirring, for about 5 minutes, until the flesh starts to look white.

5 Add the garlic halves, diluted tomato paste, tomatoes, orange zest, fennel, coarse sea salt, black pepper to taste, and chile flakes. Add the remaining 4 cups (1 l) water and bring to a boil, stirring. Boil over medium heat, stirring occasionally and skimming off the foam that rises to the surface, for 30 minutes. Remove from the heat.

6 Meanwhile, make the croutons: Preheat the oven to 325°F (160°C).

7 Arrange the baguette slices on a baking sheet and toast for 10 minutes, until mostly dried. Turn off the heat and leave the croutons in the oven until you need them.

8 Pick out and discard the garlic halves and any large pieces of bone from the soup. Using an immersion blender or stand blender, blend the soup to as fine a puree as possible; or pass it through a food mill.

9 Strain the resulting puree through a chinois (conical stainless steel strainer) or other not-too-fine strainer into a bowl or other container, working with about 1 cup (240 ml) of the soup at a time; press on the solids with a small ladle to extract as much liquid as possible, then discard the solids. (Do not use a very fine strainer or cheesecloth—the soup should have some texture rather than being a broth.) Once you have strained all the soup, add the saffron and its soaking water. Adjust the seasonings.

10 You can serve the soup now, but if you are making it ahead of time, cool it in an ice-water bath and keep in a sealed container in the refrigerator for up to 24 hours. You can also freeze this soup for up to 3 months.

11 Just before serving, bring the soup to a boil. Ladle into bowls while still very hot. Slather the croutons with the rouille, top with the cheese, and float them in the soup. They will dissolve into the soup as you eat, making it even more delicious.

SARDINES FARCIES

Stuffed sardines

Up a few steps off the Old Town's busiest pedestrian street, La Table Alziari does not immediately stand out with its ocher facade and handful of tables outside, yet this family-run bistro has long been one of the city's culinary gems. When I moved to Nice, I often ran into its founder, André, scoping out the best products at the Cours Saleya market. André still works front of house there with his daughter-in-law, Aurélie (who now takes care of the market shopping), while his son, Michel, has proudly run the kitchen for the past twenty-one years, keeping the memory of his mother, Anne-Marie, and his two grandmothers alive.

Every regular has a favorite dish from the restaurant's short repertoire: for one chef friend, it's the daube d'agneau, lamb stewed in red wine, while I inevitably order the sardines farcies, fresh sardines with a crispy, cheesy topping. Too busy to write up his recipe for the sardines, Michel invited me into his kitchen to watch him make this Niçoise classic. In a space barely large enough for two that he shares with his sous-chef, Roland, he wielded his kitchen tools like a percussionist, tending to multiple dishes at once.

Like many children of farmers and restaurateurs, Michel did not plan to go into the family business, but he found himself lured back by circumstance. He studied to be a computer engineer before coming to help out when his mother, who was then the chef, fell ill. Although running a kitchen is demanding, he has no regrets about abandoning his first career. "If I were an engineer, I would work from 7 a.m. to 9 p.m. This way, I have time off in the afternoon to spend with my children, and on quiet nights, we go home early. We don't take ourselves too seriously; in the end, we are only making food."

For Michel, "only making food" means mixing all his doughs by hand and working without a freezer. "The principle behind the restaurant is that we have a short menu using only fresh ingredients, and that's never going to change."

The stuffed sardine recipe, which came from one of his grandmothers, has a secret ingredient: Cantal cheese, which is similar to cheddar and comes from the Auvergne region in central France. "She hated revealing that," Michel says, laughing. Mixed with Emmental, it makes the filling especially cheesy and adds a touch of sharpness that cuts through the Swiss chard.

Although fresh sardines can be difficult to find in North America, I wanted to include this recipe because I love it so much, and because small, oily fish like sardines and mackerel have so much to offer in terms of flavor and health benefits. If you are lucky enough to find fresh sardines, it's worth preparing plenty of these, as I promise they will disappear quickly and convert any sardine-skeptics! They may be served as a starter, with a salad, but they can also feature as a main course if the servings are generous.

1 onion, peeled

Sea salt

2 bunches thin-stemmed Swiss chard (about 2 pounds/900 g), stems trimmed of any hard ends

1 cup (20 g) flat-leaf parsley leaves, including small stems

½ cup (about 100 g) diced salt pork or unsmoked pancetta

1⅓ cups (100 g) finely grated Emmental or Gruyère

1⅓ cups (100 g) finely grated Cantal or white cheddar

1 large egg

2 slices day-old sourdough bread or 4 slices day-old baguette (about 2 ounces/50 g), broken into small chunks and soaked in ½ cup (120 ml) whole milk for at least 15 minutes

Freshly ground black pepper

30 fresh sardines (about 2¼ pounds /1 kg), scaled and butterflied (see Cook's Note)

½ cup (60 g) fine breadcrumbs for sprinkling

Extra-virgin olive oil for drizzling

1 Parcook the onion by boiling it in a pot of water for 30 minutes, or (as Michel does) by placing it in a microwave-safe bowl of water and cooking it in the microwave for 14 minutes. Drain and set aside to cool for at least 30 minutes, then squeeze to remove most of the water.

2 Meanwhile, bring a large pot of water to a boil and salt generously. Add the Swiss chard and boil for 4 to 5 minutes, until tender. Drain in a colander, rinse under cold water, and squeeze to remove as much water as you can.

3 Roughly chop the chard with a chef's knife.

4 Using a meat grinder (ideally) or a food processor, finely mince the onion, chard, parsley, and salt pork or pancetta together and transfer to a bowl. (Or finely chop the ingredients individually with a sharp chef's knife and transfer to the bowl.) Add the grated cheeses and the egg, then add the soaked baguette, squeezing out the excess milk. Season with salt and pepper to taste and mix well to make a stuffing that holds together when squeezed between your fingers.

5 Preheat the oven to its highest setting, at least 500°F (240°C), and preferably 550°F (270°C), with a rack in the upper third.

6 Line two baking sheets with foil and arrange the sardines on the baking sheets, leaving space between them. Take a small handful of stuffing, squeeze it together, and pat it onto one of the sardines to cover the flesh with about ¼ inch (0.5 cm) of the bright green mixture. Repeat with the remaining stuffing and sardines. Sprinkle with the breadcrumbs and drizzle with olive oil.

7 Place one tray at a time in the top third of the oven and roast the sardines for 7 to 10 minutes, depending on the temperature and the size of the sardines, until the surface is nicely browned and the sardines are sizzling. Remove from the oven and let the sardines cool for 5 to 10 minutes before serving.

8 Transfer the sardines to a platter or individual plates and serve.

Cook's note

If the sardines have not been scaled and butterflied, this is how to do it:

1 One at a time, lay each sardine horizontally on a cutting board and, holding it by the head, rub a paper towel over it from the head end to the tail to remove the scales.

2 Using scissors, cut off the head, starting at the backbone, and pull away the insides that will come along with it.

3 Cut the sardine open through the belly using the scissors, staying slightly right of center to leave the spine on the left side of the fish. Clip the end of the spine just above the tail, without removing the tail.

4 Open up the sardine and pull away the bones in one swipe. Using the scissors, trim the skin on each side of the sardine to make it look neat. Your sardine is ready to stuff.

The Petits Farcis World Championships

How seriously do the people of Nice take their stuffed vegetables? So beloved is this iconic local dish that every year since 2012, the Old Town wine bar Cave de la Tour has organized the Petits Farcis World Championships, pitting amateur and professional cooks against each other to turn out the ultimate version.

Taking place in mid-May, when the vegetables traditionally used for petits farcis are at their smallest and sweetest, the competition has the ambiance of a good-humored soccer match. Hundreds of supporters in T-shirts and hats supplied by sponsors turn out to cheer on their favorite competitors, and to share their opinions about the samples that circulate on trays decorated with fresh herbs or bright zucchini blossoms.

The 2022 edition attracted nineteen entries in a competition judged by an illustrious panel of twelve that included the legendary Jacques Maximin, several chefs from local Michelin-starred restaurants, and the winemaker Gio Sergi of Clos Saint Vincent in Nice's Bellet region (see page 236). The wine bar's no-nonsense owner, Jean-Philippe Gazan, was clearly in his element as he presided over the event.

"It started as a joke," he explained. "Several of us who run businesses in the Old Town gather each Sunday to eat together, and one day the florist brought some petits farcis. They were not good, and I said we should start a competition."

Gazan calls it the "World Championships" because there is no geographical limit on who can enter. A previous winner was an Englishwoman living in Nice who had worked on her recipe for months before wowing the judges.

If everyone agrees that there are as many recipes for petits farcis as there are cooks, there are some generally accepted guidelines: The vegetables should be as small and colorful as possible, and all of them—except possibly the tomatoes—should be precooked. Veal, pork, beef, ham, and sausage are acceptable meats, with many cooks using two or three of these. The scooped-out insides of the vegetables go into the stuffing, except when they don't: "I learned to throw away the zucchini seeds and pulp and use a whole courgette de Nice [a local variety with no perceptible seeds] in the filling instead, sautéing it with onions in a frying pan and then crushing it," one mamie confided. Breadcrumbs or baguette soaked in milk often play a role, along with grated Parmesan or Sbrinz (a hard Swiss cheese favored in Nice), but add rice, and you will be laughed out of town.

What struck me about the variations I tasted was their melt-in-your-mouth quality and the subtlety of the seasonings: this thrifty dish, which started as a means to use up leftover meat, is now one in which the vegetables shine. The winner, Lucien Brych, chose to stuff red and yellow tomatoes, round zucchini, spring onions, and zucchini blossoms. As for the filling, he wasn't giving away much: "In each recipe for farcis, there is a building with several floors, several hallways, and several apartments."

LES PETITS FARCIS NIÇOIS
Little stuffed vegetables

Since I chose to name my cooking school after this emblematic dish of stuffed vegetables (*petit* means "small" and *farcis* means "stuffed"), I needed to come up with a version that would meet the approval of any mamie who might pop her head into my kitchen and quiz me about the ingredients. My recipe started with one that the chef of La Merenda, Dominique Le Stanc, shared with me during my early days in Nice. Over the years, I have made it my own, experimenting with different combinations of vegetables and meat. What makes the recipe a little unusual are the inclusion of mushrooms in the filling, which somehow enhances its meatiness, and the absence of bread, which I have come to see (controversially, I'm sure!) as unnecessary filler.

My butcher prepares a mix of ground veal, beef, and pork that is perfect for petits farcis, but I have used veal sausage, Italian pork sausage, hand-minced free-range chicken breast, and green lentils for a vegetarian version (see the Variation). Be sure to adapt the seasoning according to the meat you use; sausage meat will require less seasoning that plain ground meat. The meats are not precooked; cooking the meat inside the vegetables preserves its moisture and creates delicious pan juices for the crucial step of basting.

The vegetables used for stuffing should ideally be no larger than a golf ball; bigger ones can be cut into bite-sized pieces and hollowed out to make boats. As convivial to make (try to enlist help if you can) as it is to eat, this dish should be served warm, not hot, to best appreciate its delicate flavors.

SERVES 6

FOR THE VEGETABLES TO STUFF
6 small round zucchini or baby zucchini or 2 regular zucchini
6 round spring onions, bulbs measuring no more than 2 inches (5 cm) across, or 3 medium red or white onions, peeled but the roots left intact
6 small tomatoes, measuring about 2 inches (5 cm) across
Fine sea salt
3 mini sweet peppers or 1 red or yellow bell pepper
1 tablespoon coarse sea salt

FOR THE STUFFING
2 medium zucchini, about 6 inches (15 cm) long
15 medium button or cremini mushrooms (about 11 ounces/300 g)

2 round spring onions, white parts only, or 1 small white onion
5 tablespoons (75 ml) extra-virgin olive oil
1 teaspoon fresh thyme leaves or ½ teaspoon dried thyme
2 garlic cloves, chopped
Sea salt and freshly ground black pepper
8 ounces (215 g) ground veal or beef
8 ounces (215 g) ground pork or sausage meat
2 large eggs, beaten
⅔ cup (50 g) freshly grated Parmesan or Sbrinz
½ cup (10 g) basil leaves, thinly sliced
½ cup (10 g) flat-leaf parsley leaves, thinly sliced

FOR SERVING
6 ounces (160 g) mesclun (about 3 cups)
Everyday Salad Dressing (page 349)

To prepare the vegetables for stuffing

1 Half-fill a large saucepan with water and bring to a boil.

2 For round zucchini, cut off the caps and set aside. Hollow out the insides using a melon baller or spoon, leaving about a ¼-inch (0.5 cm) shell. For baby zucchini, cut them lengthwise in half and scoop out the seeds with a small spoon to make boats. If using long zucchini, cut each one into 2-inch (5 cm) chunks and hollow out each one from one end, leaving a ¼-inch (0.5 cm) wall at the other end. Discard the pulp and seeds.

3 If using spring onions, cut them lengthwise in half, then make a small cut next to the root and scoop out the inner layers, leaving 2 outer layers. If using medium onions, cut each one into quarters and proceed as for the spring onions. Reserve the inner layers for the filling.

4 Cut a cap from each tomato and set aside. Hollow out the tomatoes using a spoon; reserve the pulp to add to a tomato sauce or gazpacho, if you wish. Sprinkle the insides of the tomatoes with fine salt and place them upside down on a plate lined with paper towels to drain; keep the caps next to them.

5 If using mini peppers, cut them lengthwise in half and discard the core and seeds. If using a large pepper, cut it lengthwise in half, then cut each half lengthwise and then crosswise in half, to make 4 boats.

6 Add the coarse salt to the boiling water, then add the hollowed-out zucchini (and the caps for the round zucchini), onions, and peppers (cook these in batches if necessary). Bring the water back to a boil and cook for 4 to 5 minutes, until the vegetables are tender when pierced with the tip of knife but still bright colored (the onions should start to look translucent). Using a slotted spoon, transfer the vegetables to a bowl of ice water for 2 minutes, then remove and set upside down on paper towels to drain. Reserve 1 cup (240 ml) of the cooking water and discard the rest.

For the stuffing

1 Cut the zucchini, mushrooms, and onions into 1-inch (2.5 cm) chunks and place in a large bowl, along with the reserved inside layers of onion. Working in batches so as not to overcrowd the food processor, finely mince the vegetables, using the pulse button (some cooks use a meat grinder instead; in this case, set a colander in the bowl before adding the vegetables so any excess liquid can drain off). Transfer the minced vegetables to a large bowl.

2 Heat 3 tablespoons of the olive oil in a large frying pan over high heat. Add the minced vegetables, along with the thyme, and cook, stirring occasionally, until they soften, their juices evaporate, and they start to turn golden, about 10 minutes. Lower the heat to medium, add the garlic, and cook, stirring, for 2 more minutes. Season with salt and pepper to taste.

3 Transfer the vegetables to a bowl and stir in the meat with a fork, mixing thoroughly. Add the Parmesan or Sbrinz, eggs, basil, and parsley and season well with salt and pepper, going easy on the salt if you are using sausage meat.

To roast the stuffed vegetables

1 Preheat the oven to 350°F (180°C).

2 Rub a roasting pan with 1 tablespoon of the oil and arrange the vegetables in the pan. Stuff the vegetables generously with the meat mixture, but do not pack it down (you do not want a hard ball of stuffing). Top the tomatoes and the round zucchini with their caps. Drizzle with the remaining 1 tablespoon olive oil and pour ½ cup (120 ml) of the reserved vegetable cooking water around them.

3 Roast for 15 minutes, then baste the vegetables with the pan juices and roast for another 15 minutes. If the pan juices start to dry up, add a little more of the reserved cooking water. When the vegetables are browned on top, remove from the oven and baste again with the pan juices (this step is crucial).

4 Toss the mesclun with the vinaigrette. Serve the petits farcis warm, arranging the vegetables in a circle with the dressed mesclun in the middle.

Variation

For a vegetarian version, replace the meat with 1 cup (200 g) French green lentils. Place the lentils in a saucepan with 3 cups (720 ml) water, 1 bay leaf, a sprig of fresh thyme, and a crushed garlic clove. Bring to a boil, then turn the heat to medium-low and simmer for 20 minutes, or until the lentils are cooked to al dente. Drain any excess liquid from the lentils, remove the flavorings, and mix with the rest of the filling ingredients as for the meat.

161

RATATOUILLE NIÇOISE

Summer vegetable stew

Living as I do in the home of ratatouille, this is not a recipe that I take lightly. I make it only in the height of summer when tomatoes are at their peak, since they are the key ingredient in this bright-colored vegetable stew. But you can get away with making it out of season (shh, don't tell the mamies I said this!) if you use good-quality Italian passata, or strained tomatoes, especially if you have preserved them yourself during the summer (see page 337).

The name of the dish comes from the Niçoise word *rata*, or "mix," and the French word *touiller*, meaning "to stir." According to the *Larousse Gastronomique*, ratatouille once referred to "an unappetizing stew," which is exactly what happens when ratatouille is assembled hastily and cooked for too long. It's unlikely to ever taste bad if you make it with summer vegetables, but experienced Niçoise and Provençal cooks aim for clarity in the dish, preserving the taste, color, and texture of each vegetable. That means cooking the vegetables separately in olive oil and combining them only at the end. It's a time-consuming dish to make, but one so versatile that the leftovers can feed me for days.

I often poach an egg in ratatouille, shakshuka-style, or spoon it onto toasted sourdough bread and top it with the puree of garlic, fresh basil, and olive oil known here as pistou (see page 343). You can also use this ratatouille as a stuffing for round zucchini or tomatoes, or even in a variation on Stuffed Squid (page 221). The most classic way to serve it is alongside grilled meat (especially lamb), chicken, or fish; I also love it with crisp-skinned sea bream or sea bass.

In the movie *Ratatouille*, the layered vegetables emerge from the oven as a perfectly formed dome. Any Niçois would recognize the Disney version of this dish as a tian, not a ratatouille, which is more of a joyous mishmash. Feel free to vary the proportions of the vegetables, keeping in mind that the quality of the tomato coulis makes or breaks the dish.

SERVES 4

1 medium eggplant (about 1 pound/450 g), cut into ½-inch (1 cm) dice

1 teaspoon fine sea salt (optional)

5 tablespoons (75 ml) extra-virgin olive oil

3 medium zucchini (about 1 pound/450 g), cut into ½-inch (1 cm) dice

Sea salt

2 bell peppers, 1 red and 1 yellow (about 1 pound/450 g), cored, seeded, and cut into ½-inch (1 cm) dice

1 red onion, cut into ½-inch (1 cm) dice

1 to 2 garlic cloves, minced

1½ cups (375 ml) Coulis de Tomates (page 337) or store-bought passata (Italian strained tomatoes)

½ teaspoon mild to medium-hot chile powder (optional)

½ cup (about 10 g) basil leaves, roughly torn, or more to taste

Freshly ground black pepper

1 Optional but recommended step, so that the eggplant absorbs less oil and cooks a little faster: Place the diced eggplant in a colander set over a bowl. Sprinkle with the fine sea salt and toss with your hands, then cover with a plate and a small weight (such as a can of tomatoes) and set aside for 20 to 30 minutes, until the eggplant has given off some liquid. Pat the eggplant dry with paper towels or a dish towel.

2 Heat 1 tablespoon of the olive oil in a medium frying pan over medium-high heat. Add the zucchini and cook, shaking and flipping it occasionally, until golden and softened (but not mushy), 5 to 7 minutes; sprinkle with salt toward the end of the cooking time (if you salt too early, the zucchini may soften too much). Transfer to a medium saucepan (this will later hold all the ratatouille ingredients) and set aside.

3 Heat another 2 tablespoons of the olive oil in the frying pan and add the eggplant. Cover and cook over medium heat for 8 to 10 minutes, occasionally removing the lid and giving the eggplant a toss. When the eggplant is mostly golden, test a few pieces with the tip of a small knife to be sure they are soft. Transfer to the pan with the zucchini.

4 Heat another 1 tablespoon olive oil over medium heat in the same pan (or do this in a separate pan at the same time as you cook the eggplant to speed things up) and add the peppers and a little salt. Cook, stirring occasionally, until the peppers start to soften, 5 to 7 minutes, then add the onions, the remaining 1 tablespoon oil, and another pinch of salt and continue cooking until the vegetables are soft and caramelized, about 10 minutes. Add the garlic and cook over medium-low heat for another 2 minutes. Transfer the mixture to the saucepan.

5 Add the tomato coulis, chile powder, and basil to the vegetables and stir gently with a rubber spatula, so as not to break up the vegetables. Season with salt to taste, and adjust the amount of chile powder and/or basil.

6 Place the saucepan over very low heat and let the flavors combine for 5 to 10 minutes. Serve warm (not hot) or at room temperature. (Leftovers can be stored in the refrigerator for up to 3 days and served cold, at room temperature, or reheated.)

TIAN DE LÉGUMES D'ÉTÉ

Summer vegetable bake

When southern French cooks use the word *tian*, they are referring either to a round earthenware dish with handles on both sides or to whatever is inside it: usually seasonal vegetables baked with olive oil and herbs, or in a mixture of eggs and cream. Going back a couple of centuries, though, a *tian* was a conical bowl with a spout, and it served as a multipurpose vessel for everything from washing vegetables to gardening. The more tians a household displayed, the richer it was assumed to be, since that meant there was a separate tian for each task.

The tradition of cooking in tians began with communal bread ovens: as the ovens cooled off after the bread baking, villagers would bring their vegetable-filled tians to the bakery to take advantage of the slow heat, leaving them in the warm oven for hours. This is hard to replicate in a modern home, but the cooking time given here is a minimum—after you turn the oven off, you can leave the tian inside until it has cooled completely. By the end of cooking, the vegetables should be completely soft and translucent, and most of the liquid should have been absorbed.

This tian also improves on resting, and it reheats beautifully the next day, or it can be served at room temperature for a picnic. Although I've chosen to include potatoes, since they make the dish more substantial and absorb some of the excess liquid, you can leave them out. This tian is hearty enough to accompany grilled meats, but also works well with fish.

A mandoline would come in handy here for slicing the vegetables, but watch your fingers! Nearly every mandoline owner has a story to tell.

SERVES 4

1 small eggplant (about 11 ounces/300 g)

2 medium zucchini (about 11 ounces/300 g)

2 small potatoes (about 11 ounces/300 g), peeled or not

1 red onion (about 7 ounces/200 g)

2 teaspoons fine sea salt

2 beefsteak tomatoes or other ripe tomatoes (about 1 pound/450 g)

1 garlic clove

¼ cup (60 ml) extra-virgin olive oil, plus more for the casserole dish

2 teaspoons thyme leaves

2 teaspoons finely chopped rosemary leaves

Freshly ground black pepper

Fleur de sel

1   If your vegetables are not the same width, cut the wider ones lengthwise in half so that they more or less match. Then slice each vegetable ¼ inch (0.5 mm) thick, placing the vegetables in separate bowls.

2   Sprinkle the eggplant, zucchini, potato, and onion slices with ½ teaspoon salt each and toss with your hands (there is no need to salt the tomatoes). Set aside for 15 minutes.

3 Dry the salted vegetables by rolling up the slices in a dish towel or paper towels (you can use the same dish towel for all of them), one vegetable at a time.

4 Preheat the oven to 375°F (190°C).

5 Cut the garlic clove lengthwise in half and rub a 9-inch (23 cm) round tian (casserole dish) or deep-dish pie plate or an 8-by-10-inch (20 by 25 cm) gratin dish with the cut side of both halves, pressing on the garlic to extract as much juice as possible. Rub the dish with a little olive oil.

6 Arrange the slices, including the tomatoes, vertically in the dish, alternating the vegetables. Pack the slices tightly, as they will shrink during cooking.

7 In a small bowl, stir the herbs and several grinds of pepper into the olive oil in a small bowl, then drizzle over the vegetables. Sprinkle with a large pinch of fleur de sel.

8 Cover the dish tightly with foil, and bake for 45 minutes. Remove the foil and press the vegetables down with a heatproof spatula so that they are submerged in the cooking juices and oil.

9 Continue cooking, uncovered, for another 30 minutes, pressing the vegetables down once or twice more with the spatula. They should be completely soft and browned on top.

10 Turn off the oven and leave the tian in the oven, lightly covered with foil, while it cools. Or, if you want to serve the tian immediately, remove it from the oven and let it cool for at least 15 minutes. You can also serve the tian at room temperature.

PÊCHES RÔTIES À L'HUILE D'OLIVE ET AU MIEL

Peaches roasted with olive oil and honey

During my first summer in Paris, I lived at the bottom of the medieval rue Mouffetard, in a gloomy, damp apartment that was more the stuff of nightmares than of fantasy. I would walk up the cobblestone street early in the morning as the market vendors set up their stalls in front of the centuries-old Saint Médard church, bringing out boxes of downy-skinned peaches that they arranged in symmetrical rows, each cheek crease perfectly aligned. The suave and floral-scented pêche blanche (white peach), its creamy flesh tinged with pink, came as a revelation to me.

Coming back down the hill after translating a class at the Cordon Bleu, I would buy just one of these fruits, telling the vendor, *"C'est pour maintenant"* ("It's to eat right away")–a good fruit seller can predict the ripeness of a peach almost minute by minute. Home–or what passed for it– was only steps away, but I couldn't wait that long to bite into my longed-for peach, even if I knew that Parisians disapproved of eating in the street. The sight of a wide-eyed Canadian with peach juices dripping down her chin likely did little to change their minds.

White peaches are even more readily available in Nice than in Paris, but they remain sacred to me–it's rare that I eat them any other way than raw, though I do occasionally indulge in Peach Melba (page 174). For baking, I prefer yellow peaches, whose gutsy flavor can stand up to a buttery crust or cake batter.

In this recipe, delicate olive oil and mild-tasting honey enhance the peaches rather than competing with them. I usually choose lavender honey, which is easy to find in Nice and Provence, but you can use any subtle-tasting honey and add a light sprinkling of organic lavender flowers (fresh or dried), if you can find them. Thyme flowers, if you have a plant that happens to be flowering, make a nice substitute.

If possible, plan ahead when making this dessert so that you can marinate the peaches in the honey and olive oil for an hour before baking. The marinating and slow cooking gives them a texture that is almost *confit*, or candied. Serve the peaches with vanilla ice cream, if you like.

SERVES 6

6 yellow peaches, ripe but not overripe
½ cup (120 ml) mild-tasting honey, such as
  lavender or clover
½ cup (120 ml) mild-tasting extra-virgin olive oil
A few organic lavender or thyme flowers (optional)

1 Cut the peaches in half (no need to peel them) and remove the pits. Place the peach halves in a baking dish that holds them fairly snugly, with the cut side facing up.

2 If the honey is liquid (rather than crystallized), place it in a medium bowl and whisk in the olive oil bit by bit, until the mixture is smooth. At first it will seem thick and taffy-like, but it will gradually become smooth and opaque. If you pour in the oil too fast, it may separate, though, so take your time. If the honey is too thick and creamy to allow you to incorporate the oil easily, place the honey in a heatproof bowl set over a pan of simmering water and let it melt until liquid without heating it too much. Then remove from the heat and whisk in the olive oil bit by bit.

3 Pour the mixture over the peaches and sprinkle with a few lavender or thyme flowers, if using. Set aside to macerate for about 1 hour, if you can.

4 Preheat the oven to 325°F (160°C).

5 Roast the peaches for about 45 minutes, until they are very soft. Let them cool to lukewarm before serving.

Cook's note

I do not recommend softening the honey in the microwave, as it can become extremely hot extremely quickly, and that can lead to nasty accidents. I speak from personal experience!

PANNA COTTA À LA VANILLE ET AUX FRUITS ROUGES

Vanilla panna cotta with mixed berries

Although panna cotta, meaning "cooked cream," is an Italian dessert, it has crossed the border into Nice, where it is often served with the beautiful berries that reach their peak of sweetness in summer. The amount of gelatin called for in panna cotta recipes can vary wildly, but I prefer it jiggly, so I use the smallest amount and serve the dessert in a pretty ceramic or glass bowl rather than trying to turn it out. As the panna cottta contains little sugar, a fresh vanilla bean makes all the difference, adding its natural sweetness and depth to the cream (which should not be diluted with another lower-fat dairy product, such as the milk called for in some recipes). The beauty of panna cotta is that it does not require an oven, making it perfect for the hottest days of the year, and you can make it up to a day ahead.

I don't mind telling you that Jan Hendrik van der Westhuizen, who took the beautiful photos for this book, told me this was the best panna cotta he had ever tasted. "Serve this to a man, and he will ask you to marry him," he said. So think twice before making this for a first date!

SERVES 4

2 gelatin sheets (about 2 grams), preferably, or
  1 teaspoon powdered gelatin
2 tablespoons room-temperature water if using
  powdered gelatin
1 vanilla bean

2 cups (500 ml) heavy cream
¼ cup (50 g) sugar
1 cup (about 150 g) mixed berries, such as
  strawberries, blueberries, raspberries, red
  currants, and/or blackberries
¼ cup (25 g) confectioners' sugar

1 If using sheet gelatin, immerse it in a bowl of cold water for at least 5 minutes, until softened. If using powdered gelatin, place the water in a small bowl and sprinkle the gelatin on the surface, being careful not to let it clump. Set aside for at least 5 minutes to bloom.

2 Cut the vanilla bean lengthwise in half and scrape out the seeds with the back of a knife.

3 Place the cream in a medium saucepan, add the vanilla seeds, vanilla pod, and sugar, and heat over low heat, stirring occasionally, just until the cream starts to bubble around the edges. Do not let it come to a boil–if the gelatin is added to boiling liquid, it won't set. Remove the cream from the heat and fish out the vanilla bean.

4 If using sheet gelatin, squeeze out the water and add it to the cream. If using powdered gelatin, add the gelatin and its liquid. Stir to dissolve the gelatin.

5 Pour the mixture into four individual serving bowls, glasses, or jars. Let the panna cotta cool to room temperature, then chill for at least 3 hours, until set but still jiggly in the center. (Cover if you will be keeping it for longer than 3 hours before serving.)

6 Meanwhile, cut any large berries into bite-sized pieces. Gently toss the berries with the confectioners' sugar in a bowl and set aside too macerate for at least 30 minutes, and up to several hours.

7 Just before serving, top the panna cotta with the berries and their juices.

Cook's note

Vanilla beans are so precious that I never waste the pods. I wash the scraped-out bean, dry it on a paper towel, and add it to a jar of sugar to make vanilla sugar for using in cakes and crêpes, or for sprinkling over my yogurt.

Variation

For a vegetarian version of this dessert (gelatin is an animal product), substitute 1 teaspoon agar agar powder for the gelatin. Add the agar agar directly to the cold cream along with the sugar and bring the cream just to a boil.

CRÈME BRÛLÉE À LA LAVANDE

Lavender crème brûlée

When I moved to Paris in the 1990s, it seemed that crème brûlée was on the menu of every bistro. Not until it waned in popularity did I rediscover my love for it, especially once I replaced the traditional vanilla with lavender blossoms, which impart a light floral flavor to the custard. The blossoms float to the top and become part of the sugary crust, so there is no need to strain them out.

The key to great crème brûlée is to use a shallow dish; I love my porcelain crème brûlée dishes, which have a small handle on either side, but you can also look for shallow terra-cotta dishes, like the ones in which the creamy cheese Saint Félicien is sold in France. These provide a large surface area for the brittle caramel layer, resulting in the ideal proportion of crust to custard. If you don't have individual dishes, you can also make a large crème brûlée in a round or oval porcelain or glass baking dish, as long as the custard layer is no more than about ½ inch (1 cm) deep.

When baking crème brûlée in a shallow dish, there is no need to cook it in a bain marie, or water bath; keep the oven temperature low, and let it cook slowly, so that the custard never bubbles and remains wobbly in the center. Remember that it will set slightly more after you remove it from the oven, so err on the side of jiggly for perfect results.

SERVES 6

1 cup (240 ml) whole milk
1 cup (240 ml) heavy cream
2 teaspoons dried organic lavender flowers

5 large egg yolks
½ cup (100 g) sugar
6 tablespoons (90 g) raw sugar, such as Demerara or turbinado, for sprinkling on top

1 Preheat the oven to 250°F (120°C). Place six shallow round crème brûlée dishes measuring 4 to 5 inches (11 to 12 cm) in diameter on a baking sheet.

2 Pour the milk and cream into a medium saucepan and add the lavender flowers. Bring to a simmer over medium heat.

3 Meanwhile, place the yolks and sugar in a mixing bowl and whisk for 1 minute, or until the color starts to lighten. Gradually add the hot milk and cream mixture to the yolk mixture, stirring constantly with the whisk until smooth.

4 Using a small ladle, divide the mixture among the crème brûlée dishes, stirring the mixture each time before adding it to the dish. (Even if your bowl has a spout, do not pour the mixture, since the egg yolks tend to sink to the bottom and the lavender floats to the top.)

5 Place the dishes on a baking sheet and bake in the center of the oven until the custard is set but the center is still slightly jiggly, about 30 minutes. Transfer the baking sheet to a rack and let the custards cool for 15 to 20 minutes. Then refrigerate, uncovered, until chilled, at least 1 hour, and up to 24 hours.

6 If you do not have a kitchen blowtorch, preheat the broiler on its hottest setting, with a rack near the top of the oven. Sprinkle 1 tablespoon raw sugar as evenly as you can over the surface of each crème brûlée. Caramelize the sugar with a blowtorch or under the broiler until melted and golden. Serve immediately.

PÊCHE MELBA

Peach Melba

Created by the legendary southern French chef Auguste Escoffier for the Australian opera singer Dame Nellie Melba, this dessert becomes extraordinary when made with ripe summer peaches, fresh raspberries, and top-quality vanilla ice cream. The first time he presented Dame Melba with this dessert, Escoffier served it on a swan carved in ice in reference to the Swan Knight in the opera *Lohengrin* and topped it with spun sugar. At home, the spun sugar is necessary only if you have invited an opera singer to dinner. Add whipped cream, and you will have an ice cream sundae, not peach Melba; the beauty of this dessert lies in its minimalism.

Fragrant and slightly floral-tasting white peaches are best for this dessert; the flat peaches known as "donut peaches" in the United States work well, as they hold their shape. Look for peaches that give a little when lightly pressed, like a ripe avocado; too ripe, and they will fall apart in the syrup.

SERVES 4

4 ripe peaches, preferably white
4 cups (1 l) water
½ cup (100 g) sugar
A squeeze of lemon juice

1 teaspoon vanilla extract
4 scoops vanilla ice cream, the best you can find or homemade
1½ cups (about 8 ounces/225 g) raspberries
1 to 2 tablespoons confectioners' sugar

1 Cut the peaches in half and twist the halves in opposite directions to remove the pits (this should be easy to do if they are *à point*, ripe but not too soft). Place the peach halves in a large bowl and cover with boiling water. Leave for a few seconds, then remove the peaches from the water with a slotted spoon and gently peel off the skins.

2 In a medium saucepan, combine the water, sugar, lemon juice, and vanilla extract and heat over medium heat, stirring occasionally, until the sugar dissolves and the syrup comes to a simmer. Add the peaches to the syrup and poach at a very low simmer for 5 minutes. Remove from the heat and lift out the peaches with a slotted spoon, placing 2 peach halves in each of four shallow serving bowls.

3 If you have a food mill, pass the raspberries through the mill into a bowl using the finest setting, and sweeten to taste with the confectioners' sugar. If not, puree the raspberries with an immersion blender or in a food processor, then strain to remove the seeds and sweeten to taste.

4 Just before serving, place a scoop of vanilla ice cream in each dish and top with the raspberry coulis.

Exploring Nice one scoop at a time

My first apartment in Nice was around the corner from Fenocchio, an ice cream shop owned since 1966 by the family of the same name. My son was a toddler the summer we arrived, and every night we would walk past the majestic seventeenth-century cathedral on place Rossetti, with our eyes fixed on the display of up to a hundred ice cream flavors. Would we be daring and try the Swiss chard pie ice cream or the tomato-basil sorbet? Or would we stick to our favorites, which for me have always been the mandarin sorbet (made with local fruit) and ginger ice cream, and for Sam, the lemon meringue?

If I still consider Fenocchio and its mind-boggling array of flavors a must for anyone who is visiting Nice, this shop no longer has a monopoly on great ice cream. On the other side of the square, the smaller Gelato Azzuro lures customers with the scent of homemade waffle cones, and it's not a gimmick: made with natural ingredients, including bushels of melons in season, its ice creams came in second in a nationwide competition. The cassis de Bourgogne, black currant from Burgundy, takes me back to my childhood in Paris, when I fell in love with this tangy sorbet that stains your tongue deep red.

A short walk away, in a square dominated by the city's courthouse, the ever-cheerful Monica Crepaldi runs Oui, Jelato, a shop to rival any in Italy. With about thirty flavors on display during peak season, she focuses on seasonal fruits and Italian specialties like tiramisu and stracciatella, a milk-based ice cream streaked with chocolate. I often choose the chocolat extra fondant, a cocoa sorbet that pairs beautifully with almost any other flavor (try it with pistachio or mango).

Up in the Libération area, Roberto Francia brings something of a mad scientist's touch to the gelato flavors at Arlequin, which has a sister shop, César Milano, on avenue Jean Médecin. He is constantly experimenting with new combinations, and whenever I visit, he jumps out from the back and offers me samples, his eyes gleaming with enthusiasm. One of his now-classic creations is the Persepolis, a saffron, pistachio, and rosewater ice cream that is dedicated to the French actress Isabelle Adjani. In season, I can never resist the raisin framboise, a sorbet made with a rare local grape similar to the Concord.

I had one assistant who made it her mission to taste every flavor at Fenocchio, something that I have not yet accomplished. But I can vouch for the Swiss chard pie ice cream, perhaps the most Niçoise of flavors!

TARTE RUSTIQUE AUX PRUNES
Rustic plum tart

When I decided to leave the Old Town to live in the Libération area, I told a real estate agent that I wanted to be able to touch the trees from my window. She gave me a funny look and said, "I've never heard that one before." After a year of what seemed like fruitless searching, I visited a first-floor apartment in a Belle Epoque villa, hidden behind a modern building whose wood paneling and mountain mural reminded me of 1970s Banff. A small flight of steps led to a courtyard oasis whose lush vegetation included a plum tree, its leafy branches within easy reach of a bedroom window. Instantly enchanted, I made an offer so fast that the agent had to remind me to negotiate the price; never mind that my builder later summed up the state of the apartment as "Chernobyl."

I have never once regretted my choice, even during the trying period of the renovation. I can touch the plum tree from what is now my home office, and working on this cookbook, I have appreciated how its pale green leaves filter the light, keeping the room cool without air-conditioning. When its branches sagged with my biggest-yet crop of golden Mirabelles, I collected as many as I could for this tart, leaving the rest for a musical brown-feathered bird that eyed each fruit with Buddha-like patience until the skin blushed deep pink. Precisely at that moment, it pecked off the honey-sweet flesh and discarded the pit.

To make this tart, I had to pick the fruits before my discerning competitor got to them; even at this not-quite-ripe stage, their juiciness made them difficult to pit. I also make this tart with varieties like quetsche (Damson) and the golden Reine Claude (greengage), which taste even more wonderful cooked than raw. It also works well with many other fruits, such as apricots, peaches, apples, blueberries, figs, or pears (or a mix); choose a jam that complements the fruit. If you feel nervous about making your own pastry, this tart is a perfect place to start, since it doesn't aim for a perfect finish and requires no special pan, only a baking sheet.

SERVES 6

1 pound (450 g) plums

Quick Basic Pastry (page 361), chilled for at least 15 minutes

Flour for rolling the dough

¼ cup (80 g) plum jam

2 tablespoons almond meal

2 tablespoons raw cane (turbinado) sugar

2 tablespoons unsalted butter, cut into ¼-inch (0.5 cm) pieces

2 tablespoons chopped raw pistachios or hazelnuts, or slivered almonds

1   Preheat the oven to 375°F (190°C). Line a baking sheet with parchment paper.

2   Cut the plums in half and remove the pits. If the plums are large, cut the halves once more lengthwise. Set aside.

3   On a lightly floured surface, roll the dough into a 12-inch (30 cm) circle (don't worry if it's a little uneven). Sprinkle with flour, place a rolling pin near the top, and fold the top of the pastry over it. Roll the pastry up around the rolling pin, then lift it and unroll it onto the baking sheet. If the dough seems too soft and fragile at this point, place it in the refrigerator for a few minutes (not too long, or it will crack when you fold over the edges).

4   Spread the jam over the pastry, leaving 2 inches (5 cm) of bare pastry around the edges. Sprinkle the jam with the almond meal, which will soak up some of the plum juices. Arrange the plums cut side up on top of the jam and almond meal. Sprinkle with the sugar and dot the butter pieces evenly over the plums. Sprinkle with the nuts.

5   Fold the edges of the pastry up over the fruit all the way around, pleating the pastry as necessary. Gently press down on the edges to ensure that the tart holds its shape, and pinch together any small holes that may have formed.

6   Bake for 30 to 35 minutes, until the pastry is golden brown and the juices from the fruit have thickened a little (they will continue to thicken outside the oven). Remove from the oven and let the tart cool to room temperature on the pan.

7   Slide the tart, with its parchment paper, onto a cake platter or plate, then whip out the parchment paper from underneath, holding the tart in place. Cut into slices and serve.

SALADE DE FRAISES AU VIN ROSÉ

Strawberries in rosé wine

This simple dessert is popular in the Var region, west of Cannes, which produces much of the rosé sold in France. It's a perfect way to use up excess rosé (yes, there is such a thing!), though it's also worth opening a bottle to make this dessert. Darker pink rosés from Provence are usually fruitier than the pale ones, without being sweet. You might serve these strawberries with Lemon and Lavender Madeleines (page 323).

SERVES 4

1½ cups (375 ml) fruity rosé

2 tablespoons Grand Marnier or Cointreau or 1 tablespoon finely grated lemon zest (preferably from an organic lemon)

⅓ cup (80 g) sugar

1 teaspoon vanilla extract or ¼ teaspoon vanilla bean paste

4 cups (about 1 pound /450 g) strawberries, hulled and cut lengthwise in half

1 tablespoon thinly sliced mint leaves, plus 4 small mint sprigs for garnish

1 Combine the rosé, liqueur or lemon zest, sugar, and vanilla in a medium saucepan and bring to a simmer over medium heat, then turn the heat down to low and simmer for 10 minutes. Transfer the syrup to a bowl that can also hold the berries and let cool to room temperature.

2 Add the berries and sliced mint to the rosé syrup, stir, and refrigerate for at least 1 hour, and up to several hours.

3 Serve the berries in wineglasses or whiskey or sundae glasses, garnishing each one with a small mint sprig.

FALL

As French visitors head north in a tangle of traffic jams, and planes full of homeward-bound tourists leave the Baie des Anges behind, I feel like a party host bidding good-bye to a pack of boisterous, laughing guests, knowing that only a few close friends will linger in my living room. The tourist season is winding down, but not finished; those who visit at this time of year know (or quickly realize) that they are a privileged bunch.

With bright sunshine, perfect balmy temperatures, and only sporadic rain until November, fall is the perfect season for hiking along the coast or in the hills, as well as cycling (whether sporty or leisurely) and swimming. As a swimmer, I love fall best of all because the water retains much of the summer's warmth until late October, but the beaches attract mostly small groups of chatty regulars and a few tourists from more northern climates wanting to take a dip in the Med. As the days grow noticeably shorter, there are fewer evening gatherings on the beach, but more lunchtime picnics; the Niçois (whether born here or adopted) never need much of an excuse to share food outdoors.

In early September, the temperature reliably drops by a few degrees, making the kitchen inviting again; I begin to think of turning on the oven for slow-cooked tians (baked vegetable dishes) and stews. The market is also at its most glorious, since fall starts to assert itself with surprising force before summer is ready to bow out.

As early as late August, I am always surprised to see the first crop of local apples at the producers' stalls—small, red-skinned, and crunchy, these semi-wild fruits look out of place next to the voluptuous, dripping flesh of the late-season peaches and melons. Emerald trompette de Nice zucchini begin to morph into winter squash, turning first deep green and then orange as they expand to the monstrous proportions of a sprinter's thigh. Tomatoes take their last stand, as the nights grow colder. Even with wrinkly skin and bruises worthy of a boxer, they hold sugary juices that can make summer last all year if preserved wisely.

Fall is a season of weird and wonderful produce and foraged foods, so it's no wonder that cooks welcome this time of year. Mushrooms whose names translate as "sheep's hoof" or "trumpets of death" spring up in the forests after the first rains revive the parched soil, and chestnuts fall from the trees, their spiky armor cracking open to reveal mahogany treasure. Figs swell and soften on their branches, eventually dropping to the ground or withering to a semi-dried state that concentrates their sugars like jam; in a good year, they keep giving fruit until early November. Knobbly yellow-gold quinces, covered in a protective layer of fuzz, are easy to overlook but not easy to forget if you take the time to coax out their sweetness. And then there is the kaki, or persimmon, a stand-alone fruit whose jelly-like flesh should be eaten with a spoon (or your fingers, if you dare) when its texture is like that of an overripe tomato.

Knowing that nature will be less generous in winter, particularly in the snow-capped mountains, cooks from around Nice have always preserved as much of this bounty as possible in late summer and fall. Louison, a cook in her late eighties who invited me for an elaborate Sunday lunch at her home in the mountain village of Clans, proudly showed me her pantry filled with jars of preserved eggplant, wild mushrooms, and tomatoes. She harvests basil plants before their leaves turn tough and brown to make a big batch of Pistou (page 343), melts quinces into paste (page 253) and jelly (page 257), and transforms all excess fruit, especially if it is very ripe or bruised, into jam. Chestnuts simmer in sugar syrup with vanilla and perhaps a little rum to make crème de châtaignes, sweet chestnut puree. Even if there are months when only chard thrives, there is no danger of winter being a time of deprivation.

PISSALADIÈRE
Caramelized onion tart with anchovies and olives

In my classes, students often ask me which dish I like to cook the most. Though it's an impossible question for someone who loves food as much as I do to answer, pissaladière is something that I never tire of making or eating. I love the process of slapping and turning the dough by hand until it grows springy, and slowly caramelizing the onions until they turn into a golden jam that frizzles around the edges in the oven.

If you're considering leaving out the anchovies, remember that the name *pissaladière* comes from the word *pissala*, salted fish paste. Each spring, fishermen on the Côte d'Azur layer the smallest anchovies in barrels with salt, herbs, and spices. The mixture is allowed to age for forty-five days before being strained to create a potent gray paste that brings depth to anything from tomato sauce to salad dressing. A little pissala (or, in its absence, chopped anchovy) blends subtly into the onions, yet it changes everything, adding an addictive savoriness, or umami. Pissaladière without anchovy–along with a handful of Niçoise olives for more salty contrast–is simply an onion flatbread.

You can serve pissaladière hot, warm, or at room temperature, with mesclun, or cut into bite-sized pieces and pass it around as an appetizer with a glass of rosé.

SERVES 6 TO 8

¼ cup (60 ml) extra-virgin olive oil, plus more for the pan

6 large yellow onions (about 3 pounds/1.3 kg), cut lengthwise in half and thinly sliced

2 sprigs fresh thyme or ½ teaspoon dried thyme

2 bay leaves

Sea salt and freshly ground black pepper

8 anchovy fillets packed in oil, or 1 teaspoon good-quality anchovy paste and 6 anchovies

Olive Oil Bread Dough (page 357), allowed to rise until doubled

7 Niçoise olives

1 Heat the olive oil in a large frying pan or sauté pan over medium heat. Add the onions, thyme, bay leaves, and a large pinch of salt, and stir to combine. Cover with a circle of parchment paper (see Cook's Note, page 62) to keep in some of the steam and cook over medium-low heat for about 30 minutes, stirring every few minutes. At this stage, the onions will still be translucent, but the liquid should have evaporated.

2 Now turn up the heat to medium and cook the onions, without stirring, until they start to stick to the bottom of the pan, about 5 minutes. Scrape up the caramelized juices with a wooden spatula and stir into the onions. Repeat this procedure two or three times, letting the onions caramelize for 3 to 4 minutes at a time, still covered with the paper, until they are deep golden. Season with pepper to taste. →

3 Finely chop 2 of the anchovies, if not using anchovy paste. Mix the anchovy paste or chopped anchovies into the onions. Cook for another 2 minutes or so, stirring once or twice. Remove from the heat.

4 Preheat the oven to 375°F (190°C). Oil a 12-inch (30 cm) pizza pan or a 12-by-16-inch (30 by 40 cm) baking sheet.

5 Turn the dough out onto the pan and gently press out the air with your hands. Cover with a dish towel and let rest for 5 minutes.

6 Using the palms of both hands, gently stretch the dough, without tearing it, until it covers the surface of the pizza pan or makes a free-form oval about 10 by 13 inches (25 by 35 cm) on the baking sheet.

7 Spread the onion/anchovy mixture evenly over the dough, right to the edges. Bake for 20 minutes, or until the onions have started to darken around the edges.

8 Decorate the pissaladière with the remaining anchovy fillets and olives, arranging the anchovies in a starburst pattern and placing the olives between the fillets (and a final one in the center). Return the pissaladière to the oven for another 5 minutes, or until the crust has browned on the bottom. Serve warm or at room temperature. Leftovers can be refrigerated for up to 2 days and reheated in a 325°F (160°C) oven for 5 to 7 minutes.

Charcuterie Pottier-Ghibaudo

It's impossible to walk by the historic Charcuterie Pottier-Ghibaudo without noticing the pig in the display case, encased in a burnished brown rind and bulging with its chunky filling. A specialty of Nice that originated in Piedmont, porchetta ensures that no part of the animal goes to waste, incorporating its tripe, stomach, liver, and head meat, along with peppercorns, fennel, herbes de Provence, and whole garlic cloves. Once it is stuffed, the porchetta cooks slowly in a bread oven for twelve hours, before being served cold, cut into dice. Displayed complete with its ears and snout, porchetta is not for the faint of heart, but so renowned is Nicolas Pottier's version that most days, what starts out as a whole pig ends as little more than a curly tail.

Pottier-Ghibaudo has been my favorite charcuterie since my early days in the Old Town, when it was run by Laurent Pottier and his friendly American wife, Dinna, who took over from the original Ghibaudo family. When they decided to move back to her native Florida in 2014, Laurent's brother Nicolas took over the business, and he now heads a team of eleven who produce not just classic charcuterie products like the local Perugina sausages, caillette (a type of pâté from the Var region), and fromage de tête (headcheese), but also a daily-changing selection of colorful prepared meals, including sophisticated desserts like crackly-topped cream puffs, that reveal Nicolas's haute cuisine background.

When I am not in the mood for something porky, I love their take on ratatouille (in season), which Nicolas told me was inspired by puttanesca sauce. Incorporating capers, anchovies, and balsamic vinegar, with the vegetables all lightly cooked in the same pot so they retain a bite, it has an unmistakable Niçoise flavor thanks to the basil-rich tomato sauce. Best eaten at room temperature, it makes great picnic food, perhaps with a fresh goat cheese from the nearby Fromagerie Métin (see page 370).

MOSBOLLETJIES

Aniseed bread

This recipe comes from this book's photographer, Jan Hendrik van der Westhuizen, who runs the Michelin-starred Restaurant Jan in Nice. Jan has served this outrageously addictive harvest-inspired brioche in one form or another since he opened his restaurant in 2013.

Mosbolletjies is a traditional South African bread flavored with grape juice and aniseed, a spice that is also used in Nice for breads and biscuits. You can savor its soft texture warm out of the oven with churned butter, or slice it and dry it in a 325°F (160°C) oven to make rusks, which are as Niçoise as they are South African. Jan often serves it as an appetizer, to be torn apart at the table, but it is equally good for breakfast.

MAKES 1 LOAF

4 cups (480 g) all-purpose or bread flour, plus more
    for kneading

3 tablespoons sugar

1 tablespoon instant yeast

1 tablespoon whole anise seeds or fennel seeds

1½ teaspoons fine sea salt

⅔ cup (150 ml) white grape juice

8 tablespoons (1 stick/115 g) unsalted butter, plus a
    little more for the pan

½ cup (120 ml) water

¼ cup (60 ml) whole milk

1 egg, beaten, for glazing the bread

1   Place the flour, sugar, yeast, anise or fennel seeds, and salt in the bowl of a stand mixer fitted with the dough hook or in a large mixing bowl. Mix to combine using the dough hook, or use a pastry scraper or wooden spoon if you are making the dough by hand.

2   In a small saucepan, heat the grape juice with the butter over medium heat, removing it from the heat before the butter has completely melted. Let cool until warm to the touch but not hot (below 122°F/50°C, if using a thermometer).

3   Heat the water and milk in a microwave or saucepan just until warm to the touch.

4   Add the liquid ingredients to the dry ingredients and blend on low speed in the mixer, or with the pastry scraper or wooden spoon if you are mixing by hand. Add more flour as necessary so that the dough is soft but not too sticky, then knead on low speed in the mixer or by hand on the counter for 10 minutes.

5   Cover the dough with a damp dish towel and let rise in a warm place for 30 minutes, or until doubled in size.

6   Knead the dough again for at least 5 minutes, until smooth and elastic.

7 Butter a 5-by-9-inch (13 by 23 cm) loaf pan. Divide the dough into 30 pieces weighing about 1 ounce (30 g) each and roll each one on the work surface under the palm of your cupped hand to make a ball. Arrange the balls in two layers in the loaf pan.

8 Brush the beaten egg over the dough. Set aside to rise, covered with the towel, for another 30 to 40 minutes, until puffy.

9 Meanwhile, preheat the oven to 350°F (180°C).

10 Bake the bread for 30 minutes, or until the crust is deep golden. Transfer to a rack and serve warm or at room temperature.

SOUPE AU PISTOU

Fall vegetable soup with pistou

When I see the first shelling beans at the market–either the white beans known as *coco*, or the Italian beans known as *borlotti*, or *tigré* in French–I know it's time to make soupe au pistou. Named for the pesto-like sauce Pistou (see page 343) that is stirred in just before serving, this southern French take on minestrone can be made with any combination of late summer or fall vegetables. In Nice, September is prime time for green and yellow beans, as well as the flat variety known as romano, or runner beans, so I like to include as many different types of beans as I can find. The result is a soup that is hearty but light at the same time; for a more filling soup, some cooks add vermicelli or another short pasta during the last ten minutes of cooking.

Though I initially balked at the idea of cooking green or yellow beans for a long time, I have eventually come to accept that soupe au pistou is not the place for al dente vegetables. You could leave out the pancetta for a vegetarian version, but it gives this vegetable-rich soup a deeper flavor. If you have a Parmesan rind on hand, add a chunk along with the water to intensify the flavors of the soup even more.

Be prepared for a bit of fastidious vegetable cutting when you make this soup (at the markets in Nice and nearby Italy, some helpful vendors sell bags of already diced vegetables, complete with fresh or soaked beans). Once it's on the stove, it requires little attention until the end. If you don't plan to serve it right away, wait until you reheat it to add the pistou.

SERVES 4 TO 6

4 fingerling potatoes (about 8 ounces/215 g), peeled, 3 cut into ¼-inch (0.5 cm) dice, the remaining one left whole

1 large ripe tomato or 2 medium tomatoes (about 8 ounces/215 g total)

3 thyme sprigs

2 bay leaves

1 tablespoon extra-virgin olive oil

¼ cup (50 g) diced smoked or unsmoked pancetta (optional)

1 red or yellow onion, cut into ¼-inch (0.5 cm) dice

1 celery stalk, cut into ¼-inch (0.5 cm) dice

2 carrots, cut into ¼-inch (0.5 cm) dice

1 leek, white part only, cut lengthwise in half and sliced into ¼ inch- (0.5 cm) wide slices

1½ teaspoons coarse sea salt

2 small zucchini, cut into ¼-inch (0.5 cm) dice

A large handful of green beans (and/or yellow, purple, or flat beans; about 6 ounces/150 g total), cut into ¼-inch (0.5 cm) pieces

1½ cups (240 g) shelled fresh white or borlotti beans (about 1 pound/450 g in the pod)

4 cups (1 l) water

A chunk of Parmesan rind (optional)

Freshly ground black pepper

1 teaspoon red wine vinegar

Pistou (page 343), made with Parmesan

Freshly grated Parmesan for serving

1   Place the diced and whole potatoes in a small bowl of water to prevent discoloration.

2   Cut a small cross in the bottom of the tomato(es) and remove the core(s); set aside.

3   Make a bouquet garni by tying the thyme sprigs and bay leaves together with kitchen string.

4   Heat the olive oil in a large saucepan over medium heat. If using pancetta, add it and cook for about 5 minutes, stirring frequently, until golden brown.

5   Add the onion, celery, carrots, and leek, along with ½ teaspoon of the coarse salt, and cook, stirring, over low heat for 5 minutes, or until the vegetables start to soften.

6   Add the zucchini, green beans, and white beans and cook, stirring, for about 5 minutes, making sure that none of the vegetables are browning.

7   Add the drained diced and whole potatoes, the water, bouquet garni, Parmesan rind, if using, the remaining 1 teaspoon coarse salt, and pepper to taste and bring to a boil over high heat, then turn the heat down and simmer, covered, for 30 to 40 minutes, stirring occasionally, until the whole potato is cooked through and the white beans are very soft but not collapsing.

8   Add the whole tomato(es) and simmer for 2 minutes, uncovered, until the skin starts to split. Remove the tomato(es) and place on a cutting board to cool for 2 minutes.

9   Remove the whole potato and transfer to a tall heatproof container or food processor; add about ½ cup (120 ml) of the broth and vegetables.

10   Peel the tomato(es), cut into quarters, and add to the potato and broth. Blend with an immersion blender or process until smooth, then return this mixture to the soup and add the vinegar. Cook over low heat for 5 minutes, uncovered, to blend the flavors, then taste and adjust the seasonings. Remove the bouquet garni and Parmesan rind, if using. Add half the pistou to the soup and cook for another minute, stirring.

11   To serve, ladle the soup into shallow bowls and pass around a bowl of Parmesan and another one of the remaining pistou.

Cook's notes

❄

If you can't find fresh shelling beans, you can use the same amount of cooked beans—either a 15-ounce (400 g) can of beans, drained and rinsed, or ¾ cup (125 g) dried beans, soaked overnight, drained, and cooked until tender. Add the beans to the pan along with the pureed potato and tomato mixture and the vinegar in step 10 and simply heat them through before adding the pistou.

❄

Rather than trimming green beans with a knife, French cooks like to snap off both ends with their fingers, so that any string will come off along with the tips.

TIAN DE COURGE
Baked squash with Provençal breadcrumbs

For this recipe, you can use any winter squash, though I often choose courge de Nice, which starts life as the zucchini known as *courgette trompette* before morphing over the summer into an unwieldy orange-fleshed squash with a long neck and bulbous end. Crookneck, long neck, and the more common butternut squash are comparable varieties, but don't feel you need to restrict yourself to these, as southern French cooks famously make do with what they have.

Madame Luciano, a farmer based near Villefranche-sur-Mer, told me her secrets to making a great tian de courge: "I always precook the squash in a frying pan, never in water, with a minimum of olive oil. Then I mix the cooked squash with rice, Parmesan, nutmeg, and eggs. You can add a little cream, but it's really not necessary. For a change, I bake it in a piecrust."

Using these instructions, it was easy to perfect my tian de courge. For extra flavor and color I top it with Provençal breadcrumbs. Feel free to vary the recipe by mixing in a second cheese, such as Emmental or Gruyère, or fried lardons (bacon matchsticks). Serve the tian on its own with a salad, or as an accompaniment to meat.

SERVES 6

2 tablespoons extra-virgin olive oil, plus 1 teaspoon for greasing the baking dish and more for drizzling

2 pounds (900 g) squash, peeled and cut into 1-inch (2.5 cm) cubes (you should have 1¼ to 1½ pounds/560 to 675 g, or about 3 cups, prepared squash)

2 teaspoons sea salt

¼ cup (50 g) short-grain or Arborio rice

⅔ cup (50 g) freshly grated Parmesan

1 garlic clove, cut lengthwise in half

Freshly ground black pepper

¼ teaspoon freshly grated nutmeg, or to taste

2 large eggs, whisked together

½ cup (50 g) Provençal Breadcrumbs (page 354)

1 In a large frying pan, heat the olive oil over medium heat. Add the squash and 1 teaspoon of the salt, cover, and cook over medium-low heat, stirring occasionally, until the squash has softened and is starting to disintegrate, 20 to 25 minutes. If there is a lot of liquid left toward the end of the cooking, raise the heat to evaporate most of it, but the squash doesn't need to be very dry. If all the liquid evaporates before the squash has softened, add ¼ cup (60 ml) water and continue cooking, covered, until the squash is done.

2 Meanwhile, half-fill a small saucepan with water and bring to a boil over high heat. Add the rice and the remaining 1 teaspoon salt and boil, uncovered, for 10 minutes; the rice should be al dente. Drain and set aside.

3 Preheat the oven to 375°F (190°C). Rub a 10-inch (25 cm) deep-dish pie plate, preferably ceramic, with the cut garlic clove, then coat with the 1 teaspoon olive oil. →

4 Place the warm cooked squash in a large bowl and stir in the rice and Parmesan. Add pepper to taste and the nutmeg, then adjust the seasoning to your taste. Stir in the eggs quickly so that they don't scramble. The mixture might seem on the liquid side–don't be alarmed.

5 Pour the mixture into the prepared pie plate and top with the breadcrumbs and a generous drizzling of olive oil. Bake for 35 minutes, or until lightly browned on top. Serve warm.

Cook's note

⁂

I'm never entirely sure when to use the words *courge*, *potiron*, or *citrouille*, but it's some consolation that the market vendors seem similarly confused. *Courge* ("winter squash" in English) is a more general term that encompasses the potiron and citrouille–the latter of which usually refers to American-style orange pumpkins. I have read that you can recognize the citrouille by its hard stem with five distinct sides, while the potiron has a more spongy, tapered stem. This does not quite clear up the mystery, though, since butternut squash has a stem that is both five-sided and tapered. All of these can be used interchangeably in recipes that call for pumpkin or squash.

SOUPE DE COURGE À L'ORANGE

Squash soup with orange

Much as I love soup made with roasted pumpkin, subtler squash varieties such as the local courge de Nice—which comes closest in taste and appearance to butternut squash—call for gentler treatment, resulting in a more delicate soup.

In this recipe, I use a trick that I picked up from farmer Louis Berthon, thickening the soup with a mixture of crème fraîche or cream, egg yolk, and olive oil. The egg yolk gives it a silky texture, while using just a small amount of cream allows the flavor of the squash to shine through.

This soup lends itself to nearly endless possible toppings: freshly grated nutmeg, thinly sliced chives, crunchy homemade croutons, toasted pumpkin seeds, sautéed wild mushrooms, sizzled lardons (bacon matchsticks), another spoonful of crème fraîche, or—for the adventurous—fried rounds of blood sausage. Choose at least two garnishes, including some salt and crunch, for maximum wow factor.

SERVES 4

2 tablespoons extra-virgin olive oil

1 leek, white and pale green parts only, cut lengthwise in half and then into ½ inch- (1 cm) wide slices

Sea salt

1 garlic clove, chopped

1¾ pounds (800 g) butternut or other similar squash, peeled, seeded, and diced (about 1 pound 2 ounces/500 g/2 ½ cups prepared squash) (see Cook's Note)

1½ cups (360 ml) chicken or vegetable stock, homemade (page 355) or store-bought

1 tablespoon finely grated orange zest (preferably from an organic orange)

Freshly ground pepper (white or black)

1 large egg yolk

2 tablespoons crème fraîche or heavy cream

Garnishes of your choice (see headnote)

1 In a medium saucepan, heat 1 tablespoon of the olive oil over medium heat. Add the leek and a pinch of salt, turn the heat down to low, and cook, stirring, until the leek is softened but not browned, 5 to 7 minutes.

2 Add the garlic and cook for 2 minutes, stirring.

3 Add the diced squash, stir, cover, and cook for 5 to 10 minutes, stirring occasionally to prevent the vegetables from sticking and browning, until the squash has started to soften.

4 Add the stock and orange zest and season with salt and pepper to taste, taking note first of whether the stock is salty. Bring to a boil, then lower the heat, partially cover, and let the soup bubble gently until the squash has softened completely, about 20 minutes longer.

5 Meanwhile, in a small bowl, whisk together the egg yolk, crème fraîche or heavy cream, and the remaining 1 tablespoon olive oil.

6 Using an immersion blender or stand blender, blend the soup until smooth; return it to the pan if you used a stand blender. Add the egg yolk mixture, stirring to incorporate. Warm over low heat for 2 to 3 minutes to thicken the soup, being careful not to let it come to a boil. Adjust the seasonings.

7 Top the soup with your chosen garnish(es) and serve, or place some of the garnish(es) in the bottom of each bowl and pour the soup over the top in front of your guests, for the French bistro experience.

Cook's note

Peeling squash can be one of the more perilous kitchen tasks. To avoid any mishaps, first trim the base of the squash so that it can sit flat. If using butternut squash, separate the narrower top from the bulbous end. Stand the squash on the flattened end and cut off the skin from top to bottom, using a sharp knife and following its natural curves. Your other hand should stay well out of the way of the knife, holding the squash in place. Or you could choose a variety such as red kuri squash, whose skin grows tender once cooked.

MINI CITROUILLES FARCIES AUX OIGNONS, CHAMPIGNONS, ET BLETTES

Mini pumpkins stuffed with onion, mushrooms, and chard

When it's not the season for les petits farcis (see page 159), Niçoise cooks find other vegetables to stuff, often in creative ways. This recipe comes from local farmer Aimé and his Tahitian wife, Cécilia, who run an organic stall at Libération Market selling unusual vegetable varieties alongside the Niçoise stalwarts.

Bright orange mini-pumpkins—an American variety called Jack Be Little—stood out next to the deep green bunches of chard, and I asked Cécilia if they were ornamental or edible. Her eyes brightened as she told me about this recipe, whose combination of ingredients—sweet onions, earthy wild mushrooms, slightly bitter chard leaves—sounded so tempting that I rushed home to make it right away. Cheese and a touch of crème fraîche bring all the flavors together, creating a soothing fall dish that's easy enough for a weeknight but fit for a celebratory meal.

SERVES 4

Four 10- to 12-ounce (275 to 325 g) mini pumpkins
  or 2 acorn squash (1½ pounds/675 g each)
8 ounces (about 3 cups/225 g) chanterelles or other
  wild mushrooms
3 tablespoons extra-virgin olive oil
1 yellow or white onion, cut lengthwise in half and
  thinly sliced
Sea salt

1 teaspoon fresh thyme leaves or ¼ teaspoon
  dried thyme
Leaves from ½ bunch Swiss chard (about
  4 ounces/100 g), thinly sliced
½ cup (10 g) flat-leaf parsley leaves, thinly sliced
2 tablespoons crème fraîche
⅔ cup (50 g) grated Comté or Swiss cheese
Freshly ground black pepper

1 Preheat the oven to 375°F (180°C).

2 Cut the tops off the pumpkins and scoop out the seeds and fibers with a spoon; set aside.
Or, if using acorn squash, cut lengthwise in half and scoop out the seeds and fibers. Put the pumpkins or squash in a baking pan.

3 Clean the mushrooms using a brush or a damp paper towel, rather than rinsing them, to prevent them from becoming waterlogged. Cut them into bite-sized pieces.

4 In a small frying pan, heat 1 tablespoon of the olive oil over medium-low heat. Add the onion with a pinch of salt and sauté until soft and lightly caramelized, about 10 minutes.

5 Meanwhile, in a medium frying pan, heat another 1 tablespoon of the olive oil over medium-high heat. Add the mushrooms and thyme and cook, stirring, until all the liquid the mushrooms release has evaporated and they have started to brown a little, 5 to 10 minutes. Stir in a pinch of salt and transfer to a bowl.

6 Heat the remaining 1 tablespoon olive oil in the same pan, add the chard leaves along with a pinch of salt, and cook until wilted, 1 to 2 minutes.

7 Add the caramelized onions and chard to the bowl with the mushrooms, and stir in the parsley, crème fraîche, and half the grated cheese. Season with salt if needed and pepper.

8 Fill the pumpkins or acorn squash with the mushroom mixture and top them with the remaining grated cheese. Place the lids in the pan next to the pumpkins, if using them. Roast until you can easily pierce the flesh with a knife, 30 to 35 minutes for small pumpkins, or 35 to 40 minutes for acorn squash.

9 Top the pumpkins, if using, with the lids before serving.

TROUCHIA

Swiss chard omelet

The Swiss chard omelet called trouchia, made with just enough egg to bind it together, was a traditional harvest snack during grape-picking season, but it makes great picnic food or brunch fare.

The key is not to precook the chard, but to get the temperature just right so that the leaves don't give off too much water as they cook in the egg mixture. It's safest to cook this in a nonstick pan, though I've gotten away with using my well-seasoned cast-iron pan.

If you find yourself with any leftovers, try them tucked into a sandwich and enjoy, preferably standing on a mountainside with wild thyme and rosemary at your feet. You can make the trouchia in advance and set aside at room temperature for 2 hours or refrigerate for up to 24 hours; bring it to room temperature before serving.

SERVES 4

2 tablespoons pine nuts

8 ounces (225 g) tender Swiss chard leaves (about 1 pound/450 g untrimmed chard; save the stems for another use)

5 large eggs

Sea salt and freshly ground black pepper

¼ cup (5 g) flat-leaf parsley leaves, thinly sliced

¼ cup (5 g) basil leaves, thinly sliced

6 mint leaves, thinly sliced

½ cup (40 g) freshly grated Parmesan

2 tablespoons extra-virgin olive oil

1 Toast the pine nuts in a small dry frying pan over medium-low heat, stirring constantly, until golden brown, 3 to 4 minutes. Remove from the heat and set aside.

2 Make a stack of chard leaves, cut them lengthwise in half, and slice the leaves crosswise ¼ inch (0.5 cm) thick. Continue until you have sliced all the leaves. (You should have about 6 cups.)

3 In a large bowl, whisk the eggs vigorously for about 1 minute, until fluffy. Season with salt and pepper to taste, then add the chard, herbs, Parmesan, and pine nuts and fold in with a rubber spatula, mixing until the chard is completely coated with egg.

4 Heat the oil in a heavy 9-inch (23 cm) frying pan with a tight-fitting lid over medium heat. Add the chard mixture and press down with the spatula to immerse the greens in the eggs as much as possible. Cover, turn the heat to low, and cook for 12 to 15 minutes, until the bottom of the omelet is golden brown and the top looks nearly set. Keep an eye on it to be sure that it doesn't cook too quickly.

5 Invert a plate over the pan, hold it in place with your hand, and carefully flip the omelet onto the plate. (If you find this too intimidating, you can slide the omelet onto a plate and place a second plate over the top to flip the omelet.) Slide it back into the frying pan and cook for another 5 to 7 minutes, uncovered, over low heat, until lightly browned on the other side. Transfer to a serving plate. Serve the trouchia warm or at room temperature.

FLANS DE BETTERAVE, SALADE DE MÂCHE AUX NOIX

Beet flans with lamb's lettuce and walnut dressing

Beet and lamb's lettuce (mâche) is a classic French combination, which here is presented in a more elegant form than the usual cubes of beet on salad. Also known as corn salad, lamb's lettuce is related to the medicinal plant valerian, and it is rich in omega-3s and beta carotene. This winter green grows in tiny bouquets attached at the root, which I break off before washing to remove most of the dirt and separate the leaves. The dark green leaves are thick and silky-textured, with a subtle tang. If you can't find lamb's lettuce, baby spinach and/or beet leaves would make a good substitute.

I learned this recipe decades ago from the late chef Robert Reynolds, who taught produce-driven French cooking classes in San Francisco and Portland. The flans can be served on their own as a starter, but I also love them as a side dish, especially with salmon, since the contrasting colors and flavors work beautifully together. You might even convert beet-haters with this dish, as the cream and egg mellow the earthy taste of the root vegetable. But this is not the time to use fancy striped or pink beets—the classic dark purple variety tastes best and results in the most dramatic color. I cook the flans in glass ramekins, which can go from oven to table.

SERVES 4

FOR THE FLANS

2 tablespoons unsalted butter, plus more for the ramekins

1 medium beet (about 6 ounces/150 g), peeled and cut into ½-inch (1 cm) dice (about 1 cup diced)

¾ cup (180 ml) heavy cream

2 large eggs

½ teaspoon sea salt

Freshly ground white or black pepper

FOR THE SALAD

½ cup (50 g) walnuts

1 tablespoon sherry vinegar

Sea salt and freshly ground black pepper

1 tablespoon finely minced shallot

2 tablespoons mild-tasting extra-virgin olive oil

2 tablespoons walnut oil

2 cups (about 4 ounces/100 g) packed lamb's lettuce or baby spinach leaves

For the flans

1 Preheat the oven to 325°F (160°C), with a rack in the middle of the oven.

2 Butter four ⅔- to ¾-cup (150 to 180 ml) ramekins. Line the bottom of each ramekin with a circle of parchment paper if you wish to turn out the flans once they are cooked. Line a roasting pan with two layers of paper towels and set aside.

3 Put the diced beet in a saucepan with the cream, bring to a simmer, partially cover, and cook until the beet is soft when pierced with a knife, about 20 minutes.

4 Pour the beet and cream into a blender, add the butter, and blend to a smooth puree. Whisk the eggs together in a small bowl, then add them to the beet mixture, along with the salt and pepper to taste and blend well (be careful to avoid creating too much foam).

5 Fill the ramekins with the beet mixture and place them in the roasting pan. Pour enough very hot water into the pan to come halfway up the sides of the ramekins. Carefully transfer the pan to the oven and bake until a toothpick inserted in the center of a flan comes out clean, 30 to 45 minutes, depending on the depth of the ramekins. Remove from the oven and let the flans rest in the pan.

6 The flans can be served warm or at room temperature; you can prepare them up to several hours ahead of time and reheat briefly in the microwave, if you wish.

For the salad

1 Preheat the oven to 350°F (180°C).

2 Spread the walnuts on a baking sheet and toast for about 5 minutes, until they darken slightly in color (be careful not to burn them). Remove from the oven.

3 In a small bowl, whisk together the vinegar, salt and pepper to taste, and the shallot. Whisk in the olive and walnut oils 1 tablespoon at a time, whisking after each addition.

4 Toss the greens with the vinaigrette.

Presentation

Turn a flan out onto each plate (or leave them in the ramekins, if you wish), peel off the parchment, if you used it, and surround with the salad. Scatter the walnuts over the top.

Variation

※

Replace the beet with red kuri (potimarron) or kabocha squash, whose dense, not-too-sweet flesh retains its character even when mixed with cream and egg. Top the flans with sautéed wild mushrooms, such as the jet-black horns of plenty (*trompettes de la mort*, or "trumpets of death," in French).

PETIT ÉPEAUTRE AUX CÈPES, TRÉVISE, ET NOISETTES

Einkorn wheat berries with porcini mushrooms, radicchio, and hazelnuts

Driving through the lavender fields of Provence for the first time, I was struck not just by the fragrant purple blossoms but also by the fields of wheat interspersed with the neat rows of lavender bushes. I grew up in the vast flatness of Canada's wheat country, and the rolling hills of Provence were not where I expected to see the spiky ears tilting in the breeze.

It turns out that a variety of einkorn wheat known as *petit épeautre de Haute Provence*, or *engrain*, has been grown in the South of France since 9000 BC, making it one of the world's oldest wheat crops. Though the development of more productive wheat varieties has turned it into a curiosity rather than a staple food, since the 1990s, this protein-and-vitamin-rich grain has been enjoying a renaissance in the Alpes de Haute Provence, the region between Nice and Provence that is famed for its lavender. Crops of einkorn wheat are often alternated with lavender and legumes to keep the soil healthy, and although this wheat takes eleven months to reach maturity, it has the advantage of thriving in dry conditions at high altitudes.

Petit épeautre is not to be confused with spelt, also known as *grand épeautre*, though the two can be used interchangeably. Being a closer cousin of wheat, spelt is a more productive plant with a higher gluten content; einkorn is said to be easier to digest by those with wheat intolerances (but those with a true allergy should still avoid it).

Although you can theoretically cook einkorn or spelt without soaking it first, soaking the grains for 24 hours reduces the cooking time considerably and allows the nutrients to be better absorbed. There is no need to stir the einkorn constantly—I let it soften first with the lid on, then stir it toward the end. Another benefit of substituting einkorn for rice is that you can make this dish in advance; the chewy grains will retain their texture once cooked.

SERVES 4 AS A MAIN COURSE, 6 AS A STARTER

- ½ cup (15 g) dried porcini mushrooms, rinsed and soaked in 4 cups (1 l) water for at least 30 minutes (reserve the water when you drain the porcini)
- 1 tablespoon extra-virgin olive oil
- 1 onion, diced
- Sea salt
- 1½ cups (13 ounces/350 g) einkorn wheat berries or spelt berries, soaked in plenty of water at room temperature for 24 hours and drained
- ½ cup (125 ml) dry white wine or dry white vermouth
- ½ head radicchio (about 4 ounces/100 g), cut lengthwise in half and then crosswise into ⅛-inch (3 mm) wide slices
- ⅔ cup (50 g) freshly grated Parmesan, plus more for serving
- 2 tablespoons unsalted butter
- Freshly ground black pepper
- ½ cup (10 g) flat-leaf parsley leaves, thinly sliced
- ¼ cup (30 g) toasted and skinned hazelnuts, lightly crushed (optional)

1   Lift the porcini out of the water using your hands and squeeze them dry. Strain the water through a very fine strainer into another bowl, leaving any sand in the bottom of the bowl behind. If the mushrooms are larger than bite-sized, slice them into bite-sized pieces. Set the mushrooms and their soaking liquid aside.

2   Heat the olive oil in a heavy saucepan or a Dutch oven over medium-low heat. Add the onion with a large pinch of salt and cook, stirring, for 5 minutes, or until softened and translucent but not browned. Add the drained einkorn or spelt and cook, stirring, for 2 minutes, to lightly toast the berries. Add the wine or vermouth, turn the heat up to medium, and cook, stirring, until the liquid has evaporated, about 2 minutes.

3   Add the soaking liquid from the porcini along with 2 large pinches of salt, cover, and cook over low heat for 15 minutes (the liquid should bubble gently). Stir in the drained mushrooms and the radicchio, cover, and cook for 15 minutes.

4   Remove the lid, turn the heat up to medium, and let the liquid reduce for 10 to 15 minutes, stirring frequently. When the liquid just covers the bottom of the pan and appears slightly thickened and starchy (do not expect the same creaminess as risotto), turn the heat off. (If you would like to serve this dish later on, set it aside at this stage and reheat it when you are nearly ready to serve it.)

5   Add the butter and Parmesan to the hot grains. Cover with a lid and let sit for 2 minutes, then stir well. The mixture should be slightly creamy, with just a little liquid. Add more salt if necessary and season with pepper to taste.

6   Transfer the einkorn or spelt to shallow bowls and top with grated Parmesan, the parsley, and crushed hazelnuts, if using.

Cook's notes

If you can only find hazelnuts raw with their skins, it's easy enough to toast them. First taste the hazelnuts to make sure they are fresh; they should have no bitterness. Preheat the oven to 350°F (180°C), spread the hazelnuts on a baking sheet, and toast for 10 to 15 minutes, until golden and fragrant. Immediately transfer the nuts to a dish towel, roll them up in it, and set aside to steam for 2 minutes. Rub the hazelnuts in the towel with your hands to remove the skins. Remove the hazelnuts from the towel once they have cooled and discard the skins. Don't fret if some of the skins still cling to the nuts–it will not take anything away from the flavor.

To crush toasted hazelnuts, I like to use my trusty mortar and pestle, but you can also return them to the dish towel once you have discarded the skins and bash them a few times with a rolling pin or the bottom of a heavy pot.

Hunting for wild mushrooms

If you go walking in the mountains behind Nice in the late summer or early fall, you will likely see a few people sneaking around in the undergrowth, cradling flat-bottomed baskets filled with fragrant cèpes (porcini) or perhaps sanguins, orange-capped mushrooms that are named for the blood-like juice they release when cut. There is no point in asking anyone where they found these treasures, as they would not reveal this even to their closest friends (I can attest to this!). Mushroom hunters jealously guard their secret spots, returning to them year after year to collect their bounty.

This region produces a wide variety of mushrooms that are prized for their quality, thanks to the combination of intense sun and humidity. The best season for wild mushrooms is between late August and the first heavy rains, which come anytime between September and November. Though the rain encourages mushroom growth, the extra water dilutes their flavor and makes them trickier to cook, since they give off more liquid. So, during the brief window when wild mushrooms are at their peak, I try to use them as often as possible. They can be pricey, but a little goes a long way, especially when the mushrooms are not the main ingredient in a dish.

When preparing wild mushrooms, try to avoid washing them to prevent them from becoming waterlogged, though some sturdier varieties like cèpes can withstand a quick rinse. I use a slightly stiff mushroom brush to remove any earth and twigs or, failing that, a damp paper towel.

Below are a few of the wild mushroom varieties that you might come across at the market. The French and English names can be quite different once translated, but they are often equally colorful and descriptive.

CÈPE (CEP OR PORCINI)

With an aroma that can rival that of truffles, another edible fungus, cèpes have an earthy, nutty flavor and a meaty texture that stands up beautifully to grilling and to roasting in the oven (or, even better, over a wood fire) next to meat or fish. The most prized French variety is the *Boletus edulis*, or Bordeaux cèpe, with a reddish-brown cap and rounded stem; despite the name, it grows in several French regions, including the Mediterranean Alps. Dried cèpes can be as rewarding as fresh, since their flavor is so concentrated.

When buying the fresh mushrooms, check the stems for signs of worms (French vendors will often cut them open for display to show they are not infested), and avoid those with green or yellow patches beneath the cap, which will turn slimy once cooked. Though overgrown cèpes can look impressive, smaller specimens are more flavorful. If you get your hands on perfect ones the size of Champagne corks, try them shaved raw with just a drizzling of good olive oil, a generous shower of Parmesan shavings, and a sprinkling of fleur de sel.

GIROLLE (CHANTERELLE)

My favorite mushroom, both to look at and to cook, girolles have an eye-catching yellow-apricot color and a cap shaped like a flamenco dancer's skirt. More commonly associated with cooler climates, they can be found in the mountains around Nice. Look for those with firm, creamy-colored stems and unblemished caps; if they feel heavy, they may give off a lot of water once cooked. Slightly confusingly, a mushroom of the same family with a thin yellow stem and gray cap is known as *chanterelle* in French; it is very delicate, and should not be stored for long.

Mushrooms from the girolle family are best cooked slowly in butter over low heat; this way, they will retain their beautiful shape and texture. I try to choose small ones so that I can leave them whole. If they give off water, turn up the heat until it has evaporated, but try not to let the mushrooms brown. With their delicate, almost apricot-like flavor, girolles are delicious in an omelet, on top of fresh pasta or gnocchi, or alongside fish, chicken, or veal; it's best to keep things simple. I never use garlic when cooking girolles; instead I might add gentler-tasting minced shallots or spring onions, though these are barely necessary. A sprinkling of chopped flat-leaf parsley accentuates the deep orange color of the cooked mushrooms and adds a touch of freshness.

PIED DE MOUTON ("SHEEP'S HOOF"; HEDGEHOG IN ENGLISH)

With a shape reminiscent of the girolle, only chunkier, pied de mouton (or hedgehog) mushrooms grow in circles and are distinguishable by the undersides of their caps, which look like a cream-colored shag carpet. Their taste is similar to that of the girolle, with a nutty edge; being more robust in texture and flavor, they make a good addition to stews, particularly those with pork or veal. If you are sautéing hedgehogs, treat them the same way as girolles, keeping the heat low so that they soften while holding their shape. You can also get away with flambéing these mushrooms with a little brandy and dousing them in cream (or, better yet, crème fraîche) at the end of cooking; if treating them this way, I would serve them on toasted sliced sourdough.

TROMPETTE DE LA MORT ("TRUMPET OF DEATH"; HORN OF PLENTY IN ENGLISH)

Despite the sinister French name, which translates as "trumpet of death," this charcoal-colored mushroom that turns jet-back when cooked has much to offer, adding an earthy layer of flavor to simple dishes and contrasting beautifully with the season's squash. The French name is said to come from the fact that its brief appearance often coincides with All Saints Day on November 1, when the French traditionally place chrysanthemums on the graves of their ancestors. →

Growing among the damp leaves of the forest floor, these mushrooms usually need a thorough brushing to remove stray pieces of twig, leaf, and moss—try not to wash them in water, as they will absorb moisture and then spit it out in the pan. Thin and delicate, they are best treated gently in the same way as chanterelles; they also dry well in a dehydrator or very low oven. To use dried horns of plenty, you can rehydrate them in warm water, like cèpes, or grind them to a powder and sprinkle them on anything that is calling out for a deeper flavor.

SANGUIN (LITERALLY, "BLOOD"; SAFFRON MILK CAP, PINE MUSHROOM, OR ORANGE LATEX MILKY IN ENGLISH)

The French name of this orange mushroom with its parasol-like cap is descriptive, since it gives off a blood-red juice (referred to as a latex) when cut. One of the more common wild mushrooms in the Nice region—though it can easily be confused with similar-looking poisonous mushrooms, so foragers should be careful—it is often preserved in oil and vinegar with herbs and spices, to be served as an appetizer or in a salad. Saffron milk caps can also be fried like other mushrooms, in which case mild-tasting olive oil suits them better than butter, and they can stand up to a persillade (a mixture of garlic and parsley). Look for saffron milk caps that are firm and unblemished, avoiding any that are turning brown or have streaks of green mold.

VESSE DE LOUP ("WOLF'S FART"; PUFFBALL OR KING OYSTER MUSHROOM IN ENGLISH)

Another mushroom that is colorfully named in French, the puffball can look like a stray soccer ball from afar. Its Greek name, *lycoperdon*, translates literally as "wolf's fart" because of the puff of smelly powder it releases when disturbed. Because of their size, puffballs are most often sliced and fried like tofu steaks—caramelization brings out their flavor—or chopped up and added to other dishes, particularly omelets.

MOULES À LA SAUCE TOMATE SAFRANÉE

Mussels with tomato and saffron

Steaming pots of moules marinières (mussels in white wine) and their accompanying frites, or French fries, are synonymous with holidays by the sea in France. If Nice has plenty of brasseries where you can dig into this dish, few visitors realize that the mussels almost always come from the opposite end of the country.

France's most renowned mussel-producing region is the Bay of Mont Saint Michel, which spans both sides of the border between Normandy and Brittany. Here mussels are cultivated on wooden stakes called *bouchots*. This method dates back to 1235, when a shipwrecked Irishman, Patrick Walton, set up a net held by wooden posts in the hope of catching water birds. Seeing the number of mussels that collected on the stakes, he planted more stakes, until he had created the region's first mussel farm. Available from July to February, moules de bouchot are small in size but big in flavor, with slender black shells and sweet orange-gold flesh.

From May to August, a larger type of mussel known as *moule de corde* appears at the markets. Cultivated on ropes rather than stakes, mainly off the western coast of France, these mussels remain fully immersed, rather than being washed by tides like bouchot mussels. Their shells are therefore more fragile, and they taste more strongly of the sea. Although they are more work to wash than bouchot mussels, with barnacles and hipster-like beards clinging to their shells, I enjoy eating them just as much.

On Saturdays at the Cours Saleya market, a seafood stall sells mussels from around Bouzigues, on the southwest coast of France. Known as Mediterranean mussels, they are immersed in deep water using cotton nets, taking a year to mature. Available year-round, though not in large quantities, they are prized for their meatiness and rich, not-too-salty flavor.

Given that each mussel has its season(s), there is no wrong time to eat them, but I like to serve this dish in the fall, when moules de bouchot are at their most flavorful (other types of mussel also work well). Instead of the traditional accompaniment of frites, I serve these with panisses, chickpea fries, which complement the southern flavors in the sauce.

**SERVES 4 AS A MAIN COURSE,
  6 AS A STARTER**

A pinch of saffron threads

¼ teaspoon fine sea salt (optional)

1 tablespoon water

2¼ pounds (about 1 kg) mussels in the shell

3 tablespoons unsalted butter

1 yellow or red onion, diced

2 garlic cloves, minced

1¼ cups (300 ml) Coulis de Tomates (page 337) or
  store-bought passata (Italian strained tomatoes)

½ cup (120 ml) dry white wine or dry
  white vermouth

¼ to ½ teaspoon Espelette chile powder (or another
  mild to medium-hot chile powder)

A handful of flat-leaf parsley leaves,
  roughly chopped

Crusty bread or Panisses (page 239) for serving

1 Crush the saffron in a mortar with the salt (or rub the threads between your fingers to crush them and drop them into a small bowl) and add the 1 tablespoon water. Set aside for at least 15 minutes—steeping the saffron extracts more of its color and flavor.

2 Rinse the mussels in a large bowl of water and then lift them out with your hands into a colander, leaving the water and sand behind. Remove the beards (the hairy part clinging to the shell) by pulling them with your fingers. Discard any mussels with broken shells, or those that are wide open and will not remain closed when pressed shut (you should feel some resistance). Using fresh water, rinse the mussels once or twice more in the same way, until there is no sand remaining at the bottom of the bowl.

3 Place the mussels in a medium pot, cover with the lid, and cook over high heat until they open, shaking the pot occasionally; this should take no more than 3 or 4 minutes. Remove the mussels from the pot with a slotted spoon and remove and discard the empty half of each shell. Arrange the mussels in their shells on an ovenproof serving platter and cover lightly with foil. Strain the mussel juices and rinse out the pot.

4 Preheat the oven to 200°F (95°C).

5 Melt the butter in the pot over medium-low heat, then add the onion with a pinch of salt and cook, stirring, for 5 minutes, or until translucent. Add the garlic and cook for another minute or so, then add the tomato coulis, wine, and reserved mussel juices.

6 Bring to a boil and continue boiling until the liquid is reduced by half, 15 to 20 minutes (it should start to thicken like tomato sauce for pasta).

7 While the sauce is reducing, place the mussels in the oven to warm up.

8 When the sauce has reduced, stir in the Espelette or other chile powder, the saffron with its water, and the parsley; adjust the seasoning if necessary. Spoon the sauce over the warmed mussels and bring the platter to the table to serve family-style, soaking up the juices with crusty bread or panisses.

ENCORNETS FARCIS

Stuffed squid

Entering the lace-curtained Chez Palmyre is like stepping back in time: vintage ads and repurposed cooking tools brighten the wood-paneled and exposed-brick walls, and wooden bistro tables sit side by side, with polished silver cutlery and a napkin ring at each place setting. At lunch and dinner on weekdays only, the dining room fills to bursting with local and international food lovers, who marvel at the bargain three-course menu (20 euros at the time of writing) while Vincent Verneveaux toils in the kitchen, smiling at the regulars who pop their heads in to thank him.

When Vincent took over this institution, he had big shoes to fill: Tuscan-born Palmyre, who founded the restaurant with her husband, Jean, in 1926, was a beloved Old Town personality, overseeing the kitchen and greeting her adoring fans until her death at age ninety-five in 2009. Her daughters, then in their seventies, quickly realized that they could not continue without her, but they feared selling to the wrong person. With culinary credentials that included working at the Hotel Negresco under the famously demanding Jacques Maximin, cooking for President François Mitterrand, and several years as a private chef on luxury yachts, Vincent was also a regular customer with a deep respect for the restaurant's history and reputation. Chez Palmyre could not have found a better buyer, and like many who had known the restaurant during Palmyre's reign, I breathed a sigh of relief.

At the helm of a restaurant best known for its great value, the modest yet perfectionist Vincent has never cut corners. He keeps costs down by doing his own food shopping, often starting his days at dawn (which is why he closes on weekends). Instead of sticking to the same repertoire of dishes, he changes the menu every two weeks, revisiting French classics such as oeufs en meurette (poached eggs in red wine sauce) and blanquette de veau (veal stew with cream), as well as lesser-known local dishes like tripes à la niçoise (stewed tripe) and encornets farcis (stuffed squid). His wife, Sam, and business partner, Philippe Terranova, run the dining room with the same calm efficiency that he practices in the kitchen.

I had come across various versions of stuffed squid in local cookbooks, and I asked Vincent to share his recipe. Though it wasn't on the menu that week, he found time to demonstrate the dish for me, all the while telling me that his is not the definitive version. "You can use whatever ingredients you have available—squid are also delicious stuffed with a mini-ratatouille."

Don't worry about finding squid that are exactly the right size for this recipe; you can use smaller or larger squid, adapting the serving portions to their size. Larger squid may need to cook longer; you can test for tenderness with the tip of a knife. Serve this dish as a course on its own, or with new potatoes or rice. Any leftover filling can be frozen for up to a month, as long as the squid were not previously frozen.

SERVES 4

2 tablespoons long-grain white rice

1 tablespoon coarse sea salt

4 cups (120 g) spinach or Swiss chard leaves, large
    stems removed

8 cleaned whole squid, with their tentacles, bodies
    about 6 inches (15 cm) long

3 tablespoons extra-virgin olive oil, plus more
    for drizzling

1 onion, finely minced

6 garlic cloves, finely minced

1 celery stalk, with its leaves if possible, cut into
    ¼-inch (0.5 cm) dice, leaves (if you have them) cut
    into ¼-inch (0.5 cm) wide slices

Sea salt

Quick Tomato Sauce (page 339), made with basil,
    oregano, or marjoram, or 2 cups (480 ml) store-
    bought tomato sauce

½ cup (120 ml) dry white wine or dry
    white vermouth

Freshly ground black pepper

2 tablespoons roughly chopped flat-leaf parsley

1 Bring a small pot of water to a boil. Add the rice and boil for 10 minutes, uncovered. Drain in a
    sieve and set aside to cool (you will have about ¼ cup/45 g cooked rice).

2 Half-fill a large pot with water and bring to a boil. Add the coarse salt, then add the spinach
    leaves and blanch for 1 minute, or blanch the Swiss chard leaves for 3 to 4 minutes, until tender.
Drain in a colander, rinse under cold water, and squeeze dry with your hands. Finely chop the
spinach or chard; you should have ½ to ⅔ cup/80 to 100 g cooked greens.

3 Separate the tentacles and "wings" from the bodies of the squid, discarding the heads. If the
    bodies still have their outer membranes, remove them by sliding your fingers underneath the
membranes at the pointy end of the squid and pulling them down like a sock (if this does not work,
you may need to remove the membranes in strips).

4 Wash the squid and tentacles inside and out and pat dry with paper towels. Cut the tentacles
    into ¼-inch (0.5 cm) pieces and set aside. (I do not usually use the wings for the filling, but they
can be fried separately and tossed with garlic and parsley.)

5 In a medium heavy saucepan or a sauté pan, heat 2 tablespoons of the olive oil over medium
    heat. Add the onion, garlic, and celery, with a pinch of salt, and cook over medium-low heat for 5
to 7 minutes, until the vegetables are softened but not browned.

6 Add the chopped tentacles, turn up the heat to high, and cook, stirring, for about 5 minutes,
    until the liquid has evaporated. Transfer to a medium bowl and add the rice, spinach or chard,
and ½ cup (120 ml) of the tomato sauce, stirring to combine. Let the filling cool for a few minutes.

7 Transfer the filling to a pastry bag with the end cut off to create a 1-inch (2.5 cm) opening, or a
    ziplock bag with a lower corner cut off (you can also fill the squid using a small spoon, though it
helps in that case to have a second person holding the squid open!). Fill the squid bodies, inserting
the end of the bag (or spoon) well into the squid. Leave some space at the top so you can close the
bodies with toothpicks; the filling will expand a little as it cooks, so do not overfill.

8 Heat the remaining 1 tablespoon olive oil in a heavy sauté pan or Dutch oven over medium heat.
    Add the stuffed squid and lightly brown them, about 3 minutes on each side.

9 Deglaze the pan with the white wine or vermouth and let it bubble for 1 minute. Add the remaining tomato sauce and bring to a simmer. Cover and cook over low heat for 20 to 30 minutes, until the squid are tender, adding a little water if the sauce begins to dry out.

10 Serve the squid in shallow bowls, topped with a drizzle of olive oil, some pepper, and the chopped parsley.

BOUILLABAISSE DE POULET ET ROUILLE

Chicken with pastis and chile-saffron aïoli

I first tasted this dish on the tree-shaded terrace of a family-run restaurant in the hills of Nice. It has the robust flavors of the Provençal fish stew bouillabaisse—onion, tomato, fennel, saffron, and a hint of orange—but with chicken replacing the mix of Mediterranean fish, some of which can be challenging to find even in Nice. The chef wouldn't give me his recipe, but with a little research and tinkering, I came up with this version, which I love just as much.

This fricassée also goes by the name *poulet au pastis*, referring to the anise-flavored alcohol used in the marinade (plan on starting this dish the day before cooking it). Most commonly sold under the brand names Ricard and Pernod, it's an apéritif that brings up images of sun-wizened men in flat caps playing *pétanque* in a dusty village square. As a drink, pastis is diluted with plenty of water, which turns it from deep gold to an opaque pale yellow. Because it's so strong in flavor and alcohol, I mix it with white wine in the marinade—I recommend you serve the rest of the wine with the dish, so a Provence white would be ideal (or a Vermentino from Italy). Don't be put off by the strong licorice scent as you open the bottle of pastis; the anise mellows considerably as it cooks.

Like bouillabaisse, poulet au pastis is traditionally served with Rouille (page 348), aïoli turbocharged with saffron and chile pepper. This may be dabbed directly onto the chicken and slathered onto small boiled potatoes, which make the perfect accompaniment.

SERVES 4

FOR THE MARINADE

½ cup (120 ml) pastis (or other anise-flavored alcohol)

½ cup (120 ml) dry white wine

1 tablespoon extra-virgin olive oil

A pinch of saffron threads, crushed in a mortar with a little salt or crushed with your fingers

1 teaspoon fennel seeds, lightly crushed in a mortar

1 teaspoon sea salt

Freshly ground black pepper

1 free-range chicken (about 3 pounds/1.3 kg), cut into 8 pieces, or 4 free-range chicken legs (with the skin), each cut in half

FOR THE STEW

3 sprigs flat-leaf parsley, plus chopped parsley for garnish

2 sprigs fennel leaves or wild fennel (optional)

3 long strips orange zest, removed with a vegetable peeler

1 tablespoon extra-virgin olive oil

1 red onion, cut lengthwise in half and thinly sliced crosswise

1 medium fennel bulb, trimmed, cut lengthwise in half and thinly sliced crosswise

Sea salt

1¾ cups (450 ml) Coulis de Tomates (page 337) or store-bought passata (Italian strained tomatoes)

Freshly ground black pepper

FOR SERVING

1 pound (about 450 g) fingerling potatoes (10 to 12)

1 bay leaf

1 teaspoon coarse sea salt

Rouille (page 348)

For the marinade

1   In a medium bowl, stir together the pastis, white wine, olive oil, crushed saffron, fennel seeds, salt, and pepper to taste.

2   Lightly score the chicken on the skin side so that the flesh can absorb the marinade, and place it in a dish large enough to hold it in one layer, with the pieces close together.

3   Pour the marinade over the chicken and turn it to thoroughly coat the pieces. Cover with plastic wrap or a plate, and refrigerate for 12 to 24 hours; turn the chicken at least once as it marinates.

For the stew

1   Tie the parsley sprigs, fennel sprigs, if using, and orange zest strips together with kitchen string to make a bouquet garni and set aside. Remove the chicken pieces from the marinade (reserve the marinade) and dry on paper towels.

2   Heat the olive oil in a large heavy frying pan over medium heat until it is hot but not smoking. Add the chicken pieces and cook, turning occasionally, until golden brown on all sides, 10 to 12 minutes total.

3   Transfer the chicken to a large Dutch oven (or a heavy ovenproof saucepan) and reduce the heat under the frying pan. Pour away most of the fat, leaving about 2 tablespoons of it in the pan.

4   Preheat the oven to 350°F (180°C).

5   Add the sliced onion and fennel to the frying pan, along with a large pinch of salt, and cook over medium heat, stirring occasionally, until softened and pale golden, about 10 minutes.

6   Pour the reserved marinade over the onion and fennel and turn the heat up to high. Boil until the marinade has reduced and is almost syrupy, about 2 minutes, then add the tomato coulis and cook over medium heat for 5 minutes. Adjust the seasoning with salt and pepper and remove from the heat.

7   Tuck the bouquet garni in among the chicken pieces and carefully pour the tomato sauce over the chicken. Cover with a lid.

8   Transfer the pot to the oven and cook the chicken for about 45 minutes, until the meat is fully cooked. (You can also cook the chicken in a saucepan over low heat for about 45 minutes, checking that the meat is not sticking to the pan.)

9   While the chicken is cooking, place the potatoes in a medium saucepan and add the bay leaf, salt, and water to cover. Bring to a boil, covered, and cook over medium heat for 15 to 20 minutes, until a knife easily pierces the largest potato. Drain and set aside in the hot pan.

10   Divide the chicken pieces and sauce among four shallow bowls, or arrange the chicken on a serving platter with the sauce. Sprinkle the chicken with chopped parsley. Pass the rouille at the table to dollop onto the chicken and the potatoes.

MAGRET DE CANARD AU MIEL ET À L'ANIS

Duck breasts with honey and aniseed

The thick duck breasts known as *magrets* make a perfect match for deeply flavored honey, such as chestnut, *garrigue* (scrubby wild herbs that grow in the mountains), or heather. But don't worry if you can't find these–any dark but not-too-strong honey will fit the bill.

The original version of this recipe, which I found in a magazine that I have long since misplaced, called for several different spices, including Szechuan pepper. After making it a few times, I decided that green aniseed was really the only essential spice, giving the duck a distinctly Provençal flavor. Soy sauce and balsamic vinegar seem an unlikely combination, but the flavors work surprisingly well together.

I often serve these duck breasts with Panisses (page 239) and a green vegetable, such as broccoli florets, green beans, or asparagus.

SERVES 4

2 large duck breasts (magrets de canard; see Cook's Notes), 12 to 14 ounces (325 to 375 g) each

Coarse sea salt and freshly ground black pepper

2 tablespoons dark honey

2 tablespoons plus 1 teaspoon balsamic vinegar

1 teaspoon Japanese soy sauce

1 teaspoon powdered green aniseed (or substitute half a star anise, crushed)

1 teaspoon crushed pink peppercorns for garnish (optional)

1 Trim the excess fat from the duck breasts by placing them fat side down on a cutting board and cutting away any fat that extends beyond the flesh. Using a sharp knife, score the fat in a crisscross pattern, without cutting all the way to the flesh. (Be sure to do this while the magrets are still cold, or the fat will soften too much, making it difficult to score.) Season the fat side generously with coarse salt and grind some black pepper over both sides.

2 Combine the honey with 1 teaspoon balsamic vinegar, the soy sauce, and green aniseed (or star anise).

3 Place the duck breasts fat side down in a heavy frying pan that holds them fairly snugly, and place the pan over medium heat to warm it up. When the fat starts to melt, turn the heat down to medium-low and let the duck cook slowly until the fat side is well browned, spooning most of the excess fat into a bowl as it accumulates. This should take 10 to 12 minutes.

4 Turn the duck breasts over–leave about 2 tablespoons of the fat in the pan–and cook on the other side for 5 to 7 minutes. The duck should still be pink (but not raw) inside. Set aside on a plate, covered with foil, in a warm place for 5 to 10 minutes. Discard any excess fat from the frying pan. $\rightarrow$

5 Once the duck has rested, set the pan over medium heat, and add the honey mixture to it. Put the duck breasts back in the pan and turn to coat with the honey mixture as it bubbles and thickens, about 2 minutes.

6 Remove the duck breasts to a plate and add the remaining 2 tablespoons balsamic vinegar to the pan to thin the sauce. Cook for another minute, until the sauce is slightly syrupy. Strain the sauce into a small jug or pitcher.

7 To serve the duck, slice each breast lengthwise in half (half a magret is enough for one serving) or slice the whole breasts crosswise into ½-inch- (1 cm) thick slices. Arrange the duck on individual plates (next to your chosen accompaniment), sprinkle with the crushed pink peppercorns, if using, and drizzle the sauce around the plates.

Cook's notes

Duck magrets are becoming more common in American supermarkets and specialty shops, but if you can't find them locally, D'Artagnan sells them by mail order (www.dartagnan.com).

Whatever you do, don't throw away the excess duck fat. Use it to sauté potatoes, as they do in Southwest France, tossing them with chopped parsley and garlic at the end, or massage it onto your Thanksgiving turkey. Strained duck fat keeps for several months in the refrigerator in a sealed jar.

VEAU EN MIJOTÉ À LA NIÇOISE

Veal stew with tomatoes, olives, and mushrooms

I have slightly adapted this recipe from one by Laurence Duperthuy, a Niçoise who runs the cooking school Notes de Cuisine in the pretty town of La Colle sur Loup, in the hills near Saint-Paul-de-Vence. She is also the author of the beautiful blog *Variations Gourmandes*. The ingredient list sounds simple enough, but the finished dish is greater than the sum of its parts; I particularly love the saltiness the olives impart. Although it takes a couple of hours to cook, this is a wonderful make-ahead dish that tastes even better the next day. If you can't find veal shoulder or prefer not to eat veal, you can make this dish with beef or pork, using cuts that are meant for stewing.

Serve the stew with pasta, polenta, mashed potatoes, or rice.

SERVES 6

2 pounds (900 g) boneless veal shoulder, cut into 2-inch (5 cm) chunks

1 teaspoon fine sea salt

2 sprigs fresh thyme or 1 teaspoon dried thyme or oregano

1 sprig rosemary

1 bay leaf

5 tablespoons (75 ml) extra-virgin olive oil

3 onions, cut lengthwise in half and sliced crosswise ⅛ inch (3 mm) thick

3 carrots, cut lengthwise in half and sliced ⅛ inch (3 mm) thick on the diagonal

2 garlic cloves, cut lengthwise in half and sliced as thin as possible

½ cup (120 ml) dry white wine or dry white vermouth

3 cups (about 1 pound/450 g) cherry tomatoes, cut in half through the stem end, or one 14-ounce (400 ml) can diced Italian tomatoes

Freshly ground black pepper

11 ounces (300 g) cremini mushrooms, sliced ¼ inch (0.5 cm) thick (about 3 cups sliced)

½ cup (90 g) Niçoise or other flavorful black olives, pitted or not

Sea salt (coarse or fine)

½ lemon

Parsley or basil leaves for garnish

1 Trim any excess fat from the veal, without aiming to remove all the fat. Transfer the veal chunks to a bowl, toss with the 1 teaspoon fine sea salt, and leave for at least 15 minutes, and up to 1 hour, so the veal can absorb the salt.

2 Tie the thyme sprigs, if using, bay leaf, and rosemary together with kitchen string to make a bouquet garni.

3 Preheat the oven to 300°F (150°C).

4 Heat 2 tablespoons of the olive oil in a large Dutch oven or other heavy ovenproof pot over medium heat. Add the veal (cook it in two batches if necessary so that the pieces are not touching) and sear, turning once, for 3 to 4 minutes on each side, until the meat is browned and the juices have started to caramelize in the pot. Set the browned meat aside on a plate. →

5 Add another 2 tablespoons of the olive oil to the pot, then add the onions and carrots, along with a large pinch of salt, and cook, stirring, for about 5 minutes, until the onions have softened and turned pale golden. Add the garlic and cook for 1 to 2 minutes, being careful not to burn the garlic.

6 Add the white wine or vermouth and let it boil and reduce for about 1 minute, scraping the bottom of the pot with a wooden spatula. Add the tomatoes, bouquet garni, dried thyme or oregano, if using, and veal. Season with pepper, bring to a boil, cover the pot, and transfer to the oven.

7 Heat the remaining 1 tablespoon olive oil in a medium frying pan over medium-high heat. Add the mushrooms and sauté, without adding any salt, until lightly browned, about 5 minutes. Salt the mushrooms lightly once they have browned, and set aside.

8 After 1 hour, remove the pot from the oven, add the sautéed mushrooms, and stir. If the liquid level is below that of the meat, add water just to cover it. Taste the sauce for seasoning and adjust if necessary.

9 Return the pot to the oven and cook for another hour, stirring once or twice and checking the level of the liquid. About 5 minutes before the end of the cooking time, add the olives to the pot. Test the meat by removing a chunk; it should be tender enough to cut with a fork. Finish the stew with a squeeze of lemon and remove from the heat.

10 Garnish the stew with torn fresh parsley or basil leaves and serve. Leftover stew will keep for up to 3 days in the refrigerator, and it only improves with each day.

CARRÉ D'AGNEAU, CROÛTE AUX HERBES

Rack of lamb with mustard-herb crust

Lamb is a meat most often associated with spring, and particularly Easter, but it's especially flavorful in the fall, when the animals have had a chance to mature while feeding on summer pasture. Sold between September and December in France and known as *broutard*, this meat is rosy red in color (rather than pale pink) and can stand up to bold flavors like mustard and herb-rich Provençal breadcrumbs. Ratatouille (page 163) makes a perfect accompaniment, as would Slow-Roasted Potatoes with Parmesan (page 305).

SERVES 4 TO 6

2 Frenched lamb rib racks with 7 or 8 bones each
 (about 1 pound/450 g each)

1 tablespoon extra-virgin olive oil
2 tablespoons Dijon mustard
Provençal Breadcrumbs (page 354)

1 Preheat the oven to 350°F (180°C).

2 Score the fat on the lamb racks, making shallow crisscross cuts no deeper than the fat, about 1 inch (2.5 cm) apart.

3 Heat the oil in a large frying pan over medium-high heat. Add the racks flesh side down and sear for 4 to 5 minutes, until golden brown.

4 Transfer the racks to a roasting pan, turning them flesh side up, and roast for 20 minutes. Remove the lamb and let it cool for 5 minutes.

5 Using a brush, spread the mustard over the meat, except for the ends. Place the breadcrumbs in a large shallow bowl and press the flesh side of the rack into the crumbs so that they stick. (At this point, you can set the racks aside for up to 2 hours at room temperature before returning them to the oven to finish cooking them.)

6 Return the racks to the oven at and roast for another 15 to 20 minutes for medium-rare meat. (If you are using a thermometer, the internal temperature should be between 150°F and 160°F/60°C and 70°C.) Remove from the oven and allow to rest, loosely covered with foil, for 10 to 15 minutes before slicing into individual chops. →

Cook's notes

When I moved to Nice, I noticed that lamb racks sold in butcher shops were only partially trimmed (or Frenched), with just the top half of the rib bones scraped clean of meat. In keeping with the region's more rustic style of cooking, the fatty meat surrounding the bone is also valued, and the trimmed portion is usually provided along with the rack. Known as the *épigramme* or *haut de côtes*, this thin, fatty, but flavorful piece is best suited to slow cooking, though I sometimes roast it with potatoes after having trimmed off some of the fat. The part that stays on the bone while the rack of lamb roasts is the very best part for gnawing on—so don't hesitate to pick up the chops with your hands and savor every last bit of meat.

For food safety reasons, any leftover breadcrumbs should be thrown away after you have coated the lamb, unless you decide to make Provençal Tomatoes (page 241) or Baked Squash with Provençal Breadcrumbs (page 201) and use the crumbs right away.

Bellet: France's only urban wine region

Joseph Sergi's vineyard is only a twenty-minute drive from the center of Nice, but it feels anything but urban: a series of bumpy lanes ends abruptly in front of a small parcel of grapevines with a sweeping view of the surrounding hills. His wines are sold under the name Clos Saint Vincent at the most prestigious restaurants along the Côte d'Azur. Beyond the region, only the savviest wine specialists know of them.

Joseph, better known as Gio, is the spokesperson for eight wine producers who cultivate some 140 acres (56 hectares) of land in the western hills of Nice, making Bellet France's only wine region within a large urban center. Bellet obtained the AOC label guaranteeing the origin of its wines in 1941, but wine has been produced on these slopes since Roman times. So steep are the hills that you are often looking at a sheer drop, making the grapevines hard to spot–mechanical harvesting is impossible here. To make the winemaker's job even more difficult, the land is divided into tiny parcels, often some distance apart.

Bellet's producers are passionate about their wines–if they weren't, they would have long ago sold their property to developers rather than tending rare grape varieties on arid soil made up of sand and pudding stone. Until the disease phylloxera wiped out most of the vines in the nineteenth century, Bellet covered 2,500 acres (1,000 hectares) of land. Now producers who wish to expand pay up to $300,000 for a single hectare (2½ acres). At the vineyard Domaine de la Source, among the smallest AOC wine producers in France, Carine Dalmasso told me that her family once grew carnations in greenhouses before planting vines in the 1980s.

All of the wine producers in Bellet have the organic label, and some, such as Clos Saint Vincent and Domaine de la Source, go one step further, reducing treatments to a bare minimum and harvesting their grapes according to the cycles of the moon. These ancestral biodynamic methods suit their ancient grape varieties, which include the unpredictable Folle noire for the reds and Braquet for the rosés. Bellet is best known for its elegant, cherry-like reds and deep pink, rose-scented rosés, but the whites are crisp and fruity, and Domaine de la Source now produces a sparkling wine using the traditional method from the Champagne region. Several of the winemakers also grow the small black olives known as Caillette, producing golden olive oil with the AOP Nice label.

Although some winemakers, including Gio, have invested in tasting rooms to welcome the public, visiting the smaller vineyards in Bellet remains a down-to-earth experience; the first time I found my way to Clos Saint Vincent nearly twenty years ago, he had to call off his Dobermans, Margaux and Pétrus. The biggest and slickest among the region's winemakers are the four-centuries-old Château de Bellet, named after the family that gave the Bellet region its name, and the rococo Château de Crémat, designed in the 1920s, whose double-C logo is said to have inspired Coco Chanel when she attended one of its legendary parties.

If you want to taste Bellet wines without visiting the vineyards, La Cave de la Tour in Nice Old Town stocks wines from all of the producers from Bellet in its back room, and the historic wine shop Caves Caprioglio also has a good selection. Most of the higher-end restaurants in and around Nice have at least one Bellet wine on the menu. Given the small production, Bellet wines cost about twice as much as those from Provence, but they are worth it; try them with food, especially meat dishes like Rack of Lamb with Mustard-Herb Crust (page 233) or Veal Stew with Tomatoes, Olives, and Mushrooms (page 229), to best appreciate their complexity.

Carine Delmasso

PANISSES

Chickpea fries

Like their cousin, Socca (page 268), panisses are made with a simple mixture of chickpea flour, water, olive oil, and salt. But instead of being cooked in the oven at a high temperature, the mixture is stirred in a saucepan, polenta-style, before it is cooled until set, cut into strips, and fried.

In fresh pasta shops around Nice, you can recognize panisses by their saucer-like shape. When Genoese immigrants brought this recipe to Nice in the nineteenth century (they originally used a mix of corn and chickpea flours), home cooks improvised by pouring the hot chickpea mixture into saucers to set, and the round shape became standard in this area. Farther along the coast in Marseille, the panisse batter is shaped into cylinders (originally using a dish towel), which are cut into rounds before being fried. I use round crème brûlée dishes in place of saucers, but the quickest (if nontraditional) way to make panisses is to pour the cooked batter into an oiled baking pan, which allows you to cut it into even-sized strips once it is set.

Panisses are most often served as an accompaniment to meat or mussels, like French fries, but they can also be a snack or even a dessert: my friend Karine remembers her grandmother sprinkling them with powdered sugar to create a sweet after-school snack. Some local pasta shops offer a variation with olives, which is particularly good alongside lamb. If you find yourself craving a dip, Rouille (page 348) makes a perfect accompaniment, or you can improvise by adding your favorite chile paste to some mayonnaise.

Note that you will need plenty of oil for the shallow-frying, so be sure you have at least 2 cups (500 ml) on hand. I have a preference for peanut oil, which seems to produce the crispiest panisses. You can also replace about a quarter of the oil with olive oil, to enhance the flavor.

SERVES 6 TO 8

¼ cup (60 ml) extra-virgin olive oil, plus 2 teaspoons for the saucers or baking pan

2 cups (200 g) chickpea flour

4 cups (1 l) water

1½ teaspoons sea salt

1 teaspoon herbes de Provence

At least 2 cups (500 ml) peanut or sunflower oil for shallow-frying

Fine sea salt and freshly ground black pepper

1 Using the 2 teaspoons olive oil, lightly oil six 5-inch (12 cm) saucers or crème brûlée dishes or an 8-by-11-inch (22 by 30 cm) baking pan.

2 Sift the chickpea flour into a medium bowl.

3 In a medium saucepan, bring the water to a boil, then add the salt, herbes de Provence, and the remaining ¼ cup (60 ml) olive oil. Slowly sprinkle in the chickpea flour, whisking constantly →

(it's easier if one person sprinkles and another whisks). Then turn the heat down so that the mixture bubbles slowly, and stir constantly with a wooden spoon for 5 minutes, being careful not to burn your hand, or until the mixture is very thick and smooth. Remove from the heat.

4 Working quickly before the mixture sets, fill the saucers (or dishes) to the brim with this mixture (about ½ inch/0.5 cm deep), or spread it out in the baking pan. Dip your fingers in cold water to press the batter into the saucers or pan and flatten the surface. Let cool for at least 1 hour before proceeding, placing the saucers or pan in the refrigerator once the mixture has cooled to room temperature. (The panisses can be made ahead and kept refrigerated, covered, for up to 3 days.)

5 Turn the panisses out onto a work surface, easing them from the saucers or baking pan with a round-tipped table knife, and cut into fries about ½ inch (1 cm) wide and 4 inches (10 cm) long (the lengths will vary if you used saucers).

6 Place a large frying pan over high heat and pour in about ½ inch (1 cm) of oil. Heat the oil until the surface shimmers (if using a thermometer, the temperature should be 375°F/190°C).

7 Working in batches, add the panisses to the pan without crowding them (there should be at least 1 inch/2.5 cm between the panisses): To avoid splattering, place the end closest to you in the hot oil first, then gently lower the opposite end into the oil. Fry the panisses for 4 to 5 minutes, until browned on the first side, then carefully turn them with tongs and fry until browned on the other side, another 4 to 5 minutes. If they seem to be browning faster than that, adjust the heat.

8 Meanwhile, line a wire rack placed over a baking sheet with paper towels. Transfer the fried panisses to the paper towels to drain. Sprinkle with fine sea salt and pepper, and serve hot. (If you are cooking the panisses in batches, you can keep the first batch in a warm oven [150°F/65°C] on the prepared rack while you cook the second; add more oil to the frying pan as necessary.)

9 Remove the pan from the heat and strain the frying oil once it has cooled; keep it in a glass jar in a cool, dark place for the next time you make panisses.

Variation

To make olive panisses, add ½ cup (90 g) pitted wrinkly black olives, roughly chopped, to the batter along with the chickpea flour.

Cook's notes

If you don't plan to eat all the panisses right away, fry only what you plan to serve and keep the rest, covered, in the refrigerator. Slice and fry the remaining panisses just before serving.

You can reheat panisses for 5 to 7 minutes in a preheated 350°F (180°C) oven, though they will not be quite as crispy as when freshly fried.

TOMATES PROVENÇALES
Provençal tomatoes

Tomatoes are still plentiful in the early fall but have lost some of the sweetness that makes them heavenly in salads. This is when I like to cook them slowly in the oven under a layer of bright green Provençal breadcrumbs. Meltingly soft but crunchy, with an almost candied quality, these tomatoes can accompany any meat or fish, and they make a colorful addition to a vegetarian plate.

SERVES 4

2 beefsteak tomatoes (about 8 ounces/225 g each)

1 teaspoon sugar

2 tablespoons extra-virgin olive oil

¼ cup (40 g) Provençal Breadcrumbs (page 354)

1 Preheat the oven to 350°F (180°C).

2 Core the tomatoes and cut each one horizontally in half. Gently squeeze out most of the seeds and juice into a small bowl, without damaging the tomatoes. Sprinkle the cut sides lightly with the sugar.

3 Heat a medium frying pan over medium-high heat and add 1 tablespoon of the olive oil. Place the tomatoes cut side down in the pan and cook for 2 to 3 minutes, without moving them, until the cut sides start to brown; turn the heat up if they are giving off a lot of juice. Remove from the heat.

4 Arrange the tomatoes cut side up in a baking dish that holds them snugly. Spread 1 tablespoon of the breadcrumbs over each tomato half, and drizzle with any juices from the pan and the remaining 1 tablespoon olive oil.

5 Bake for 1 hour, or until the tomatoes have collapsed and the breadcrumbs have browned. Remove from the oven and allow to cool for at least 10 minutes before serving. (If you'd like to make them a few hours ahead, these tomatoes reheat very well in a preheated 350°F/180°C oven for about 10 minutes.)

TARTE AUX FIGUES À LA CRÈME D'AMANDE ET AU MIEL

Fig tart with honey-almond cream

Can anything beat a fig bursting out of its skin, picked warm from the tree and gobbled up within seconds? Probably not, but that doesn't stop me from setting some of the bulging fruits aside for this typically southern French tart.

In Nice, figs come in three colors: pale green, known as *figues blanches*, or white figs; green streaked with purple, referred to as *violets*; and deep purple, called *figues noires* (black figs). The smaller, more acidic "black" fruits, which release deep purple juice as they cook, are my choice for baking, although any fresh fig will work here as long as it's ripe. A small amount of honey enhances their natural sweetness in this tart.

SERVES 6 TO 8

Quick Basic Pastry (page 361), chilled for at least 15 minutes

FOR THE FILLING
1 large egg
2 teaspoons cornstarch
⅓ cup (80 ml) heavy cream

½ cup (50 g) ground almonds
2 tablespoons sugar
1 teaspoon pure vanilla extract or ¼ teaspoon vanilla bean paste
3 tablespoons mild-tasting honey, such as lavender or acacia
4 tablespoons (55 g) unsalted butter, melted
12 to 15 ripe figs, washed and cut in half lengthwise

1 On a floured work surface, roll the pastry out to an 11-inch (28 cm) circle about ⅛ inch (3 mm) thick, flouring the work surface and the surface of the pastry lightly as necessary to prevent it from sticking.

2 Roll the pastry up around the rolling pin, then unroll it into a 9-inch (23 cm) tart pan, preferably with a removable base (or a metal pastry ring placed on a parchment-lined baking sheet). Use a small ball of excess dough to press the pastry into the corners. Then cut the overhang off with a swipe of the rolling pin. If the pastry tears, just press it back together, using stray pieces of dough to reinforce any weak spots.

3 With your thumb, press the pastry up against the sides of the tart pan (or ring) so that it comes very slightly above the rim. Place in the refrigerator to chill for at least 30 minutes before baking.

4 A few minutes before the end of the resting time, preheat the oven to 400°F (200°C), with a baking sheet on the middle rack if using a tart pan. →

Fill and bake the tart

1 In a medium bowl, whisk together the egg and cornstarch. Whisk in the cream, ground almonds, sugar, vanilla, and 2 tablespoons of the honey. Stir in the melted butter.

2 Pour the almond cream into the tart shell and arrange the figs on top, cut side up so that the juices do not run into the filling. Drizzle with the remaining 1 tablespoon honey.

3 Place the tart pan on the preheated baking sheet, or slide the pan holding the ring straight onto the middle oven rack. Bake for 10 minutes, then lower the heat to 350°F (180°C) and bake for 30 minutes longer, or until the pastry is crisp and the filling is brown on top.

4 Remove the tart from the oven and let cool for 10 minutes. If the pan has a removable base, place the pan on a small bowl and let the rim drop, then transfer to a serving plate (you can leave the tart on its metal base). Serve warm. (Leftovers can be served at room temperature or rewarmed in a 350°F/180°C oven for a few minutes.)

Variation

⁂

In summer, I like to replace the figs with apricots and sprinkle the tart with fresh lavender flowers before baking.

TARTE TATIN

Upside-down apple tart with lemon and olive oil

This caramelized apple tart is not a Niçoise dessert—it comes from the forested Sologne region south of Paris, and is a bistro favorite all over France—but I have been making it since I was a teenager working in a French tearoom in Canada. During apple season in Nice, I couldn't resist giving it a local twist with a touch of olive oil and lemon zest.

Since the aroma of apples cooking in butter and sugar is the most rewarding part of making this tart (along with successfully flipping it onto a plate), I did not want to eliminate the butter altogether. Instead, I combined it with a delicate olive oil, as in my Lemon Tart (page 307). Lemon zest brings sunshine to this rich dessert, though I have reduced the fat and sugar as much as I deemed reasonable.

In Canada, we used Red Delicious apples for this tart; most French pastry chefs choose either the easily available Golden Delicious or the more tart-tasting Granny Smith, because they hold their shape and absorb flavor so well. I suggest starting with one of these varieties until you have perfected the recipe, then branching out into less predictable heirloom apples if you wish—some will collapse as they cook, or not produce enough pectin to stay in place when the tart is turned out. Remember that this is intended to be a rustic dessert, so be kind to yourself if it does not come out picture-perfect.

I once visited the birthplace of tarte Tatin to investigate the legends behind this dessert. Even then I did not get to the bottom of how one of the Tatin sisters, working in a hotel kitchen, was said to have invented the tart by accident. According to *Larousse Gastronomique*, it was a great PR stunt, long before the days of social media, for a regional dessert that already existed!

SERVES 6 TO 8

Quick Basic Pastry (page 361), chilled for at least 15 minutes

FOR THE FILLING
6 Golden Delicious apples (about 3 pounds/1.3 kg)
1 tablespoon freshly squeezed lemon juice (zest the lemon first)

½ cup (100 g) sugar
1 tablespoon finely grated lemon zest (preferably from an organic lemon)
3 tablespoons unsalted butter
2 tablespoons fruity, mild-tasting extra-virgin olive oil

1 Peel the apples. Core them using an apple corer, or cut into quarters and remove the cores. If you used an apple corer, cut the apples into quarters. Toss the apple quarters with the lemon juice in a large bowl.

2 In a small bowl, rub the sugar and lemon zest together with your fingertips for about 30 seconds, to release the essential oils. →

3 Cut the butter into chunks and place in a cast-iron or other ovenproof 9-inch (23 cm) frying pan. Spread the lemon sugar evenly over the bottom of the pan (on top of the butter).

4 Arrange the apple quarters, on their sides, in concentric circles in the pan, packing them as tightly as possible (they will lose volume as they cook). Drizzle the olive oil over the apples.

5 Place the pan over medium-low heat and cook the apples in the butter, olive oil, and sugar for about 30 minutes, rotating the pan every few minutes, until the liquid thickens and turns golden brown. Baste the apples now and then using a turkey baster, a silicone basting brush, or a spoon. There should be about ½ inch (1 cm) of caramel on the bottom of the pan. Do not let it get too dark, as the color will deepen in the oven.

6 Meanwhile, preheat the oven to 400°F (200°C). Line a baking sheet with parchment paper or foil.

7 When the juices are golden, roll out the pastry to a round at least 10 inches (25 cm) in diameter, sprinkling both the pastry and your work surface lightly with flour. The pastry should be a little thicker than for a normal tart, as it needs to hold its shape when you flip the tart over. Place a 9-inch (23 cm) lid or cake pan on the pastry and, using a small knife, trim it to a circle slightly larger (by about ¼ inch/0.5 cm) than the lid or pan.

8 Place the rolling pin at the top of the pastry and roll up the pastry on the rolling pin, then unroll it over the apples. Tuck the edges in around the apples as best you can, being careful not to burn yourself. Place the pan on the lined baking sheet, as the juices may bubble over.

9 Bake the tart for 25 to 30 minutes, until the pastry is golden. Remove from the oven and let stand for at least 5 minutes. (You can also let the tart cool completely in the pan, then warm it for a couple of minutes on top of the stove to melt the caramel before unmolding it.)

10 Turn the tart out onto a plate that is just a little larger than your pan: Run a knife around the edges of the tart to release any caramel that has hardened. Place the plate upside down over the pan, hold the pan and plate tightly together using two oven mitts, and flip it over confidently. Lift off the pan, and rearrange any apple slices that have stuck to the pan on top of the tart.

Cook's note

I have invested in a copper tarte Tatin pan, which distributes the heat perfectly, but for many years I used a cast-iron skillet with great results. A good-quality round cake pan (not with a removable base) can also work.

FLAN PÂTISSIER

Vanilla custard tart

Sold in gargantuan wedges for a token sum at nearly every bakery in France, this French classic has long been a favorite of my son, Sam, who started asking for it as a toddler. I took much longer to come around to flan pâtissier, thinking of it as heavy and one-dimensional. Then I tasted a version by Corsican baker Michel Fiori, who runs one of my favorite boulangeries in Nice, and marveled at the still-wobbly custard generously flecked with vanilla seeds. Michel turns out pistachio, black sesame, and tiramisù versions, but any novice flan-maker should begin with vanilla before experimenting with other flavors. (See the Variations below for other options.)

Start making the tart well in advance of when you plan to serve it, since you will need to let the pastry rest, and the dessert is best served a few hours to a day after it is made. If you really think ahead, you can infuse the vanilla bean in the milk and cream overnight for an even deeper flavor.

Serve this tart from the refrigerator as a *goûter* (afternoon snack), or as a dessert after a light meal. The dough is similar to my Quick Basic Pastry (page 361) but a little sweeter, because the filling is not too sweet.

SERVES 10

FOR THE PASTRY

8 tablespoons (1 stick/115 g) unsalted butter, cut into ½-inch (0.5 cm) dice, at cool room temperature

1 cup (100 g) confectioners' sugar

2 cups (240 g) all-purpose or cake flour

1 large egg

1 large egg yolk

FOR THE VANILLA PASTRY CREAM

3 cups (720 ml) whole milk

1 cup (240 ml) heavy cream

2 vanilla beans or 1 vanilla bean plus 2 teaspoons vanilla extract

3 large eggs

3 large egg yolks

1 cup (200 g) sugar

½ cup (60 g) cornstarch

For the pastry

1 In the bowl of a stand mixer fitted with the paddle attachment, beat together the butter and confectioners' sugar on low speed until smooth and creamy. Add the flour and continue mixing until the mixture looks crumbly. Add the whole egg and egg yolk and mix just until the pastry comes together.

2 Turn the pastry out, shape it into a disk, and wrap in plastic wrap. Chill for at least 1 hour, and up to 24 hours.

3 If the pastry is too firm to roll out, let it soften at room temperature for 15 minutes. On a lightly floured surface, roll out the pastry into a ⅛-inch- (3 mm) thick round about 16 inches (40 cm) in

diameter. Fit it into a 9-inch (23 cm) springform pan, pressing it over the bottom and up the sides and leaving a 1-inch (2.5 cm) overhang all around. If your pastry is a little too warm, this could get messy–patch it as you need to and don't panic. Trim the pastry so that it is even with the rim of the pan, then press it with your thumb all the way around the sides of the pan so that it comes slightly above the rim. Place the pastry shell in the freezer while you make the filling.

4 Preheat the oven to 350°F (180°C).

For the vanilla pastry cream

1 Combine the milk and cream in a pitcher or jug. Slit the vanilla bean(s) lengthwise in half, and scrape out the seeds using the back of a small knife. Add the vanilla seeds and pod to the milk and cream and stir to distribute the seeds (you can do this step up to 1 day ahead to infuse the vanilla); cover and refrigerate.

2 In a mixing bowl, whisk together the whole eggs, egg yolks, sugar, vanilla extract, if using, and cornstarch. Add ½ cup (120 ml) of the cold milk and cream and whisk until smooth; set aside. Pour the remaining milk and cream into a medium-large saucepan and bring to a simmer.

3 Pour one third of the hot milk and cream over the egg mixture and whisk until combined. Pour the remaining milk and cream into the bowl, stirring constantly, then pour the mixture into the saucepan.

4 Place the saucepan over medium heat and bring the milk mixture to a boil, stirring at first and then whisking as it starts to thicken (this will take some effort!). When the mixture reaches a boil, after 2 to 3 minutes, it should be thick like pudding. Remove from the heat.

Assemble and bake the tart

1 Remove the pastry shell from the freezer. Whisk the pastry cream again to remove any lumps, and pour it into the pastry shell. It will not fill the pan entirely; the pastry will shrink slightly and the filling will puff up as the tart cooks.

2 Place in the oven and bake for 40 minutes, or until the surface of the filling turns a deep golden brown. It will bubble as it bakes; do not be alarmed by this. When you remove the tart from the oven, the filling will still appear to be liquid, but it will set as it cools. Let the tart stand for 15 minutes.

3 After 15 minutes, release the sides of the pan and let the tart cool to room temperature on a rack. Transfer to the refrigerator for at least 4 hours, until fully chilled, before slicing and serving. $\rightarrow$

Flan pâtissier (page 248) from Michel Fiori's bakery

Variations

✳

To make a pistachio flan, add ½ cup (100 g) unsweetened, unsalted pistachio paste to the finished filling, along with a few drops of green food coloring if you like. For a cheesecake variation, add 4 ounces (110 g) cream cheese to the pastry cream after removing it from the heat.

POIRES POCHÉES AU VIN ROUGE ET AUX ÉPICES

Pears poached in red wine with spices

I love the moment in fall when French pears start to appear at the Cours Saleya market, with names like Williams, Passe-Crassane, Louise Bonne, Comice, and Conférence. For this recipe, I use the fragrant and sweet Bartlett (known as *poire Williams* in France), which holds its shape when cooked—you can also make this with the similarly sturdy Bosc or Concorde pear. Be sure to choose pears that are neither too hard nor too ripe—the flesh should give just a little when you press it.

If you are able to cook the pears a day before serving them, you will be rewarded with fruits that are red to the core. With no fat and not much sugar, this dessert is perfect when you want something light to finish off a meal, but you can make it richer by serving it with scoops of vanilla bean ice cream. Or you can go in the other direction and serve slices of these pears alongside roasted pork, duck, or game meat. In Nice, these pears are traditionally served as part of the "thirteen desserts" at Christmas (see page 320).

SERVES 4

4 medium pears, such as Williams (in France) or
    Bartlett (in the U.S.)
4 cups (1 l) fruity red wine, such as Beaujolais (not
    Beaujolais Nouveau) or Pinot Noir
½ cup (100 g) sugar
1 vanilla bean
2 cinnamon sticks

1 star anise
A strip of orange zest about ½ inch (1 cm) wide and
    3 to 4 inches (8-10 cm) long, removed with a
    vegetable peeler
A strip of lemon zest about ½ inch (1 cm) wide and
    3 to 4 inches (8-10 cm) long, removed with a
    vegetable peeler
A few thin slices of fresh ginger

1 Peel the pears, preferably using a vegetable peeler rather than a knife for a more even result. Leave the stems intact and cut a small slice from the bottom of each so that the pears stand up straight.

2 In a saucepan that will hold the pears snugly, stir together the wine and sugar (off the heat) until the sugar is dissolved. Add the pears, which can be either upright or on their sides, as long as they are covered with the wine.

3 Slit the vanilla bean in half lengthwise and, using the back of a small knife, scrape out the seeds.

4 Add the vanilla bean and seeds, cinnamon sticks, star anise, citrus zests, and ginger to the pan with the pears. Bring to a simmer and cook the pears at a simmer for 30 to 40 minutes, until tender; test with the tip of a sharp knife. (At this point, the pears can be set aside in the pan for several hours or overnight, allowing them to soak up more wine.) →

5 Remove the pears to a plate using a slotted spoon. Turn the heat up and bring the liquid to a boil. Let it boil and reduce for about 30 minutes, until it thickens to a light syrup consistency. You should have about 1½ cups (360 ml) liquid. Let the liquid cool to room temperature.

6 Place the pears in shallow bowls and top with the syrupy sauce. The zests and spices will have become candied, and you can use them as garnishes.

Cook's note

To remove a long strip of zest from a citrus fruit, use a vegetable peeler. The French like to use a peeler called an *économe* (I am fond of the inexpensive and classic Nogent brand), which requires you to peel toward yourself while using your thumb as leverage. There is a knack to finding the right angle, but once you've mastered it, the économe offers you more control and—as its name suggests—is an economical way of peeling fruits and vegetables, since it removes only a very thin layer.

PÂTE DE COINGS

Quince paste

Green-golden, cheekily curvaceous, and downy skinned, with a delicate rose-and-citrus scent, quinces beg to be picked up and caressed or captured in a still life. But peeling and cutting them is a less romantic proposition. Surely the most stubborn and resistant of fruits, quinces–like love–are a pleasure that has to be earned. No wonder they are the symbol of Venus, who is always portrayed holding a quince.

Quinces are too hard and astringent to eat raw, requiring at least a quarter of their weight in sugar before they melt into syrupy sweetness on the tongue. They can be poached in a syrup with spices and rose petals to complement their floral fragrance, stewed alongside meat (they go especially well with duck and lamb), or transformed into this sweet paste, known as *membrillo* in Spanish and *pâte de coings* in French. It's traditionally served with cheese, especially goat cheese in the South of France or Manchego in Spain, but it can also be eaten as a sweet on its own or as part of a spread, such as the "thirteen desserts" at Christmas (see page 320).

Although they start out with ivory flesh like an apple, the longer quinces cook, the pinker their color, eventually deepening to an orangey red. This is due to compounds known as anthocyanins, which in quinces are released with a combination of heat and acid.

Ninety-year-old Louison from the town of Clans dictated this recipe to me over the phone, providing tips that I had never seen in any book. It is amazing that, starting with two chubby fruits, I could produce a tray of quince paste and two jars of jelly (page 257). In typically thrifty Niçoise style, no part of the fruit is wasted. I have added lemon juice to the recipe, since I discovered through trial and error that, without it, some quinces never darken to the orange (or deep red) color that makes them so magical.

Quince trees are rare in North America, so most quinces that you find in the shops (if you're lucky) are imported. If you can get your hands on freshly picked quinces, don't be in a hurry to cook them, as they benefit from ripening once picked. Place them in a fruit bowl and enjoy their potent scent for up to two weeks before cooking them.

MAKES 36 SQUARES; SERVES 12

2 large or 3 medium quinces (about 1 pound 11
    ounces/750 g)
4 cups (1 l) water
3 tablespoons freshly squeezed lemon juice
2¼ cups (450 g) sugar

1 Line an 8-inch (20 cm) square pan with parchment paper so that the paper covers the sides as well as the bottom.

2 Wipe any downy fuzz off the quinces using a dry cloth, then wash them and wipe dry. Peel the quinces using a vegetable peeler, setting aside the peels. Cut the fruit into quarters and carefully cut out the cores, using a small sharp knife. Place the cores and peels on a square of cheesecloth, lift up the corners, and tie them together to make a bundle.

3 Cut each quince quarter crosswise into 3 pieces and place them in a medium saucepan, along with the cheesecloth bundle. Pour in the water, which should just cover the quinces, and add 2 tablespoons of the lemon juice.

4 Bring the water to a boil, then lower the heat and cook at a steady boil, uncovered, for 10 to 15 minutes, until the quince pieces feel soft when pierced with a knife. Scoop the quinces into a strainer placed over a bowl. Reserve the liquid for Quince Jelly (page 257) and discard the bundle of peels and cores. Let the quinces drain for at least 30 minutes; reserve the liquid.

5 Using a food mill, immersion blender, or food processor, puree the quinces. Transfer the puree to the saucepan and add the sugar and the remaining 1 tablespoon lemon juice. Cook over low heat, stirring frequently, for 45 minutes, or until the puree has thickened to a paste that holds its shape and is coming away from the sides of the pan. At first the mixture will spit and need to be stirred constantly, but as it thickens, it will bubble slowly, like a thick porridge. Depending on the quinces, the color may range from golden-pink to deep orange-red.

6 Transfer the paste to the prepared pan, using a heatproof spatula, and smooth the surface.

7 Traditionally this paste is dried at room temperature for 4 to 5 days, turning it over each day. However, I use a slightly faster method from Alice Waters: Preheat the oven to 200°F (95°C), then turn it off. Place the pan in the oven and leave it there for 7 to 8 hours.

8 Remove the pan from the oven and, using the edges of the paper as handles, flip over the quince paste. Peel off the paper and discard. Preheat the oven to 200°F (95°C) again, turn it off, and place the paste in the oven for another 7 to 8 hours, or longer if it still feels sticky to the touch. I sometimes leave the quince paste in the oven for another 2 to 3 days to dry, since the enclosed space protects it from inquisitive flies. Just be sure to remove it if you need to use your oven for something else!

9 Remove the paste from the pan, place on a cutting board, and cut it into 6 strips. Cut each strip into 6 squares, or, if you don't plan to eat the paste immediately, wrap the strips tightly in plastic wrap and keep in the refrigerator for up to a month or in the freezer for several months; cut into squares to serve.

GÉLÉE DE COINGS

Quince jelly

If you have already gone to the trouble of making Quince Paste (page 253), you will want to go all the way and turn the poaching liquid into quince jelly. It requires no more work than adding sugar and letting the syrup boil down until thickened, and the rose-orange color is irresistible. Although it is undeniably high in sugar, quince jelly is said to be good for digestion because of its high pectin and tannin content; I like to mix it into my morning yogurt. Like quince paste, it also makes a great match for most cheeses; try it with blue cheese.

MAKES 2 SMALL JARS
 (1⅔ CUPS/400 ML TOTAL)

2½ cups (625 ml) poaching liquid reserved from
   making Quince Paste (page 253)
2½ cups (500 g) sugar

1 To sterilize your jars: Preheat the oven to 350°F (180°F). Wash the jars and lids in soapy water and rinse well. Arrange the jars and lids on a clean tray and place in the oven. Heat for 15 minutes, then turn off the oven and leave the jars there until needed.

2 Place a small plate in the freezer (for testing the consistency of the jelly later).

3 Pour the quince poaching liquid into a medium saucepan, add the sugar, and bring to a boil, stirring to dissolve the sugar, over high heat, then continue boiling until the liquid has reduced by about half and begun to thicken, 30 to 45 minutes. The color will deepen to a reddish orange when the syrup is nearly ready.

4 Place a small spoonful of the syrup on the cold plate. If it begins to set after 1 minute, the jelly is ready. If not, continue boiling the mixture for a few more minutes, then test again.

5 Pour the jelly into the hot jars and cover with the lids, without tightening them immediately. (If the jars are very hot, the jelly might start to bubble as you pour it in. Wait for it to settle before adding more.) When the jelly has cooled a little, 10 to 15 minutes, seal the lids. The jelly is ready to eat once it has cooled and fully set, which will take 3 to 4 hours.

CONFITURE DE TOMATES VERTES AU GINGEMBRE ET À LA VANILLE

Green tomato jam with ginger and vanilla

Local tomato season is slow to begin in Nice because of the cooler nights in the hills, but it's also slow to end–I often see tomatoes at the market stalls as late as October. These heat-deprived green tomatoes can't compare to the summer's flamboyant display, but the locals have found ingenious uses for them, as in this green tomato jam, which is zingy with fresh ginger and fragrant with vanilla. I first came across it spooned onto the fresh sheep's-milk curds known as *brousse* at Nadim Beyrouti's olive oil shop and restaurant, Oliviera. Farmer Louis Berthon told me that he loves to encase a small spoonful of this jam in the dough for *ganses*, or sweet fritters (see page 325), before frying them. Of course, you also can't go wrong by spreading it on warm, crusty baguette or on a buttery croissant.

MAKES FOUR 12-OUNCE (360 G) JARS

4½ pounds (2 kg) green tomatoes

1 vanilla bean

2 pounds (4½ cups/900 g) sugar

A 2-inch (5 cm) chunk of fresh ginger, peeled and finely grated

¼ cup (60 ml) freshly squeezed lemon juice (preferably from an organic lemon)

1 To sterilize your jars, follow the instructions in the recipe for Quince Jelly (page 257). Place a small plate in the freezer (for testing the consistency of the jam later).

2 Cut the tomatoes horizontally in half and squeeze out most of the seeds. Cut the tomatoes into ½-inch (1 cm) dice.

3 Slit the vanilla bean lengthwise in half and scrape out the seeds with the back of a small knife.

4 Place the green tomatoes, sugar, ginger, vanilla bean and seeds, and lemon juice in a large nonreactive saucepan or a copper jam basin, if you have one (the high concentration of sugar prevents the acidity of the fruit from reacting with the copper). Bring to a boil, stirring, then reduce the heat and let the jam bubble happily and reduce until thickened, stirring more frequently toward the end of the cooking time to prevent it from sticking. It should look like thick, syrupy green tomato sauce, which can take up to 2 hours.

5 Place a small spoonful of the jam on the cold plate. If it begins to set after 1 minute, the jam is ready. If not, continue boiling the mixture for a few more minutes, then test again.

6 Pour the jam into the hot jars and cover with the lids, without tightening them immediately. (If the jars are very hot, the jam might start to bubble as you pour it in. Wait for it to settle before adding more.) When the jam has cooled a little, 10 to 15 minutes, seal the lids. The jam is ready to eat once it has cooled and fully set, which will take 3 to 4 hours.

Variations

You can use the same proportions of fruit, sugar, and lemon to make jam with any fruit; I especially like to make plum and apricot jams when the fruits are in season, since they contain plenty of pectin and set beautifully. The riper the fruit, the better, as that intensifies the sweetness. Depending on the width of your pan and the quantity and type of fruit used, the jam may take between 1 and 2 hours to set; keep stirring it every few minutes, and don't rush the process, or you may burn the jam.

WINTER

If the festive atmosphere of summer drew me to Nice, it's the bright winters that keep me here. Reliable stretches of vivid sunshine during the shortest days of the year attracted the first British tourists in the eighteenth century, initially inspired by curmudgeonly Scottish writer Tobias Smollett's descriptions in his 1766 book *Travels Through France and Italy*. The Russians soon followed, and in the nineteenth century, the city rapidly expanded thanks to its popularity with British and Russian aristocrats, who took advantage of the new train line from Paris. Until the Americans arrived in the 1920s, January to May was peak tourist season, with restaurants closing in the summer when the population once again became sparse. Recently, UNESCO awarded World Heritage status to Nice as a "Winter Resort Town of the Riviera," paying tribute to the way this early influx of tourists shaped the city we know today.

As we soak up the sun on café terraces or picnic on the beach with palm trees in the background, the snow-capped mountains in the distance remind us that we don't need to go far to experience a different kind of winter. An hour and a half from Nice, the dry and rocky landscape abruptly turns a brilliant white as you drive into Gréolières-les-Neiges, where I snowshoed for the first time in my life, despite having grown up in Canada. It's one of several ski resorts, including La Colmiane, Auron, and Isola 2000, that attract snow-seekers from December to March. The colder climate calls for heartier food, and while most high-altitude restaurants serve crowd-pleasing basics like cheese fondue and pizza, a few draw on the local produce to prepare dishes worth climbing a mountain to taste. In home kitchens, energetic mamies turn out rustic fare like Daube de Boeuf (page 295), Quiques (page 280), ravioli, and winter tians; each village has its own variations of these dishes, inspiring a fierce but friendly rivalry.

Closer to the coast, the mild weather conditions guarantee that the market stalls are never short of local vegetables: I look for pointy-tipped romanesco broccoli, beets in shades of pink and orange, squeaky-fresh bunches of spinach, purple-topped turnips, and broad beans that make an early appearance in December before coming back again in the spring. This is peak season for citrus fruit—not just the lemons for which the Côte d'Azur is famed, but also fragrant mandarins, lip-tingling grapefruits, and kumquats so addictive that I pop them in my mouth like jelly beans. If winter naturally lends itself to the slow-cooked dishes that are central to Niçoise cuisine, I also love to use the season's bitter greens, sweet root vegetables, and zingy citrus to make salads that jolt the palate out of its carbohydrate-rich stupor. There is no denying that Swiss chard features heavily in the winter cooking around Nice; if I had included every recipe, I could have subtitled this "the chard chapter."

Winter eating reaches its peak during the holidays, or *les fêtes*, a time for indulging in luxury foods, but also for observing more modest traditions that date back to Roman times. In February, Nice begins to anticipate spring with a lavish yet tongue-in-cheek Carnival that has its roots in the Middle Ages, while down the coast in Menton the same month, some 140 tons of citrus fruit star in an over-the-top Lemon Festival. February can be a gray and rainy month (comparatively speaking), but there is never a lack of color, and the moodier skies create stunning sunsets over the Baie des Anges. For those of us who live here, winter—once the city's raison d'être—is now a secret we are reluctant to share with the rest of the world.

Clockwise from top left: Carnival fritters (page 325);
Chocolate mousse with olive oil (page 314); Beef stew
(page 295); Naked ravioli (page 297); Semi-salted cod with
caper, lemon, and chile sauce (page 78); Lemon tart with
olive oil (page 307); Stuffed cabbage (page 289)

The socca wars: Who makes the best chickpea pancake in Nice?

One New Year's Eve, I was riding the tram home with one of my favorite socca vendors, who had attended the same party as me. Sensing an opportunity, I asked him what made his socca so addictive. Loose-lipped from the Champagne, he leaned in and whispered, "Let the batter rest for a really long time. Forty-eight hours is best." The 100-year-old Chez Pipo has another trick: before the batter has completely set on top, the cook pulls the copper tray out of the fire and runs a metal spatula over it to give the surface more texture and crunch. Considering how few ingredients go into this savory street-food pancake, it's remarkable how it can vary from one vendor to another.

Socca probably arrived in Nice along with Genoese laborers who came to work in southern French shipyards in the late nineteenth century. Called *farinata* in nearby Liguria, the chickpea pancake came to be known as *socca* in the local language for reasons that remain unclear, though the name may refer to the burnt edges. Nice's first street food vendor, Theresa, further popularized this snack in the early 1900s by wheeling her portable oven through the Old Town and along the Promenade, tempting workers with the scent of freshly fired pancakes. Socca became an essential part of *la merenda*, the midmorning or late afternoon snack enjoyed by manual laborers and anyone else who might be experiencing a hunger pang. Once wedged between slices of bread to make a filling sandwich, socca is now served on its own, with nothing more than a sprinkling of black pepper to enhance its flavor.

Names that often come up during animated discussions (which could be mistaken for arguments) about the best socca in Nice are Chez Pipo and Socca d'Or near the port; Receta de Jou and Socca Tram in the Libération area; and La Socca du Cours on Cours Saleya. In the Old Town, René Socca and Chez Theresa, its name descended from Theresa herself, also attract long lines. Some, but not all of these, have wood-fired ovens; more important is the quality of their ingredients, simple as they might be, and the care the vendors take in resting and cooking the batter. Since I like my socca extra-crispy, I have a penchant for Chez Pipo's version, but the only way to find your favorite is to try them all, being sure to eat them piping hot.

LA SOCCA

Chickpea pancake

When I tell locals that I make this emblematic Niçoise street food at home, most of them look puzzled, if not downright disapproving. "You need a wood-fired oven to make socca," they say. While the result might not be exactly the same, my life is better with homemade socca in it, and I'm willing to bet yours will be too.

Look for chickpea flour in natural food stores and Middle Eastern or Indian markets; the more finely ground, the better for this recipe. If you visit Nice, Liguria, or Tuscany, you might want to invest in a beautiful tin-lined copper pan for cooking socca or farinata, but a pizza pan, cake pan, or cast-iron frying pan works almost as well.

Be sure to eat the socca piping hot, with your fingers—the Niçois do not condone dipping it in anything, but I have used the cooked pancake as a gluten-free base for Pissaladière (page 191) and served it with Eggplant Caviar (page 123). In the unlikely event that you find yourself with leftovers, they reheat best in a frying pan with a little more olive oil. Plan on letting the batter rest for at least 2 hours, and if you are organized enough to make it the day before (I rarely am), you will be rewarded with socca that is especially tender and flavorful.

Oh, and to pronounce the name correctly, say "sock-a," with the emphasis on the sock!

SERVES 4 TO 6

1½ cups (200 g) chickpea flour, preferably Italian

2 teaspoons fine sea salt

½ teaspoon herbes de Provence or finely chopped rosemary

2 tablespoons extra-virgin olive oil, plus ¼ cup (60 ml) for the pan

2 cups (480 ml) water

Freshly ground black pepper

1 Sift the chickpea flour into a bowl and, using a whisk, mix in the salt and herbes de Provence or rosemary. Add the olive oil and about half the water and whisk until you have a thick, smooth batter. Add the remaining water and whisk again until smooth.

2 Let the batter rest, covered, for at least 2 hours at room temperature, and up to 48 hours in the refrigerator—the longer, the better, because the chickpea flour will absorb more of the water, resulting in a more crisp-tender texture when the socca is cooked.

3 Preheat the oven as hot as it will go, at least 500°F (260°C) and up to 550°C (275°C), with a rack in the top third of the oven.

4 Place a 12-inch (30 cm) socca or pizza pan or a 9-inch (23 cm) round cake pan or cast-iron frying pan on the top oven rack. (If you are using the smaller pan, you will need to cook the socca in two batches.) Heat the pan for 10 minutes.

5 Carefully remove the very hot pan from the oven and pour in the ¼ cup (60 ml) olive oil (or 2 tablespoons oil if you are using the smaller pan). Use the back of a metal spoon to spread the oil over the surface of the pan.

6 Whisk the batter again for a few seconds, since it will be thicker at the bottom of the bowl. Pour all the batter into the 12-inch (30 cm) pan or half of it into the 9-inch (23 cm) pan.

7 Using the whisk, stir the batter with the oil that rises to the surface until the surface is covered with swirls of oil (the batter should be no thicker than ¼ inch/0.5 cm).

8 Carefully transfer the pan to the oven (this can be tricky if the pan has a small lip). Bake for 15 to 18 minutes, shaking and turning the pan to distribute the oil after the first 5 minutes, when the pancake has set.

9 Remove the socca when it is deep golden in color. Let it rest for 5 minutes, then sprinkle with pepper and cut into rough pieces. Serve hot, and eat with your fingers. (If you used the smaller pan, bake the second socca now, or save the batter in the refrigerator to use within the next 2 days.)

Rosé revelations

Nothing says summer in the South of France like a chilled glass of pale rosé, alongside a saucer of tiny black olives or a few rough slices of socca. Yet sommelier Viktorija Todorovska, who teaches wine and cooking classes at Les Petits Farcis, firmly believes that there is no wrong time to drink Provence's signature wine.

Viktorija's revelation came during a trip to Marseille, where as part of a group of wine experts she tasted rosés with a series of dishes. "I remember being surprised by how well they went with the food," she said. "We paired mussels with white wine from Cassis and with rosé, and I liked them best with the rosé. Before that, I had thought of rosé as a glass of wine, not something that would necessarily go with food."

During this trip, Viktorija also came to understand the significance of rosé in Provence. "I usually drank rosé only in summer, and did not associate it just with Provence. I discovered that, since 90 percent of the region's production is rosé, every aspect of their winemaking is done with rosé in mind. In other French regions, rosé is an afterthought, never the focus."

Back in Chicago, where she lived at the time, Viktorija discovered that Provence rosé could help her through the gloomy winters, transporting her to a place where the sun was shining. "To me, rosé is not just a drink, it's a lifestyle." She credits her decision to move to France largely with the appeal of this lifestyle.

Viktorija readily admits that her love for rosé is unusual among sommeliers. "In sommelier circles, rosé is not seen as being complex, valuable, or prestigious enough. Wine that does not age is not deserving of attention."

Though it's true that most rosés are served within a year or two of being produced, two regions offer an exception to this rule: Bandol, near Marseille, and Bellet (see page 236), in the hills of Nice. Working with historic grape varieties–Mourvèdre for Bandol and Braquet for Bellet–winemakers in these regions produce darker, fruitier rosés that are best enjoyed with food and can be aged for several years.

When selecting a rosé, Viktorija advises looking for an alcohol content of no more than 13.5 percent, to keep it light, and avoiding bottles that are nonstandard sizes or shapes, "or you will be paying for the bottle rather than what's inside." Generally rosés that are lighter in color will be more dry and crisp, while darker rosés will have robust and fruity qualities, complementing heartier foods. Examples of foods that Viktorija likes to pair with rosé are fresh goat cheese, octopus salad, marinated fish dishes like ceviche, and anything spicy, from zucchini sautéed with chile to Korean dishes. Much as she loves rosé, she prefers a light red with pizza because of the strength of the tomato sauce, and she avoids serving pink wine with red meat.

Even if rosé is still struggling to win the respect of professionals, Viktorija believes its skyrocketing popularity over the past fifteen years is well deserved. "Rosé is the hardest wine to make, because you need to extract flavor and minerality without extracting color, but advances in technology have made this easier. Plus, rosé comes with a story: its color makes you think of this sky and sea."

Viktorija Todorovska

SALADE D'ORANGES AUX OLIVES ET À LA MENTHE

Orange salad with olives and mint

This simple but exquisite salad made its way to Nice via North Africa and Sicily, thanks to the larger-than-life chef Marco Folicaldi, who ran the vegetarian restaurant Zucca Magica. His restaurant no longer exists, but a version of the salad lives on in my kitchen. If you happen to come across blood oranges, which appear fleetingly in winter, they are ideal for this recipe because of their balance of acidity and sweetness and their stunning color.

SERVES 4

4 medium oranges, the freshest and juiciest you can find

½ white onion, sliced paper-thin with a mandoline or sharp knife

6 tablespoons (90 ml) delicate-tasting extra-virgin olive oil

24 pitted Niçoise olives, cut lengthwise in half

Leaves from 1 sprig mint, thinly sliced

Sea salt and freshly ground black pepper

Ground cinnamon for dusting

1 Cut off the top and bottom from each orange, so that the flesh is exposed and the fruit can sit flat on one end. Using a small sharp knife and working over a shallow bowl to catch the juices, cut off the peel from top to bottom, following the curve of the orange and removing all the bitter white pith. Trim off any remaining pith. Slice each segment away from the membranes on either side to release it. Transfer the orange segments and their juice to a shallow serving dish.

2 Arrange the onion over the oranges. Drizzle the olive oil over the salad, scatter with the olives and mint leaves, and season with salt, pepper, and a light dusting of cinnamon, to transport you to North Africa. Serve within the hour, as the salt will draw juice out of the oranges and eventually make the dish soupy.

Variation

You can add thinly shaved fennel to this salad, for a welcome crunch and slight anise flavor; if you want to highlight perfect oranges, though, it's better to leave the fennel out.

CAROTTES RÂPÉES, AVOCAT, ET PAMPLEMOUSSE

Carrot, avocado, and grapefruit salad

Carottes râpées–which I first tasted at my middle school cafeteria in Paris–is a classic French salad, usually consisting of nothing more than grated carrots in a lemony dressing, with a hint of orange or lemon. This is a slightly more elaborate version, which I often throw together for lunch when I don't want to interrupt my work for too long, varying the nuts, seeds, and dried fruits according to what I have on hand.

Avocados are not a traditional part of the local diet, but the climate lends itself perfectly to this fruit, as proved by the avocado tree that has found a home in our shared courtyard. It has grown tall and unwieldy, and I can only gaze longingly at the out-of-reach fruits until they drop with the lightest thud from the tree. If a treasure happens to land within reach, I have to jump on it quickly before the birds start pecking at its buttery flesh. The avocado season coincides with that of grapefruit, which might explain why they make such a perfect match; pink grapefruits bring sweetness to this salad, while the yellow ones create a mouth-puckering experience (I can appreciate both).

For this recipe, I like to use big, juicy carrots, which are easier to grate and often more flavorful than the skinny carrots that appear in spring. If the avocado tree has not cooperated, I look for the lighter green thin-skinned avocados at the market, which I find silkier and nuttier-tasting than the standard imported Hass. Since I often eat this as a solo lunch, the quantities given are for one person, but you can easily scale it up. If you want to turn it into a more complete meal, you can add sliced chicken breast or cubes of fried tofu.

SERVES 1

1 large carrot (about 4 ounces/110 g), coarsely grated

1 ripe but firm avocado, halved, pitted, and cut into ½-inch (1 cm) dice

1 small pink or yellow grapefruit (about 8 ounces/225 g)

1 tablespoon sunflower seeds, pumpkin seeds, or chopped walnuts

1 tablespoon dried cranberries or raisins

1 tablespoon thinly sliced cilantro or flat-leaf parsley leaves

1 tablespoon extra-virgin olive oil

1 teaspoon balsamic vinegar

Sea salt and freshly ground black pepper

1 Place the carrot and avocado in a shallow serving bowl.

2 Cut off the top and bottom of the grapefruit, so that the flesh is exposed and the fruit can sit flat on one end. Using a small very sharp knife, cut off the peel from top to bottom, following the curve of the grapefruit and removing as much of the bitter white pith as you can. Trim off any remaining pith. Slice each segment away from the membranes to release the grapefruit segments. Place the segments in the bowl with the carrot and avocado, then squeeze any remaining juice from the membranes into the bowl. Don't be tempted to skip this step, as grapefruit membranes can be bitter and tough.

3 Toast the seeds or nuts in a dry frying pan over medium heat for 3 to 4 minutes, stirring, until fragrant. Remove from the heat.

4 Add the seeds or nuts, cranberries or raisins, cilantro or parsley, olive oil, balsamic vinegar, and salt and pepper to taste to the salad and toss everything together. Serve immediately, or let the flavors blend for up to 1 hour before serving.

BAGNA CAUDA

Warm anchovy and garlic dip

A potent anchovy fondue that originated in northern Italy during the grape harvest, bagna cauda is traditionally served as part of the "lean" Christmas Eve dinner (see page 320), with a colorful array of raw vegetables for dipping. Italian and southern French cooks like to dispute whether bagna cauda should contain butter or even hazelnut oil–a product of Piedmont–but the standard Niçoise version reflects olive oil's dominance. If you are put off by the idea of an anchovy-heavy dip, keep in mind that their fishy flavor is softened by the slow cooking in oil, as is the strong flavor of the garlic. If you adore garlic, by all means use more than I have suggested, but be careful who you kiss afterward!

The fondue pot that might be lurking in the back of your cupboard would be ideal for keeping the dip warm–you can also use a portable burner on the lowest setting, or place your saucepan or cast-iron frying pan on a trivet or steaming rack set over a candle.

Leftover bagna cauda makes an addictive sauce for meat, boiled potatoes, fried polenta, fresh or wilted greens, or eggs, to name a few possibilities. Leftovers will keep for up to a week in a sealed jar in the refrigerator.

SERVES 4

1 cup (240 ml) extra-virgin olive oil

8 to 10 anchovy fillets packed in oil or salt (if using salted anchovies, soak them in water for 30 minutes and remove any bones)

3 garlic cloves, cut lengthwise in half and any green sprouts removed

2 slices sourdough or other rustic white bread (50 g), preferably stale, crusts removed

1 cup (240 ml) whole milk

RAW VEGETABLES FOR DIPPING,
    SUCH AS:

Baby artichokes, trimmed of their tough outer leaves and choke (see page 55), thinly sliced, and tossed with a little lemon juice to prevent discoloration

Carrots, cut lengthwise in half or into quarters

Bell peppers, cored, seeded, and cut into thin strips

Celery, cut into long, thin sticks

Radishes

White mushrooms, cut into halves or quarters

Fennel, cut into sticks

Kohlrabi, peeled and cut into sticks or thin slices

Beets, preferably pink or striped varieties, cut into thin slices

Cardoons (see box, page 279)

1 Warm the oil in a heavy saucepan or fondue pot over low heat until it reaches a simmer.

2 Chop the anchovies and thinly slice the garlic. Add to the saucepan and let them infuse for 30 minutes, still over low heat; the oil should simmer very gently but not boil, to prevent the garlic from burning.

3 Meanwhile, soak the bread in the milk for at least 15 minutes until soft. Remove the bread from the milk and squeeze out the milk.

4 With the pan still over the heat, mash the anchovies and garlic with a potato masher to dissolve them in the oil. Add the bread, tearing it up with your fingers, and continue mashing until the bread is incorporated. At this point, you can keep the bagna cauda warm on the stove (at barely a simmer) or in the oven at 175°F (80°C) for up to 30 minutes, or let it cool and rewarm it when you need it.

5 Arrange the vegetables artistically on a platter, rather than on individual plates, since, like cheese fondue, this is a dish made for sharing. I always aim for a colorful array of vegetables.

6 Keep the bagna cauda warm (see headnote) while everyone dips the vegetables into the sauce.

Learning to love cardoons

Cardoons, a wild relative of the artichoke, are synonymous with bagna cauda in northern Italy and southern France. A member of the thistle family, they have long, gray-green stalks, festooned with small spikes like a dragon's tail. In North America, you might spot them in specialty shops or Italian markets during the winter.

The older inhabitants of Piedmont and the mountains around Nice have an uneasy relationship with this vegetable, as it brings back memories of poverty. Springing up by the sides of country roads, cardoons were traditionally considered a food of necessity rather than pleasure, though many cooks now appreciate their artichoke-like flavor. Vegetables like cardoons, Jerusalem artichokes, kohlrabi, and parsnips are often referred to as *légumes oubliés*, or forgotten vegetables, but they are now making a comeback at the markets, with prices to match their newly fashionable status.

The fully grown stalks of cardoons can taste bitter, and they require peeling and boiling for 20 to 30 minutes to become tender and palatable. Like artichokes, they will discolor once peeled, so immerse them in a bowl of water with lemon juice as you work, and then use this lemon water (with salt added) to cook them. Bagna cauda would originally have been served with young, tender stalks that did not require cooking, but these are difficult to find even in Europe.

QUIQUES, SAUCE AUX NOIX

Rustic green pasta with walnut sauce

This recipe comes from my great friend and fellow cooking teacher Karine Brun, who works magic with the wild plants that grow around her home in the mountain village of Saint-Etienne-de-Tinée. To make this pasta, she often uses various combinations of wild spinach, nettles, dandelion, parsley, and scallion greens, depending on the season. The standard green to use is Swiss chard, preferably the smaller-leaved varieties, which are more tender.

Although I am using the word *pasta* here, quiques are almost more of a dumpling, with a chewy texture that is reminiscent of the spätzle found in Germany and Alsace. They are less fussy to make than pasta, and if you get children involved, they might end up loving greens (it worked for Karine!). The walnut sauce, although dairy-free, has a surprising creaminess that comes from the nuts, bread, and olive oil. Quiques can also be served with tomato sauce; mountain cooks love to add mushrooms and/or crumbled sausage to make the dish even heartier.

This dish is quite rib-sticking, so serve it in small portions unless you are living in the snowy mountains, like Karine!

SERVES 4 TO 6

FOR THE WALNUT SAUCE

1 slice sourdough or other rustic bread (25 g), preferably stale, cut into ½-inch (1 cm) cubes

¾ cup (180 ml) vegetable stock, homemade (page 355) or store-bought, warmed

1 cup (120 g) walnuts

1 garlic clove, smashed with the flat side of a knife and peeled (or 2 to 3 roasted garlic cloves, prepared as in Semi-Salted Cod with Garlic Confit, page 78)

½ cup (40 g) freshly grated Parmesan or aged pecorino

A pinch of dried marjoram or oregano

Sea salt and freshly ground black pepper

5 tablespoons (75 ml) extra-virgin olive oil

FOR THE QUIQUES

6 ounces (160 g) Swiss chard leaves (the leafy part from 1 bunch) or other tender greens of your choice (to yield about 2 packed cups chopped greens)

2½ cups (300 g) Italian 00 flour or all-purpose flour

2 large eggs

A pinch of freshly grated nutmeg

½ teaspoon fine sea salt

2 tablespoons extra-virgin olive oil, plus a drizzle for cooking the pasta

3 to 4 tablespoons (45 to 60 ml) room-temperature water

Coarse sea salt

For the walnut sauce

1. In a small bowl, soak the bread in the warm vegetable stock until the bread is completely soft. Squeeze out the bread over a bowl and set aside ¾ cup (180 ml) of the soaking liquid to add to the sauce as necessary.

2 In a food processor or blender, combine the soft bread with the walnuts, garlic, cheese, marjoram or oregano, salt and pepper to taste, and olive oil and process until smooth. Add enough of the reserved stock to make a thick sauce, like a runny mayonnaise. Taste to adjust the seasoning. Set the sauce aside until ready to serve (you can make it up to a day ahead and keep it in the refrigerator).

For the quiques

1 Chop the Swiss chard leaves or other greens as fine as possible. A mezzaluna would be a perfect tool for this, but a chef's knife also works well.

2 Place the flour in a large mixing bowl or on your work surface and make a well in the middle. Add the chopped greens, eggs, nutmeg, salt, and olive oil and mix with a fork or pastry scraper to break up the eggs and start bringing in the flour. When it becomes too difficult to mix with your tool, bring everything together with your hands, adding 3 to 4 tablespoons water as needed, to make a fairly stiff dough that is not sticky. Knead the dough on the counter for 2 to 3 minutes, until smooth with specks of green. Set aside at room temperature, covered with a bowl, for 30 minutes (you can make the sauce while the dough rests).

3 Divide the dough into 4 pieces. One at a time, roll out each piece about ⅛ inch (3 mm) thick, using flour as necessary so that it doesn't stick. Using a fluted pastry wheel or a pizza cutter, cut the sheet of dough into strips about ½ inch (1 cm) wide, then cut these into 2-inch (5 cm) lengths. Spread out on a baking sheet and sprinkle with a little more flour to keep them from sticking together. (At this stage, you can cover the quiques and leave them at room temperature for up to 2 hours, or freeze them on the baking sheet; once they are frozen hard, transfer the quiques to freezer bags. To cook from frozen, add the quiques directly to the boiling water and boil for 4 to 5 minutes, until tender.)

4 Bring a large pot of water to a boil and add a handful of sea salt and a drizzle of olive oil. Add the quiques and boil for 3 to 4 minutes, stirring occasionally, until tender (sample one to be sure that it does not have a raw flour taste). Remove the pot from the heat. Scoop out a ladleful of the pasta water, swish it around on a serving dish to warm it, then discard the water.

5 Place the walnut sauce in the bowl, scoop out the quiques with a slotted spoon, and transfer them to the serving dish (it's okay if a little water comes with them). Stir to combine, adding a little more cooking water if the sauce seems too thick, and serve immediately.

Cook's note

You can also make this dough by first roughly chopping the chard, then combining everything in the food processor and processing until a smooth green dough forms. But I like to see the green flecks from hand-chopped chard, and the dough comes together quickly enough by hand. Cook's choice!

BRANDADE DE CABILLAUD DEMI-SEL AU CITRON CONFIT ET AUX HERBES

Semi-salted cod mashed with potatoes, preserved lemon, and herbs

The French name of this dish comes from the Provençal word *brandar*, which means "to stir." During the eighteenth century, French fishermen began trading tons of cod from their long Atlantic excursions for sea salt from the southern French port of Aigues-Mortes, which allowed them to preserve the fish on their boats. Salt cod became an important part of the diet in Provence and the Niçoise region, since it did not spoil in the hot, dry climate and made fish readily available to those who lived far from the coast.

The invention of brandade is credited to an unnamed woman in the nearby town of Nîmes, who had the idea of pounding rehydrated salt cod with the herbal-tasting local olive oil in a mortar. The potent paste was eaten as an appetizer, often spread on thin slices of toasted baguette. Over the centuries, brandade evolved into a more complete dish made with potatoes, garlic, and cream—a kind of southern French fish pie.

Purists maintain that true brandade should contain no potato and can only come from Nîmes, but once you taste this version, I think you too will be willing to bend the rules. I first had it at the excellent bistro La Table du Chef in Cannes, whose chef at the time, Bruno Gensdarme, generously shared the recipe (which I have since slightly adapted to my own taste). I love his addition of cilantro and preserved lemon, which give the brandade a subtle North African twist. If lemons preserved in salt brine (a North African and Middle Eastern ingredient) are difficult to find, you can substitute lemon zest. A topping of sautéed cherry tomatoes and arugula adds color and brightness to this otherwise rich wintry dish.

SERVES 4

1 cup (280 g) coarse sea salt

One 1-pound (450 g) fresh cod fillet, 1 to 1½ inches thick

2 bay leaves

1 sprig thyme

8 to 10 small new potatoes (1 pound/450 g), peeled and sliced ¼ inch (0.5 cm) thick

1 cup (240 ml) heavy cream

1 cup (240 ml) whole milk

2 garlic cloves, chopped

Sea salt and freshly ground black pepper

¼ teaspoon Espelette chile powder or other mild chile powder

FOR THE CHERRY TOMATO TOPPING

2 cups (8 ounces/225 g) cherry tomatoes, cut in half

1 tablespoon extra-virgin olive oil

1 teaspoon sugar

A pinch of sea salt

⅓ cup (80 ml) extra-virgin olive oil , plus more for drizzling

½ preserved lemon, rind only, cut into small dice (or 1 tablespoon grated lemon zest, preferably from an organic lemon)

½ cup (10 g) cilantro leaves, roughly chopped

A handful of arugula leaves for garnish

1 Spread half the coarse salt in a dish that can hold the cod, place the fish on the layer of salt, and cover it with the rest of the salt. Refrigerate for 30 minutes, then wash the cod under cold running water to remove the salt.

2 Half fill a large saucepan with water and add the bay leaves and thyme. Bring to a boil and add the cod, then turn off the heat and leave for 7 to 10 minutes, covered, until the cod is white all the way through and flaky. Drain the cod.

3 Place the potatoes in a saucepan, along with the cream, milk, garlic, a pinch of salt, and pepper and Espelette or other mild chile powder to taste. Bring to a simmer, then reduce the heat to low, cover the potatoes with a circle of parchment paper (see Cook's Note, page 62) to keep the steam in, and cook for 20 to 25 minutes, until the potatoes are tender. Remove from the heat.

4 Meanwhile, make the cherry tomato topping: Heat the olive oil in a medium frying pan or sauté pan over medium-high heat. Add the cherry tomatoes, sugar, and salt and cook, shaking the pan occasionally, until the tomatoes collapse and their juices thicken and begin to stick to the pan, about 10 minutes. Remove from the heat.

5 Once the potatoes are cooked, break the cod into flakes. Using the large holes of a food mill, puree the cod and potatoes with their cream into a bowl, or mash them with a potato masher in a flat-bottomed bowl. Mix in the olive oil, preserved lemon, and cilantro, using a spatula or wooden spoon. Adjust the seasoning if necessary.

6 Preheat the broiler to its highest setting. Transfer the brandade to a medium baking dish (I use an oval one) and smooth the surface. Place 3 to 4 inches (8 to 10 cm) below the heating element and broil until the surface has browned, 4 to 5 minutes. Remove from the heat.

7 Arrange the tomatoes in a diagonal strip across the surface of the brandade, top with the arugula leaves, and drizzle them with olive oil.

ENDIVES CARAMÉLISÉES À L'ORANGE ET AU MIEL, COQUILLES SAINT JACQUES

Belgian endives caramelized with orange and honey, with seared scallops

In winter, bitter greens take over the market stalls in Nice, from cream-and-crimson radicchio to pale green, pointy-tipped Belgian endive. In this recipe, orange juice and honey infuse the endives with sunshine, balancing their bitterness with sweetness and acidity. Serving them with seared scallops elevates this to a dinner party dish, but they would also be delicious on their own as part of a vegetable spread or alongside roast chicken.

SERVES 4

FOR THE ENDIVES

6 Belgian endives (1½ pounds/700 g)

2 tablespoons unsalted butter

1 tablespoon extra-virgin olive oil

⅔ cup (150 ml) freshly squeezed orange juice (from 2 to 3 oranges)

Sea salt

1 tablespoon mild-tasting honey, such as acacia or clover

FOR THE SCALLOPS

12 large fresh sea scallops

Sea salt and freshly ground black pepper

2 tablespoons unsalted butter

1 tablespoon extra-virgin olive oil

For the endives

1 Remove any outer leaves that are streaked with brown and cut the endives lengthwise in half (do not remove the cores, as they will hold the leaves together).

2 In a large sauté pan or frying pan, melt the butter with the olive oil over medium heat. Place the endives cut side down in the fat and brown on both sides, 3 to 4 minutes on each side.

3 Add the orange juice, a pinch of salt, and the honey to the pan and cover with a circle of parchment paper (see Cook's Note, page 62). Cook for about 15 minutes, until the endives are very soft and caramelized. If there is still liquid in the pan, remove the paper and turn up the heat to let the excess water evaporate until the sauce looks syrupy. Remove from the heat.

For the scallops

1 Season the scallops on both sides with salt and pepper to taste. Melt the butter with the olive oil in a medium frying pan over medium-high heat. Add the scallops and cook for 1 to 1½ minutes on each side, until pale golden but still springy to the touch. Remove from the heat.

2 Arrange 3 warm endive halves on each plate and top with 3 seared scallops. Serve immediately.

TAGINE DE POULET AUX ORANGES CARAMÉLISÉES

Chicken tagine with caramelized oranges

Chicken with preserved lemon and olives is an internationally known Moroccan dish, but I had never heard of this orange variation until I met my friend Fouad Zarrou. Growing up in northern Morocco, Fouad learned Berber cuisine by watching his mother cook for their family of ten. The first time I tasted this dish, I found it so astonishing that I could barely speak as I scraped the earthenware tagine clean; it has now become my firm favorite in the Moroccan repertoire, making the most of the citrus season in Nice.

This dish is not complicated to make once you have marinated the chicken (you can also boil the oranges several hours or up to 2 days ahead of time). Moroccans would cook this dish in an earthenware tagine with a cone-shaped lid that distributes the steam, but a Dutch oven also works well. The key to a great tagine is to cook it for long enough that the juices reduce and the meat begins to stick to the bottom of the pot, creating irresistible caramelized juices. Keep the spice jars and extra herbs handy, as you may wish to add more during cooking.

SERVES 4

FOR THE MARINADE
Grated zest of 1 orange (preferably organic)
½ cup (120 ml) freshly squeezed orange juice (from 2 to 3 oranges)
½ cup (10 g) cilantro leaves, lightly chopped
½ cup (10 g) flat-leaf parsley leaves, lightly chopped
A pinch of saffron threads
A pinch of freshly ground black pepper
1 teaspoon ground ginger
1 teaspoon ground cumin
2 teaspoons sea salt
2 cinnamon sticks
1 teaspoon paprika

4 free-range chicken legs and thighs (or 2 legs and 2 bone-in breasts)

FOR THE CARAMELIZED ORANGES
2 oranges, preferably organic, scrubbed
2 tablespoons unsalted butter

3 tablespoons honey
Ground cinnamon, to taste
3 tablespoons orange flower water
1 tablespoon toasted sesame seeds

FOR COOKING THE CHICKEN
¼ cup (60 ml) extra-virgin olive oil
3 medium onions, cut lengthwise in half and thinly sliced lengthwise
2 medium tomatoes, cored and diced
6 carrots, cut lengthwise in half and then into 2-inch (5 cm) pieces
⅓ cup (60 g) unpitted green olives, such as Cerignola
¾ cup (about 110 g) dried fruits, such as prunes, apricots, and/or raisins

FOR THE FRIED ALMONDS
About ¼ cup (60 ml) vegetable oil
½ cup (65 g) blanched whole almonds

Cilantro sprigs for garnish

Make the marinade and marinate the chicken

1 In a bowl that can hold all the chicken, combine all the marinade ingredients. Place the chicken in the marinade, turning it to coat, and cover. Marinate the chicken for at least 30 minutes at room temperature, or, preferably, overnight in the refrigerator.

2 When ready to cook the chicken, transfer it to a plate; reserve the marinade.

Prepare the oranges

1 Place the oranges in a medium saucepan and cover with water. Bring to a boil and cook at a low boil for 30 minutes, or until soft all the way through. Remove from the heat.

2 Once the oranges have cooled enough to handle, cut them crosswise, peel and all, into slices about ½ inch (1 cm) thick. In a large frying pan, melt the butter over medium-high heat. Add the oranges, honey, and cinnamon and fry the oranges, turning once, until golden on both sides. Add the orange flower water and let it evaporate.

3 Transfer the orange slices to a plate and sprinkle with the sesame seeds.

For the tagine

1 Heat the olive oil in a tagine or Dutch oven over medium heat. Add the chicken pieces and lightly brown them for about 10 minutes, turning occasionally. Add the sliced onions and cook for another 5 minutes, stirring occasionally, until soft.

2 Add the tomatoes and carrots, along with the reserved marinade, cover, and cook for about 20 minutes, checking occasionally to make sure that the pot is not too dry; add a little water if necessary.

3 Meanwhile, soak the dried fruits in hot water for 10 minutes. Save a handful for garnish, and add the rest to the stew after the tomatoes and carrots have cooked for 20 minutes.

4 Cook for 10 more minutes, or until the chicken is completely tender and caramelizing on the bottom of the pot. Toward the end of the cooking time, taste and, if necessary, adjust the spices and herbs to your liking.

For the almonds

While the tagine is cooking, cover the bottom of a small frying pan with a ¼-inch (0.5 cm) layer of vegetable oil and heat over medium-high heat. Add the almonds and cook, stirring, for about 5 minutes, until golden brown. Remove with a slotted spoon and drain on paper towels.

Finish the dish

Garnish the tagine with the caramelized orange slices, fried almonds, and cilantro sprigs.

CHOUX FARCIS

Stuffed cabbage

Wherever cabbages grow, there is stuffed cabbage, it seems, so it's hard to say where the Niçoise version originated–though I like to think it was the Russian aristocracy who introduced the dish when they began spending winters here in the nineteenth century. Most likely it was a recipe of necessity–another way of stretching out small amounts of meat with readily available vegetables to create a dish that feels celebratory.

Known as *lou capoun* in the local language, the Niçoise version usually contains sausage meat, which creates flavorful juices as it cooks inside the cabbage leaves. This being Nice, some cooks like to add a few leaves of Swiss chard, but these are optional, since the cabbage already provides plenty of greens for the filling.

This recipe from my friend and fellow cooking teacher Hélène Albou is different from many, in that she does not add stock when cooking the cabbage in the oven. This way, the cabbage retains its bright color and texture, and the resulting dish is not soupy. Hélène uses a mixture of sausage meat and ground veal, but since veal can be hard to find in North America, I have simplified the filling. She cooks a tomato coulis separately and adds it at the table, but you can also pour it over the cabbage during the last few minutes of cooking. Crinkly-leaved Savoy cabbage is ideal for this dish–if it comes with beautiful dark-green outer leaves, be sure to stuff those rather than throwing them away. If you can't find Savoy cabbage, Napa cabbage also works, but you will only need to blanch the leaves for a few seconds, as they are more delicate, and you may need two heads to have enough large leaves to stuff.

I like to serve the stuffed cabbage as part of a meal that might start with soup or a winter salad, but you could boil or mash potatoes to serve along with it.

SERVES 4

1 Savoy cabbage (about 2¼ pounds/1 kg)

Sea salt

¼ cup (50 g) long-grain white rice

1 cup (20 g) flat-leaf parsley leaves

5 Swiss chard leaves, ribs removed (optional)

1 onion, minced

2 garlic cloves, minced

⅔ cup (50 g) freshly grated Parmesan

11 ounces (300 g) sweet Italian sausage meat

1 large egg

¼ cup (60 ml) extra-virgin olive oil, plus more for the baking pan

Freshly ground black pepper

½ cup (120 ml) water or vegetable stock, if necessary

FOR SERVING

Quick Tomato Sauce (page 339), made with oregano, warmed

1 Bring a large pot of water to a boil. Remove the core from the cabbage and separate the leaves; wash any dirt from the outer leaves. Reserve the 12 largest leaves to stuff, and heap all the inside leaves together.

2 When the water reaches a boil, salt it generously (as for pasta). Add the 12 large cabbage leaves, and once the water returns to a boil, set the timer for 3 minutes. Prepare a large bowl of ice water. Using tongs, transfer the blanched leaves to the ice water. After 1 minute, remove the cabbage leaves, drain them well in a colander, and spread them out in one layer on a large dish towel.

3 Add the remaining cabbage leaves to the boiling water and set the timer for 4 minutes once it comes back to a boil. Refresh in the ice water and drain as for the outer leaves. Once the inner leaves have cooled, squeeze them with your hands to remove most of the water (you don't have to remove every drop) and set aside.

4 Bring a medium pot of water to a boil and salt it lightly. Add the rice and cook for 10 minutes. Drain and set aside.

5 Preheat the oven to 375°F (190°C).

6 Finely chop the leaves for the stuffing, as well as the parsley and chard leaves, if using. Place in a large bowl and add the onion, garlic, Parmesan, rice, sausage meat, egg, 2 tablespoons of the olive oil, and salt and pepper to taste (use more or less salt depending on the saltiness of your sausage). Mix well (use your hands for this), until you can form a ball with the mixture.

7 Oil a 9-by-13-inch (23 by 33 cm) baking pan. Divide the stuffing among the 12 leaves, shaping it into an oval at the bottom of each leaf; I find it helpful to use a ⅓-cup (80 ml) measure to divide the filling. Fold the bottom of each leaf up over the stuffing, then fold over the sides and roll up. Arrange the cabbage leaves seam side down in the baking pan, fitting them snugly together. Drizzle with the remaining 2 tablespoons olive oil.

8 Bake the cabbage rolls for 45 minutes, or until beautifully browned. Check that there are still some juices in the pan after 30 minutes; if not, add the water or vegetable stock.

9 Baste the stuffed cabbage with the cooking juices, turn off the oven, and leave it in the oven for another 15 minutes.

10 To serve, divide the tomato sauce evenly among four shallow bowls, and top with the stuffed cabbage. (Any leftover stuffed cabbage can be reheated in a frying pan on the stovetop in a little water, or in the leftover tomato sauce, with a little extra water added.)

Cook's note

⁂

If you don't eat pork, you can use any other ground meat for this dish as long as it is not too lean. For a vegetarian version, you can add extra vegetables, such as sautéed carrot and leek, and double the amount of egg and olive oil. In that case, add 1 cup (240 ml) vegetable stock to the pan at the beginning of the baking time.

LENTILLES SAUCISSES

Lentils with sausages

I can't resist the small, round Perugina sausages hanging in long links from hooks at traditional butcher shops in Nice. Usually flavored with garlic, pepper, and/or fennel, they can be used fresh or allowed to dry, in which case they are eaten like salami. The sausages can be grilled, but the most popular way to cook them is braised with lentils. You can replace the Perugina with any good-quality Italian sausages (including spicy ones) or smoked sausages, or leave them out altogether—the lentils and chard will still be delicious. Don't be tempted to brown the sausages before adding them to the stew—the point of this dish is to infuse the lentils with all their flavor as they cook.

The type of lentil makes a difference here: French green lentils, the most prized of which is the lentille du Puy, from the Auvergne region, will hold their shape once cooked and bring a slightly nutty taste to the dish.

SERVES 4 TO 6

2 bay leaves
2 sprigs thyme
2 sprigs flat-leaf parsley
1 tablespoon extra-virgin olive oil
1 small onion, diced
1 medium carrot, cut into ¼-inch (0.5 cm) dice
1 celery stalk, cut into ¼-inch (0.5 cm) dice
1 medium leek, cut lengthwise in half and thinly sliced
2 garlic cloves, minced

Sea salt
1½ cups (8 ounces/210 g) French green lentils, such as lentilles du Puy, rinsed
6 cups (1.5 l) water or vegetable stock
6 Swiss chard leaves (with their stems)
6 Italian sausages (about 3 to 4 ounces/80 to 110 g each)
Freshly ground black pepper
Excellent extra-virgin olive oil for serving
Chopped flat-leaf parsley for garnish

1 Tie the bay leaves, thyme, and parsley together with kitchen string to make a bouquet garni.

2 In a medium-large heavy saucepan, heat the olive oil over medium heat. Add the onion, carrot, celery, leek, garlic, and a pinch of salt and cook, stirring, until the vegetables turn pale golden, 8 to 10 minutes.

3 Add the bouquet garni, lentils, and water or stock and bring to a boil, then partially cover the pan, lower the heat, and allow the liquid to bubble gently for 20 to 30 minutes, until the lentils are near the point of being completely soft but retain a bite (think of al dente pasta).

4 In the meantime, separate the chard leaves from the stalks. Cut the leaves into slivers and the stems into thin slices.

5 Add the sausages and chard stems to the lentils and simmer for 10 minutes.

6 Add the chard leaves and continue cooking for about 5 minutes; the lentils should be soft but still hold their shape. Season generously with salt and pepper, remove from the heat, and remove the bouquet garni.

7 To serve, remove the sausages from the pan and slice them, or cut them lengthwise in half. Ladle the lentils into shallow bowls and top with the sausages. Drizzle with your best olive oil and sprinkle with chopped parsley.

DAUBE DE BOEUF NIÇOISE

Beef stew cooked in red wine with porcini and orange zest

Fragrant with wild herbs, strips of orange zest, and porcini mushrooms, daube de boeuf is the southern French answer to beef bourguignon. The original cooking vessel was a pot-bellied earthenware *daubière*, with a spout for releasing the steam. These days, most cooks use an enameled cast-iron pot for the slow cooking the dish requires.

One of the best versions of this I have tasted was at the bistro La Merenda, which has a cult following in Nice and far beyond. When I asked chef Dominique Le Stanc for the recipe, he wrote it out for me in beautiful handwriting. I have slightly adapted his daube to my taste, cooking the carrots separately with butter and honey so that they add a pop of color and sweetness. I also marinate the beef and aromatics overnight in the red wine to deepen the stew's flavor even more.

In the countryside around Nice, this dish had particular importance because few people could afford pricier cuts of meat. As always, locals found ingenious ways to transform the leftovers, stretching out the meat with Swiss chard to make Niçoise ravioli, or pelotons, also known as "naked ravioli" (page 297). Any leftover sauce can be served with Gnocchi (page 67).

Serve the daube with boiled potatoes, polenta, or Panisses (page 239).

SERVES 6

2 sprigs fresh or dried thyme

2 bay leaves

2 sprigs flat-leaf parsley

3 strips mandarin or orange zest, about 3 inches (8 cm) long and ½ inch (0.5 cm) wide, removed with a vegetable peeler

1 dark green leek leaf (optional)

1 bottle (750 ml) full-bodied fruity red wine, such as Côtes du Rhône

2¼ pounds (1 kg) stewing beef, cut into 2-inch (5 cm) cubes and trimmed of most of its fat

1 onion, cut lengthwise in half and thinly sliced crosswise

4 garlic cloves, cut lengthwise in half and thinly sliced

1 teaspoon sea salt, plus more to taste

Freshly ground black pepper

½ cup (⅓ ounce/10 g) dried porcini mushrooms

½ cup (120 ml) warm water

2 tablespoons extra-virgin olive oil

1 tablespoon tomato paste

FOR THE GLAZED CARROTS

1 bunch slim carrots (about 8 carrots)

1 tablespoon unsalted butter

1 teaspoon honey

½ teaspoon sea salt

1 The day before cooking the daube, make a bouquet garni by tucking the thyme, bay leaves, parsley, and citrus zest into the leek leaf, if using, and tying it at either end with a piece of kitchen string, criss-crossing it in the middle; if you don't have a leek leaf, just tie the herbs together in the same way.

2 Pour the wine into a large bowl and add the beef, onion, garlic, bouquet garni, salt, and pepper to taste. Cover and refrigerate overnight to develop the flavors. →

3   The next day, drain the meat and vegetables in a colander set over a large bowl; reserve the wine. Separate the meat from the other ingredients, reserving the bouquet garni, onion, and garlic. Dry the meat with paper towels.

4   Soak the porcini mushrooms in the warm water in a small bowl for 15 to 20 minutes, or until soft. Lift the mushrooms from the soaking liquid, squeezing the excess liquid back into the bowl. Strain the liquid through a fine strainer to remove any sand, and reserve the mushrooms and liquid.

5   Preheat the oven to 300°F (150°C).

6   Heat a large Dutch oven or other heavy ovenproof pot over medium heat and add the olive oil. Add the meat and brown the pieces on all sides (cook in two batches if necessary so that the pieces are not touching as you sear them). Wait for each piece to turn deep golden brown before turning it (4 to 5 minutes), or it may stick to the pot. Set the meat aside on a plate.

7   Add the reserved onion and garlic to the pot, turn the heat to medium-low, and cook until soft and pale golden, stirring occasionally, about 5 minutes. Add the bouquet garni and tomato paste and stir for 1 minute to cook the tomato paste.

8   Pour in the red wine, scraping the bottom of the pot with a wooden spatula to release any caramelized juices. Add the browned meat.

9   Add the porcini and the reserved soaking liquid to the pot. Brush the sides of the pot with a pastry brush dipped in water to prevent any splashed juices from burning in the oven.

10   Cover the pot with the lid and transfer to the oven. Cook for 3 to 3½ hours, checking a few times to make sure that the meat is still covered with liquid and adding a little water as needed. The daube is done when the meat almost collapses when you poke it with a knife. Don't worry if the meat seems slow to soften; the transformation comes almost from one moment to the next. Once the meat has softened, do not let it cook longer, or it could fall apart and become fibrous.

While the daube is cooking, make the glazed carrots

Scrub the carrots and peel them only if the skin seems thick. If they are very skinny, leave them whole; if not, cut them lengthwise in half. Place the carrots in a sauté pan or frying pan large enough to hold them in one layer and add just enough water to cover. Add the butter, honey, and salt, bring to a boil, and cook at a fast boil until the water has evaporated and the carrots are tender when poked with a knife, shaking the pot every 2 to 3 minutes. Let the carrots glaze in the butter and honey until shiny but not browned. Remove from the heat.

Serve the daube

When the daube is cooked, add the carrots to the pot and shake it gently to incorporate them into the stew. Taste the sauce, adjust the seasonings, and serve.

PELOTONS, SAUCE TOMATE

Naked ravioli with tomato sauce

Peloton means "ball" in French—hence the name for groupings of cyclists in road races like the Tour de France, and the popular exercise bike. In this recipe, leftover meat from Daube de Boeuf Niçoise (page 295) is combined with Swiss chard, Parmesan, and egg and shaped into little balls that are rolled in flour before being boiled like gnocchi. It's typical of the mountains behind Nice, where cooks often found ingenious ways to stretch leftovers. Despite being meat-based, these pelotons are surprisingly light, their thin skins melting on the tongue. If you don't happen to have extra daube meat lying around, be creative like a Niçois, using whatever meat you have available; you can also substitute spinach for the chard.

This dish is also known as "naked ravioli" because the same mixture can be wrapped in pasta dough to make ravioli Niçois. I learned it from Franck Bermond, a local chef and cooking teacher who is passionate about preserving lesser-known recipes from the region. The day he taught me this dish, he was also working on updating an old recipe for latticed jam tart. "The day you stop experimenting is the day you lose interest in cooking," he said. The first time I made pelotons, I went a little overboard with the pepper and nutmeg; now I have decided I like them best that way.

SERVES 4

1 pound (450 g) Swiss chard or spinach leaves, without the stems (from 2 to 3 bunches)

1¼ cups (about 300 g) leftover meat from Daube de Boeuf Niçoise (page 295), drained (or other leftover braised beef or other meat)

⅔ cup (50 g) freshly grated Parmesan

1 tablespoon extra-virgin olive oil

2 large eggs

Sea salt and freshly ground black pepper

Freshly grated nutmeg to taste

Up to ¼ cup (50 g) dry breadcrumbs if the mixture is too wet

1 cup (120 g) all-purpose flour for coating the pelotons

Quick Tomato Sauce (page 339), warmed

1 Bring a large pot of water to a boil. Immerse the Swiss chard or spinach leaves in the boiling water and blanch for 2 minutes, then drain in a colander and immediately rinse under cold water; drain. When the leaves are cool enough to handle, press out as much water as you can, working with a tennis-ball-sized handful at a time. Set aside.

2 Run the meat through a meat grinder, or chop it by hand very finely. (Franck prefers not to use a food processor to chop the meat. But if you opt to save time by doing so, I promise not to tell!)

3 Very finely chop the Swiss chard or spinach. →

4   In a medium bowl, combine the chopped meat and chard, Parmesan, olive oil, and eggs. Season to taste with salt, pepper, and nutmeg.

5   Check to see whether a heaped teaspoon of the mixture holds together if you rub it in a circle in the palm of one hand, using the fingers of your opposite hand. If the mixture is too sticky, add enough of the breadcrumbs so that you can shape it into balls. At this stage, the pelotons may not hold together well. If this is the case, place the mixture in the refrigerator for 30 minutes before continuing.

6   To shape the pelotons, place the flour in a baking pan. As you form the balls, using a heaped teaspoon of the mixture for each one, toss them into the flour. Shake the pan occasionally to coat the balls with the flour as you roll them around.

7   Bring a large pot of water to a boil. Warm the tomato sauce to a simmer in a frying pan or sauté pan that is large enough to hold the pelotons, then turn off the heat.

8   Using a slotted spoon, transfer the pelotons to the boiling water, working in batches so as not to overcrowd the pot. Cook for 2 to 3 minutes, until they float to the surface and the flour no longer looks white. Remove them with the slotted spoon and transfer to the pan with the tomato sauce. If your pelotons burst open as they cook, it means they contained too much moisture. Don't worry, they will still be delicious.

9   Serve immediately. Or, if you want to serve the pelotons up to an hour later, gently reheat them with the sauce in the frying pan. You can also store them in the refrigerator for up to 2 days and reheat them in the sauce in a frying pan on the stove when needed.

Cook's note

꙳

If you are using leftover meat from the Daube de Boeuf Niçoise (page 295) to make pelotons, you can serve the remaining daube sauce and vegetables with fresh pasta or the Green Gnocchi (page 67).

Maison Barale: Reinventing ravioli

Nathalie Barale was up to her elbows in raw artichokes when I stopped by the Old Town institution Maison Barale to learn more about her family history. Deftly trimming the tough leaves, she told me that her Piedmontese great-grandparents, Matteo and Erminia Barale, founded the shop in 1892, at first selling dried pantry staples like beans and lentils alongside fresh pasta. The handmade products soon pushed aside the others, and Barale has been known for its ravioli, gnocchi, tagliatelle-style noodles, and Panisses (page 239) ever since, drawing a line of patient pasta-lovers that extends down the block on weekends.

Maison Barale retains its charming retro facade, but while I was living down the street from this shop, I watched the interior transform. Nathalie was working as an accountant in Paris when she met her husband, Eric, and together they decided to take over the family business, with Eric heading up the kitchen. Over the past two decades, they have modernized the kitchen and shop, adding new products like pedigreed cheeses, hand-churned butter, and wine and Champagne from small producers, selected by their sommelier son, Hugo. It takes a team of thirteen to keep the kitchen and pocket-sized boutique running, starting before the street-sweepers have finished clearing the previous night's debris.

Most interestingly, the fourth-generation Barales have departed from Niçoise tradition by introducing ravioli with innovative fillings like lemon-ginger, pistachio-arugula, and tapenade and truffle oil. "We don't use any artificial colorings," Nathalie told me. "Instead, we rely on spices like turmeric and vegetable juices." At first, the shop's loyal customers were taken aback, "and then they tasted them," she said with a smile. If the classic Niçoise ravioli, filled with daube meat (page 295) and spinach, remains their best seller, the lemon-ginger version now appears on the blackboard list of specials almost every day, often selling out before I can get to it.

Barale's secret to success is simple: "We make ourselves happy," Nathalie said. This must have rubbed off on their son Thomas, who after traveling the world and working with star chef Alain Passard in Paris, joined Barale's team a year ago. "I followed my parents' lead and did not pressure him," Nathalie said. "His path is for him to decide." And with that, she picked up another artichoke from the seemingly endless heap and continued trimming.

ALOUETTES SANS TÊTE

Stuffed beef rolls cooked in red wine

In French, the name of this dish translates as "headless larks," because the beef rolls have the shape of tiny birds without their heads. Since I had seen various versions of this recipe in cookbooks, I asked my butcher at the family-run Carlicchi Zelino if he could share a recipe. "My grandmother is the expert," he said, telling me to come back on the weekend, when she works at the stall (French butchers don't seem to have a retirement age).

As opinionated as any Niçoise mamie, Janine pointed to the *paleron* (beef chuck or shoulder), telling me this is the best cut to use because it does not dry out during the slow cooking. "You can fill the alouettes with ground veal and pork–which will keep the filling juicy–mixed with garlic and parsley," she said. She then detailed how to make the red wine sauce, advising me to add tomato paste for a richer color and more intense flavor.

After she had thinly sliced the beef by hand, scooped up a small amount of ground meat for the filling, and demonstrated how to roll and tie the alouettes using kitchen twine, I told her that I would let her know how it went. "You have no excuse to mess it up!" she exclaimed. I'm not sure I would admit it to Janine, but it did take me a couple of tries to get this apparently simple dish right.

If ground veal and pork are not easily available, you can use a small amount of diced salt pork, as many local cooks do. Fresh pasta, polenta, or potatoes complete this dish, soaking up the sauce rich with wine and herbs. Like all slow-cooked dishes, alouettes can be made a few hours to a day ahead and reheated.

SERVES 4 TO 8

FOR THE FILLING

1 cup (about 6 ounces/160 g) mixed ground veal and pork, or 4 ounces (110 g) salt pork, cut into ¼-inch (0.5 cm) dice

2 garlic cloves, minced

2 tablespoons chopped flat-leaf parsley

Sea salt and freshly ground black pepper

8 slices beef chuck, cut ¼ inch (0.5 cm) thick and pounded to ⅛ inch (3 mm) thick (your butcher might be able to do this for you); 3 to 4 ounces (80 to 100 g) each

2 sprigs thyme

1 sprig rosemary

1 bay leaf

2 tablespoons extra-virgin olive oil

1 onion, diced

Sea salt

2 tablespoons all-purpose flour

2 tablespoons tomato paste

1½ cups (360 ml) full-bodied fruity red wine, such as Côtes du Rhône

½ cup (120 ml) water, plus more if needed

Freshly ground black pepper

Chopped flat-leaf parsley for garnish

1 To make the filling: In a medium bowl, stir together the ground meat or salt pork, garlic, and parsley, seasoning the mixture with salt (if using ground meat) and pepper.

2 Lay one slice of beef on a cutting board and place 2 tablespoons of the filling at one narrow end. (There is no need to season the beef, as it will absorb flavor from the filling and the sauce.) Roll the meat up around the filling and tie each end with string, crisscrossing the string in the middle.

3 Tie the thyme, rosemary, and bay leaf together with kitchen string to make a bouquet garni.

4 Heat the olive oil in a Dutch oven or other large heavy pot over medium heat. Add the beef rolls and brown on both sides, 3 to 4 minutes on each side. If the meat sticks to the pot initially, it will release easily once it has browned, so don't rush it.

5 Set the beef rolls aside on a plate and add the onion to the pot with a pinch of salt. Stir for 4 to 5 minutes, until the onion is translucent and caramelized from the pan juices. Add the flour and stir for 1 minute, then add the tomato paste and stir for another minute.

6 Add about ½ cup (120 ml) of the red wine and cook, stirring, until the sauce thickens. Stir in the rest of the red wine and the water and season generously with salt and pepper. Return the beef rolls to the pan. The liquid should almost cover the meat; add a little more water if needed.

7 Bring the liquid to a boil, then cover and cook over low heat for 1 to 1½ hours, with the sauce bubbling gently, turning the beef rolls occasionally, until the meat feels very tender when pierced with the tip of a small knife and the sauce has thickened like gravy. Toward the end of the cooking time, taste and adjust the seasonings. Sprinkle with chopped parsley before serving.

POMMES DE TERRE RÔTIES AU PARMESAN

Slow-roasted potatoes with Parmesan

Viktorija Todorovska, who teaches cooking and wine classes at Les Petits Farcis, makes entertaining look effortless. Whenever I attend one of her legendary dinner parties, she pulls spoon-tender roast meat and crispy-edged vegetables from the oven claiming she has done nothing but glance at them once or twice as they cooked. "It's all about the ingredients," she says. These miraculous slow-roasted potatoes appear frequently on her table, and they are always gobbled up within seconds. The light sprinkling of Parmesan makes the potatoes especially irresistible, without asserting its flavor too strongly. The only difficulty with this recipe is planning in advance, since the potatoes take a little more than an hour and a half to cook (though you can make them well ahead and serve them at room temperature). Serve these potatoes with Daube de Boeuf Niçoise (page 295), Rack of Lamb (page 233), or any other stewed or roasted meat.

SERVES 4

4 medium Yukon Gold potatoes or other waxy variety (about 1¾ pounds/800 g)

Fine sea salt

¼ cup (60 ml) extra-virgin olive oil

2 tablespoons freshly grated Parmesan

1 Preheat the oven to 225°F (110°C).

2 Peel the potatoes and cut them into bite-sized pieces. Place in a baking dish large enough that you can spread them out without the pieces touching too much. Sprinkle with fine salt, drizzle with the olive oil, and toss so that the potatoes are coated with the oil and evenly seasoned.

3 Roast the potatoes for 1 hour and 15 minutes (they will be soft but not browned). Raise the oven temperature to 400°F (200°C) and continue cooking until the potatoes start browning around the edges, about 20 minutes longer.

4 Sprinkle the potatoes with the Parmesan and return them to the oven for another 2 to 3 minutes, until the cheese melts. Serve hot or at room temperature.

TARTE AU CITRON À L'HUILE D'OLIVE

Lemon tart with olive oil

I first came across a version of this recipe in French *Elle* magazine and, intrigued by the presence of olive oil in both the pastry and the filling, tweaked the tart until it became my own. Niçoise olive oil is ideally suited to desserts because of its buttery, almond-like quality, but you can use any mild-tasting, fruity olive oil.

If you are a pastry novice, this is an ideal dough to start with because you can treat it like Play-Doh, pressing it into the pan with your fingers and patching any holes. Unlike pure butter pastry, it needs no resting time, and it shrinks very little in the oven. The olive oil gives it a light, crumbly texture, like shortbread. I learned the trick of whisking lemon curd until fluffy while taking a macarons class in Paris, and here the airy filling makes a perfect match for the delicate crust.

My son has eaten this lemon tart countless times, yet this is the dessert that he still asks for on his birthday and whenever he comes home from college. You can bake the pastry shell several hours ahead of time; once assembled, the tart is best eaten the same day.

SERVES 6 TO 8

FOR THE PASTRY

4 tablespoons (60 g) unsalted butter, at room temperature

¼ cup (30 g) confectioners' sugar

1½ tablespoons almond meal

¼ teaspoon fine sea salt

1 cup (120 g) all-purpose flour

1 large egg yolk

3½ tablespoons delicate-tasting extra-virgin olive oil

FOR THE FILLING

¾ cup (150 g) sugar

2 teaspoons cornstarch

1 tablespoon grated lemon zest (preferably from an organic lemon)

2 large eggs

2 large egg yolks

¾ cup (180 ml) freshly squeezed lemon juice (from 3 to 4 lemons)

4 tablespoons (60 g) unsalted butter

2 tablespoons delicate-tasting extra-virgin olive oil

For the pastry

1 Preheat the oven to 375°F (190°C).

2 In a mixing bowl, combine the butter, confectioners' sugar, almond meal, salt, and 2 tablespoons of the flour and blend until creamy with a pastry scraper or a fork. Add the egg yolk, olive oil, and the remaining flour. Mix again with the scraper or fork until the dough forms a smooth ball. (You can also make the dough in a food processor or a stand mixer fitted with the paddle attachment, starting with cold butter so that the mixture doesn't become too soft to work with.) →

3   With your fingers, press the dough as evenly as possible into the bottom and up the sides of a 9-inch (23 cm) tart pan, preferably with a removable base. (It's normal for the dough to be very soft at this point, but if it's too sticky to work with, flatten it with your hands to about ½ inch/1 cm thick in the tart pan and refrigerate for 15 to 20 minutes before proceeding.) Press the dough against the sides of the pan so that it extends at least ½ inch (1 cm) above the rim, then cut off the excess with one swipe of a rolling pin across the top. Press the pastry lightly with your thumb all around the sides so that it comes slightly above the rim, to compensate for any shrinkage as it bakes.

4   Place the tart pan on a baking sheet and bake for 12 to 14 minutes, until the pastry is golden brown all over, turning the pan after 8 minutes if it seems to be browning more on one side. Remove the tart pan from the oven and set it on a rack to cool completely.

For the filling

1   Place the sugar and cornstarch in a mixing bowl. Rub the lemon zest into the sugar with your fingertips to extract its essential oils.

2   Add the eggs and egg yolks and whisk until well combined. Gently whisk in the lemon juice.

3   Transfer the mixture to a heavy saucepan and cook over medium-low heat, whisking vigorously in a side-to-side motion to lighten the mixture and prevent lumps from forming. After about 5 minutes, the curd should start to thicken like pudding and the foam on the surface will start to disappear. Let the curd come just to a boil (you should see a few big bubbles when you stop whisking), then turn off the heat.

4   Add the butter in pieces, whisking until melted. Add the olive oil and whisk until completely incorporated.

Assemble the tart

Using a heatproof spatula, scrape the hot filling into the cooled crust, working quickly, as the filling will begin to set almost immediately. Place in the refrigerator to set for at least an hour. (If you are in a hurry, you can pour the filling into a still-hot crust, but you will need to allow more time for the tart to set.)

Serve the tart

If your pan has a removable bottom, place it on a small bowl so that the rim falls down, and transfer the tart (on its metal base) to a plate. Otherwise, serve the tart from the pan without attempting to remove it, as the crust is very fragile.

SOUFFLÉ AU CITRON

Lemon soufflé

When I was working at the Cordon Bleu, I rented a room in an apartment with a narrow L-shaped kitchen equipped only with two electric burners and a toaster oven. This did not deter me from practicing what I learned each day in scaled-down versions. One of my greatest challenges, I thought, would be the soufflé: could I make it work in a doll-sized oven? Towering proudly above its ramekin, my first Paris soufflé proved that this dish is harder to mess up than people think.

In Nice, I discovered an almost-miraculous three-ingredient lemon version from local chef Christian Plumail, which uses egg yolks whipped with sugar and lemon zest as a base rather than the traditional heavier pastry cream. Much of the flavor comes from the zest of the lemons that grow everywhere here in winter; be sure to choose organic fruits or scrub them before zesting. You can prep the ingredients in advance, and coat the soufflé dishes with the butter and sugar, but you will need to mix and bake the soufflé just before serving it. For a pretty presentation, I like to bake it in ovenproof glass ramekins.

SERVES 6

2 tablespoons unsalted butter

⅓ cup (65 g) sugar plus 1 tablespoon, plus 2 tablespoons for the ramekins

4 large eggs, from the refrigerator

2 tablespoons grated lemon zest (from 2 lemons, preferably organic)

¼ cup (60 ml) freshly squeezed lemon juice

1 tablespoon confectioners' sugar

1 Preheat the oven to 375°F (190°C); do not use the convection setting, as it could cause the soufflés to tilt as they rise.

2 Melt the butter in the microwave or in a small saucepan. Using a pastry brush, butter six individual ramekins, ideally measuring 3 inches (8 cm) across and 2 inches (5 cm) tall and holding 6 ounces (160 ml). Use an upward motion on the sides, and pay special attention to the rims.

3 Place the ramekins in the refrigerator for the butter to set, then brush a second coating of butter up the sides and over the rims (no need to redo the bottoms). One at a time, coat each ramekin with sugar, turning it to evenly cover the sides and bottom and then tapping any excess sugar into the next ramekin. Place the ramekins on a baking sheet.

4 Separate the eggs, being careful not to let any egg yolk fall into the whites, and transfer the yolks to the bowl of a stand mixer fitted with the whisk attachment; set the whites aside. Whisk the egg yolks with ⅓ cup (65 g) of the sugar on high speed for about 1 minute, until the mixture thickens and lightens in color. Whisk in the lemon zest briefly, so as not to liquefy the mixture too much. Transfer the mixture to another bowl. →

5 Wash the whisk and bowl thoroughly, so that no trace of yolk remains. Place the egg whites in the clean bowl and start beating them on low speed, gradually increasing the speed to high over 1 minute. Once soft peaks start to form, add the remaining 1 tablespoon sugar, then drizzle in the lemon juice, still mixing on high speed but stopping as soon as all the lemon juice has been incorporated.

6 Remove the bowl from the mixer stand. Using a rubber spatula, fold one third of the egg whites into the egg yolk mixture. Add the rest of the egg whites, folding them in gently from bottom to top, turning the bowl as you fold.

7 Fill the ramekins to the top and smooth the surface with the back of a knife. Sprinkle the soufflés with the confectioners' sugar. Immediately transfer the baking sheet to the preheated oven.

8 Bake for 7 to 8 minutes, until the soufflés are well risen and lightly browned on top. Serve immediately—a soufflé waits for no one!

Cook's notes

At the Cordon Bleu, I picked up a few egg-separating tricks. First, have three clean bowls ready—a small one that can hold a single egg white, and two large enough to hold all the yolks and all the whites once separated. Tap an egg on the counter rather than the edge of the bowl, to prevent the broken shell from piercing the yolk. Then break it open and let the white run into the small bowl, dropping the yolk back and forth between the two half shells until all the white has run out. Place the yolk in one of the larger bowls, and transfer the white to the other (discard the white if any yolk has fallen into it). Repeat with the next egg. By transferring the whites one by one from the small bowl to the larger one, you will ensure that no stray yolk will contaminate the whole batch.

If a shell fragment falls into the whites, use a half shell to scoop it out—eggshells have a magnetic attraction to each other.

GÂTEAU À L'ORANGE CARAMÉLISÉE
Caramelized orange cake

Around the corner from my studio, Vietnamese-French cook Thi-hieu (known as You) Nguyen works magic in the closet-sized kitchen of her restaurant, Banh Mei. Originally a modest street food spot serving little more than banh mi and bo bun, Banh Mei has evolved into a bistro/wine bar with a modern Asian-Mediterranean menu that changes weekly, inspired by You's finds at the nearby Cours Saleya market. Although for a while she talked about moving to a more spacious location, somehow You has found freedom in the constraints of her tiny kitchen. She has even started producing baked goods, from rum-spiked chocolate chunk cookies worthy of a New York City bakery to banana pudding.

This cake is typical of You's style: it looks simple, but it has extra depth thanks to the caramelized oranges and orange syrup. I have thought about drizzling dark chocolate ganache over it but have stopped myself, because it really needs no adornment. I did add orange zest to You's recipe to make the orange flavor even more intense. Using cake flour makes the texture lighter, but if you only have all-purpose, don't let that stop you from making this cake.

SERVES 6 TO 8

FOR THE CAKE

11 tablespoons (150 g) unsalted butter, plus 2 teaspoons for the loaf pan

2 tablespoons raw sugar, such as turbinado or Demerara

2 medium oranges, preferably organic, scrubbed

½ cup (100 g) granulated sugar

2 large eggs

1 cup (120 g) cake or all-purpose flour

1 teaspoon baking powder

Pinch of fine sea salt

FOR THE ORANGE SYRUP

Juice of 1 medium orange

¼ cup (25 g) confectioners' sugar

For the cake

1 Preheat the oven to 400°F (200°C). Grease a 5-by-9-inch (12 by 23 cm) loaf pan with the 2 teaspoons butter and sprinkle the bottom with the raw sugar.

2 Cut 4 horizontal slices about ⅛ inch (3 mm) thick from one of the oranges, then cut these in half. Arrange the orange slices in the bottom of the loaf pan, without overlapping them. Place in the oven and bake for 10 to 15 minutes, until the oranges are caramelized.

3 Meanwhile, melt the remaining butter in a saucepan or in the microwave and transfer to a medium bowl. Add the granulated sugar and whisk until the mixture is smooth. Zest and juice the second orange (you should have about 1 tablespoon zest and ⅓ cup/80 ml juice) and add this to the butter-sugar mixture, then whisk in the eggs one by one. →

4   Sift the flour, baking powder, and salt into the bowl and stir with a rubber spatula until you have a smooth batter (be careful not to overmix).

5   Pour the batter over the oranges and bake for 10 minutes (the cake will not be very tall at this point, which is fine). Lower the oven temperature to 350°F (180°C) and bake for another 15 to 20 minutes, until the cake is browned on top and a toothpick inserted in the center comes out clean. Remove from the oven.

6   Let the cake cool for 10 minutes, then run a knife around the sides and turn it out onto a rack. If the cake sticks to the pan, you can warm the bottom of the pan slightly on the stovetop to melt the orange caramel.

To soak the cake

1   While the cake is still warm, mix the orange juice with the confectioners' sugar in a small bowl, stirring until the sugar has dissolved.

2   Place a plate over the cake and flip it so that the orange slices are on the bottom. Use a toothpick or skewer to poke holes about 1 inch (2.5 cm) apart in the cake, then pour the syrup over top. Let stand for at least 1 hour.

3   Before serving, flip the cake onto another plate so that the orange slices are on top. Cut into slices and serve. (Store any leftover cake in the refrigerator, covered, and let it come to room temperature before serving.)

MOUSSE AU CHOCOLAT À L'HUILE D'OLIVE

Chocolate mousse with olive oil

As in my Lemon Tart (page 307), the surprise ingredient in this chocolate mousse is olive oil, which replaces the traditional butter. I use either the delicate Nice olive oil, which has a buttery quality, or a smooth-tasting oil known as *fruité noir*, made with wrinkly black olives from Provence. Feel free to experiment with different oils, but avoid any that are too bitter or pungent.

    I love the "chew" that chocolate mousse develops with a longer resting time, so you can plan on making this dessert several hours or up to a day ahead of serving it. Be sure to use very fresh free-range eggs, since the eggs are not cooked in this recipe. With very little sugar and no cream (which has no place in traditional chocolate mousse!), this is a grown-up dessert that is light enough to serve at the end of a hearty meal.

SERVES 6

6 ounces (165 g) good-quality bittersweet chocolate, with 60 to 70 percent cocoa solids, chopped

6 tablespoons (90 ml) delicate, fruity-tasting extra-virgin olive oil

6 large eggs, separated (see Cook's Note, page 312)

2 tablespoons sugar

A pinch of fleur de sel or flaky sea salt, plus more for garnish

Cocoa powder for sprinkling

1   In a large heatproof bowl set over a saucepan of simmering water, or in a bowl in the microwave, melt the chocolate with the olive oil. Remove from the heat just before the chocolate has completely melted and stir to melt the last lumps. Let the chocolate cool until it is warm rather than hot, about 5 minutes (if you want to use a thermometer, the temperature should be around 105°F/40°C).

2   Place the egg yolks in a medium bowl and whisk lightly. Add about 2 tablespoons of the melted chocolate and stir with a rubber spatula until smooth. Then add this mixture to the remaining chocolate and stir to combine.

3   In the bowl of a stand mixer fitted with the whisk attachment, beat the egg whites on medium speed until they start to turn white. Add the sugar, turn the speed up a notch, and continue beating until the egg whites form soft peaks. You should be able to turn the bowl upside down without the egg whites sliding out.

4   Add one third of the egg whites to the chocolate mixture and stir with the spatula to lighten the mixture. Carefully fold in another third of the egg whites, then add the rest of the egg whites and the pinch of fleur de sel or flaky sea salt and fold very gently until combined.

5   Transfer the mousse to individual ramekins or a large serving dish, cover with plastic wrap, and chill for at least 2 hours, and up to 24 hours, before serving.

6   Serve the mousse sprinkled with cocoa powder and topped with a few more crystals of fleur de sel.

TOURTE DE BLETTES SUCRÉE

Sweet Swiss chard pie

When I first moved to Nice, I lived upstairs from the now-defunct bakery Espuno, which had been run by the same family for generations. I would wake up to the scent of rustic loaves emerging from their wood-fired oven, but it wasn't just the bread that captured my attention when I went into the shop. This bakery had none of the elaborate pastries I had grown used to seeing in Paris; instead, next to the croissants and brioches, it showcased square slabs of pie with a dark green filling, the top crust sprinkled with a thick coating of sugar.

This was my first exposure to tourte de blettes sucrée, the iconic Niçoise dessert that is sold in most local bakeries and is, for many children, including my son, a primary source of greens in their diet. Filled with a sweetened mixture of Swiss chard, rum-soaked raisins, pine nuts, apple, and perhaps grated Parmesan or Sbrinz (an aged Swiss cheese), this dessert does not appear anywhere else in France, although Tuscan cooks make a similar pie using vin santo instead of rum. It was born of an abundance of Swiss chard; in winter, when local fruit was scarce, cooks used what they had available to satisfy a sweet craving. The coating of sugar–originally granulated, but now almost always powdered–distinguishes it from the savory Tourte de Blettes Salée (page 73), which is filled with a mixture of Swiss chard, rice, bacon, Parmesan, and egg.

Tourte de blettes sucrée is a traditional part of the Niçoise Christmas table and its thirteen desserts (see page 320); at this time of year, families might make the pie themselves rather than purchasing it from a bakery. There are as many variations on this dessert as there are families in Nice, but I like this one adapted from a recipe by Hélène Barale, who once ran a famous Niçoise restaurant named after her. Her use of apricot jam adds another fruity element besides the apple, without oversweetening the pie.

If you're serving this to children, don't worry about the rum–the alcohol cooks off in the oven. The quality of the rum does make a difference in the final taste of the pie, though, so use one that you would happily drink. And soak the raisins overnight if you can.

SERVES 8

FOR THE PASTRY

2 cups (240 g) all-purpose flour, plus more for
  rolling the dough

½ cup (50 g) confectioners' sugar

1 teaspoon baking powder

½ teaspoon fine sea salt

7 tablespoons (100 g) cold unsalted butter, cut into
  small pieces

1 large egg

2 to 4 tablespoons (30 to 60 ml) whole milk

1 tablespoon rum

1 tablespoon grated lemon zest (from 1 lemon,
  preferably organic)

FOR THE FILLING

¼ cup (30 g) pine nuts

1 pound (450 g) Swiss chard leaves without stems
  (from 2 bunches)

⅓ cup (50 g) golden raisins, soaked overnight if
  possible, or for at least 1 hour, in ¼ cup (50 ml)
  dark or light rum

½ cup (100 g) apricot jam, homemade or store-
  bought (such as Bonne Maman)

¼ cup (20 g) freshly grated Parmesan or
  Sbrinz (optional)

¼ cup (50 g) granulated sugar or packed
  brown sugar

1 large egg, lightly beaten

1 large apple (any variety), peeled, cut in half, cored,
  and thinly sliced (optional)

1 egg, beaten, for egg wash (optional)
Confectioners' sugar for sprinkling

For the pastry

1 Place the flour, sugar, baking powder, and salt in the bowl of a stand mixer fitted with the paddle attachment and mix for a few seconds on low speed. (Or combine in the bowl of a food processor and pulse for a few seconds.) Add the butter and mix (or pulse) until fine crumbs form. Add the egg, 2 tablespoons milk, the rum, and lemon zest and mix on low speed (or pulse) until you have a soft dough. If the dough does not come together, add another 1 to 2 tablespoons milk.

2 Turn the dough out and knead lightly by hand for about 20 seconds, then divide it into 2 pieces, one twice as large as the other one. Flatten them into disks about 1 inch (2.5 cm) thick. Wrap each piece in plastic wrap and refrigerate for at least 30 minutes, and up to 24 hours.

For the filling

1 Toast the pine nuts in a small frying pan over medium heat; remove from the heat and set aside.

2 Bring a large pot of water to a boil. Add the chard leaves, bring back to a boil, and cook for 1 minute. Drain in a colander and rinse the leaves well under cold water. Squeeze out the leaves with your hands, one half at a time—you should end up with two baseball-sized balls of chard.

3 Finely chop the chard (do not use a food processor for this, which would turn the chard into a puree).

4 In a large bowl, combine the chard, the raisins and their soaking liquid, the toasted pine nuts, apricot jam, Parmesan or Sbrinz, if using, and sugar. Add the egg and mix well.

Assemble and bake the tart

1 Preheat the oven to 400°F (200°C).

2 If you let the dough rest for longer than 2 hours, knead it again for 20 to 30 seconds, adding a little flour if it feels sticky, before rolling it out–otherwise, it may easily tear.

3 On a floured surface, roll out the larger disk of pastry to an 11-inch (28 cm) round about ⅛ inch (3 mm) thick, using as much flour as you need so that it doesn't stick. Fit it into a 9-inch (23 cm) tart pan, pressing it against the bottom and up the sides, letting the excess dough hang over the sides.

4 Spread the chard mixture evenly over the pastry, then top with the apple slices, if using, arranged in a spiral.

5 Roll out the second piece of pastry to a 10-inch (25 cm) round and place on top of the filling. Pinch the edges of the dough together, then trim the edges with scissors to ½ inch (1 cm) wider than the pan and crimp all the way around. Make a few slits in the top crust using scissors or a small knife, or prick in a few places with a fork. Brush the top of the tart with the egg wash, if using.

6 Bake the tart for about 35 minutes, until well browned on top. Cool on a rack.

7 Sprinkle the top of the tart generously with confectioners' sugar before serving. (Store any leftovers in the refrigerator for up to 3 days.)

Les fêtes

In Nice, *les fêtes* (the holidays) are a time when modest local traditions meet the French penchant for luxury foods. If the abundance on display in Paris can seem over the top, Nice strikes a happy balance between foods that are accessible on the average budget–Bagna Cauda (page 275), Le Grand Aïoli (page 85), fresh sheep's-milk brousse (curds) drizzled with chestnut honey–and occasional indulgences such as heritage poultry or truffled Brie.

When I first moved to Nice, I was fascinated to learn about the *souper maigre*, or "lean supper," a concept I had not encountered in Paris (where the word *lean* could never be associated with holiday eating). Descended from the Romans, this Christmas Eve tradition is closely related to the *vigilia*, or Feast of the Seven Fishes, a seven-course meal that originated in southern Italy and lives on in some Italian American communities. In the Niçoise language, the word for Christmas, *calena*, refers to the beginning of the Roman calendar year.

Since fresh fish was not easily available in the hills and mountains, the Niçoise version of the lean supper always includes salt cod and preserved anchovies in some form, along with vegetable tians (gratins) and pasta or polenta. When it comes to dessert, the word "lean" is forgotten, as there should be no fewer than thirteen, representing Christ and the twelve apostles (with dried fruits also symbolizing different religious orders). Tourte de blettes sucrée (page 317), fougasse scented with orange flower water (page 358), candied oranges, quince jelly (page 257), and pears poached in wine with spices (page 251) are traditional inclusions in the Nice area. The sweet display stays out for three days, while on the main dining table, three tablecloths are laid on top of each other, to be progressively removed for each meal (because the eating continues at lunch and dinner Christmas Day).

The farther inland you go, the more likely you are to find families who observe the complex rituals of the Christmas meal, but these days, most people borrow from tradition rather than following it slavishly. My longtime accountant told me that she loves to prepare a dessert spread for Christmas that includes her own favorites, like chocolate mousse and tiramisù. As in the rest of France, butchers do a roaring trade in specially bred poultry at this time of year, displaying ducks, geese, capons, and guinea hens complete with feathers and feet to show off their quality. In the days before Christmas, anyone who has not staked their claim on a bird may be out of luck.

No French feast would be complete without cheese, and this is the season when *fromagers* bring out their ooziest Vacherin, a cheese from Savoie or Switzerland that is best eaten with a spoon, and fill split wheels of Brie with a thick layer of truffled mascarpone. Comté aged for thirty-six months emerges from the cellar for the *fêtes*; its complex, nutty flavor and slightly crunchy texture make it a cheese to savor on its own. Locally, this is the season for fresh ewe's cheeses, whose mild, milky (and sometimes slightly funky) flavor makes a perfect foil for a flavorful honey or sweet quince jelly.

The New Year's Eve meal is not specific to Nice, but one shared with the rest of France: seafood plays a key role, particularly oysters, scallops, and smoked salmon. Foie gras might make an appearance: although not produced in this region, it's all the more special here for being a rare treat. For the host, the key to a successful *réveillon du nouvel an* is to serve a multitude of courses—accompanied by Champagne or carefully chosen wines—to draw out the dinner for as long as possible.

To assume that the indulgence ends with the beginning of the new calendar year, though, would be to underestimate the French. No sooner have the bakeries sold their last bûches de Noël (Christmas log cakes) than they bring out the galettes des rois (Epiphany cakes). Officially celebrated on January 6, Epiphany really serves as an excuse to extend the festivities for another month. The southern French version of this cake—also found in Spain and Portugal—is a crown-shaped brioche studded with candied fruit whose origins also date back to the Romans, while in the rest of France, it's all about the galette frangipane, puff pastry with a buttery almond filling. Pâtisseries in Nice display both, with the brioche gradually being nudged out by its frangipane rival, a true test of a pastry chef's skill. Both of these cakes come with a small porcelain figurine embedded in them: whoever finds it in their slice is declared king or queen for the day.

However you choose to mix and match traditions, there is no wrong way to celebrate in this Mediterranean port that has always attracted a blend of cultures: for me, the holiday season would not be complete without mince pies and Christmas pudding, which I make with the local persimmons. My son and I also celebrate Hanukkah, using vegetable oil for frying and delicate-tasting Nice olive oil for baked goods and last-minute drizzling. What I like best is that all of these celebrations center around food rather than a frenzy of gift-giving—is there any better way to bring people together?

MADELEINES AU CITRON ET À LA LAVANDE

Lemon and lavender madeleines

Scalloped on the bottom and with a characteristic bump on top, the madeleine might seem a modest creation compared to more elaborate French pastries. Yet this is the cake that inspired one of Marcel Proust's greatest displays of literary acrobatics in his epic novel *In Search of Lost Time*. As macarons and éclairs soak up their moment in the sun, the madeleine seems to coast above fashion, often appearing at the end of a multicourse meal like the final word.

The chief concern for bakers is how to achieve the elusive bump, which gives the madeleine its rustic feminine charm. Adding baking powder increases your chances of achieving a satisfying hump, though if you are willing to let the batter rest in the refrigerator overnight, you can do without it. Experts agree that madeleines should be cooked in the top third of the oven.

There are many ways to dress up a madeleine, such as adding honey to the batter, browning the butter, or dipping the finished product in citrus glaze or dark chocolate. I flavor mine with lemon zest and a sprinkling of lavender blossoms to evoke my adopted home. The quality of the butter will make a crucial difference to the flavor, so use the best that you can afford.

Because I am an impatient baker, my recipe calls for butter that is softened but not melted, to avoid having to let the batter rest for hours in the refrigerator. Folding the butter into the fluffy batter can be a little tricky, but there is no need to worry about small lumps, which create appetizing air pockets in the finished cake. Feed these to your children, and you might awaken their literary souls.

**MAKES 24 MADELEINES
(OR 48 MINI MADELEINES)**

10 tablespoons (1¼ sticks/125 g) unsalted butter, cut into ½-inch (1 cm) dice, at warm room temperature, plus melted butter for the pan(s)

⅔ cup (135 g) granulated or raw (Demerara) sugar

1 tablespoon grated lemon zest (preferably from an organic lemon)

3 large eggs, at room temperature

Pinch of fine sea salt

2 tablespoons freshly squeezed lemon juice

1⅓ cups (160 g) all-purpose or cake flour

1 teaspoon baking powder

About 1 tablespoon organic lavender flowers for sprinkling (optional)

1 Preheat the oven to 410°F (210°C), with a rack in the top third. Using a pastry brush, butter a madeleine mold or cupcake pan with melted butter, and place in the refrigerator. (Use two pans if you have them, or bake the madeleines in batches.)

2 In a small bowl, rub the sugar and lemon zest together with your fingertips to release the essential oils from the lemon zest. →

3 In the bowl of a stand mixer fitted with the whisk attachment, or in a large bowl, using a handheld electric mixer, beat the eggs, sugar–lemon zest mixture, salt, and lemon juice until foamy, thick, and pale. Remove the bowl from the mixer stand, if using.

4 Sift the flour with the baking powder and fold into the egg mixture. Using a rubber spatula, in a medium bowl, beat the butter until smooth and creamy, like mayonnaise, then fold into the batter, breaking up any large pieces (small lumps of butter are all right).

5 Transfer the batter to a pastry bag. (At this stage, you can refrigerate the batter for up to 48 hours.) Using the pastry bag, fill the cavities in the mold or pan three-quarters full. (If you don't have a pastry bag, you can fill the mold using two spoons.) Sprinkle each madeleine with a few lavender blossoms, if using.

6 Bake the madeleines for 5 minutes, then lower the oven temperature to 350°F (180°C) and bake for another 10 minutes, or until puffed and golden. Let cool in the mold or pan for 5 minutes, then remove the madeleines with a round-tipped table knife and transfer to a rack to cool. (Reheat the oven to 410°F/210°C if baking a second batch of madeleines.) Serve warm or at room temperature.

Cook's notes

If you are investing in a madeleine pan, I have a strong preference for the traditional metal ones, rather than silicone, which create a crunchier and more evenly browned crust. Mini madeleines make a delightful little mouthful with coffee or tea, especially when served warm out of the oven.

To soften the butter, you can use the defrost setting of the microwave for up to 30 seconds, or place the butter in a plastic bowl in the oven at 95°F (35°C) for 10 to 15 minutes (don't worry, at this temperature, the plastic won't melt). Don't use a metal bowl for this, as it will retain more heat and the butter could melt.

Madeleines taste best the day they are made, but they freeze well. Place them straight from the freezer into a 325°F (160°C) oven until warmed through, about 10 minutes.

GANSES DU CARNAVAL

Carnival fritters

During the Carnival season in February, bakeries display heaps of sweet fritters sprinkled with powdered or granulated sugar—historically, a last oily treat before the lean days of Lent. If Lyon is known for its bugnes, which have a soft, donut-like texture, Nice is famed for ganses, which are thinner and crunchier. The name refers to the neckerchief that men wore as part of the traditional Carnival costume, since the dough is tied like a scarf. Local chef and cooking teacher Franck Bermond, who taught me this recipe, says you can make the ganses even crunchier by leaving out the baking powder and rolling the dough thinner, but I like them as they are here—crunchy on the outside and slightly soft inside.

If you can't find orange flower water, lemon zest will add a slightly less mysterious but equally delicious flavor. And, as Franck says, ganses are not just for Carnival: they can be enjoyed as a morning or afternoon snack at any time of year—children especially love them.

MAKES 30 TO 35 FRITTERS

2 cups (240 g) all-purpose flour, plus more for
  rolling the dough
¼ cup (50 g) sugar
1 teaspoon baking powder
2 large eggs
5 tablespoons (2½ ounces/75 g) unsalted butter,
  cut into 1-inch (2.5 cm) chunks, at cool
  room temperature

1 tablespoon orange flower water or 1 tablespoon
  grated lemon zest (preferably from an
  organic lemon)
Up to 3 tablespoons whole milk if needed
Up to 4 cups (1 l) sunflower or peanut oil for frying
Confectioners' or granulated sugar for sprinkling

1 Place the flour, sugar, baking powder, and a pinch of salt in the bowl of a stand mixer fitted with the dough hook (you can also make the dough by hand in a large bowl, using a pastry scraper to mix). Add the eggs, butter, and orange flower water or lemon zest and mix on low speed (or mix with the pastry scraper) until a soft dough forms. If the dough does not come together, add up to 3 tablespoons milk, mixing until a soft but not sticky ball of dough forms.

2 Knead the dough for 1 minute on low speed (or for 20 to 30 seconds by hand). Turn the dough out and divide it in half. Shape each half into a disk about 1 inch (2.5 cm) thick and wrap in plastic wrap. Let the dough rest in the refrigerator for at least 1 hour (you can make the dough up to 2 days ahead, or freeze it for up to 2 months; thaw it in the refrigerator for several hours or at room temperature for 1 hour).

3 On a lightly floured surface, roll the dough out into a rectangle about ⅛ inch (3 mm) thick. Using a fluted pastry wheel, cut the dough into vertical strips about 1½ inches (4 cm) wide, then make diagonal cuts 1½ inches (4 cm) apart at a 45-degree angle to create diamond shapes. →

4 Make a 1-inch (2.5 cm) slit lengthwise down the middle of one diamond, then take one pointy end and fold it over to thread it through the hole. Gently pull on both ends of the dough to finish shaping the ganse, and place it on a baking sheet lined with parchment paper. Repeat with the remaining diamonds. Roll out any dough scraps and continue shaping the ganses until no dough remains.

5 Pour at least 3 inches/8 cm) of oil into a deep fryer and heat to 375°F (190°C), or heat 2 cups (500 ml) of oil in a sauté pan or medium saucepan over medium-high heat; use a thermometer to check the temperature if you have one (if not, a cube of fresh bread will brown in 1 minute when the oil is hot enough).

6 Carefully drop the ganses a few at a time into the oil, so as not to overcrowd the fryer or pan, and cook for 1 to 2 minutes on each side, until golden. Drain on paper towels.

7 Once the ganses have cooled, transfer to a platter and sprinkle generously with confectioners' or granulated sugar (remember the dough is not very sweet).

Cook's note

❋

Leftover ganses can be frozen and then reheated in a 325°F (160°C) oven for 7 to 8 minutes. Sprinkle them with confectioners' sugar just before serving.

Le Carnaval

I have lived in Nice long enough to think of the annual Carnival in February as more of an inconvenience than a celebration; only when traffic suddenly halts to let the satirical floats trundle by on their way to the parade do I take the time to admire their garish creativity. Yet the Nice Carnival, whose pagan roots date back to the Middle Ages, is not something we should take for granted. If today much of the show takes place behind walls constructed to maintain security and keep nonpaying spectators out, when I came to live in Nice, it still had a spontaneous side that occasionally resurfaces with impromptu parades of costumed locals throwing flour and eggs, as in the past.

Until the nineteenth century, the Carnival involved costumed balls at key locations in the city. A 1539 decree divided the partygoers into four groups: gentlemen, merchants, artisans, and farmers. The only way to crash the dance of a group you did not belong to was in disguise, which allowed for rarely seen social mingling.

In 1873, a Festival Committee was formed to turn the Carnival into a larger event, introducing the first floats bearing papier-mâché caricatures. Each year a symbolic Carnival King was declared from among these, to be burned at sea on the last day (a tradition that is maintained today). The writer Alphonse Karr dreamed up the Bataille des Fleurs (Flower Battle), introduced in 1876, during which performers in vivid flower-themed costumes throw armfuls of locally grown blossoms at the crowds.

My friend Céline, who grew up in the 1980s, remembers the Carnival as a festival that was mainly for children. "The parades took place all over town," she recalls, "and our parents would send us out of the house in costume, which gave us an incredible sense of freedom." Then, as now, the children would return home with their clothes covered in confetti, which would litter the house for weeks to come.

Carnival coincides with peak citrus season on the French Riviera, and down the coast in Menton, the Lemon Festival provides an eye-popping spectacle with its tons of citrus fruits transformed into elaborate sculptures and floats. Although Menton is famous for the quality of its lemons, the quantity produced locally is so tiny that all the lemons used in the festival are imported. At least the Mentonnais do not throw them at each other, as in the messy and perilous Battle of the Oranges in the northern Italian town of Ivrea!

NICE COOKIES

When I was growing up in Canada, I only needed to nibble on a coconut-flavored "Nice Biscuit" to imagine myself in a more exotic place–I couldn't guess that I would one day live in the city that inspired this popular cookie, which came in shiny turquoise packets adorned with palm trees. It's unclear who invented the Nice Biscuit, but the British company Huntley & Palmers was producing it as early as 1904, and in Australia, it has been part of the Arnott's Biscuits range since 1922. The Dutch company Verdake has also manufactured a Nizza cookie since 1910, and it introduced a cinnamon version in 2010 to celebrate its 100th anniversary.

Never mind that coconuts don't grow in the South of France–it's the word *Nice* printed in sans-serif capitals on each cookie that evokes the retro elegance of the French Riviera. Until recently, it had never occurred to me to make these cookies, but their delicate, shortbread-like crumb calls for only a few ingredients and the dough comes together in minutes. I added lemon zest to evoke the French Riviera even more. To give mine an authentic look, I had a "NICE" stamp made using a 3D printer.

Given their British origins, these cookies are perfect next to a cup of tea, but with coffee they are also "as delightful as the town for which they are named," to quote the 1929 Arnott slogan. This recipe is adapted from one on the website NibbleMyBiscuit.

MAKES ABOUT 20 COOKIES

8 tablespoons (1 stick/115 g) unsalted butter, at cool room temperature

⅓ cup plus 2 tablespoons (90 g) sugar

1 tablespoon grated lemon zest (preferably from an organic lemon)

A pinch of sea salt

1¼ cups (150 g) all-purpose flour

⅓ cup plus 2 tablespoons (35 g) finely shredded desiccated unsweetened coconut

1   Preheat the oven to 325°F (160°C). Line two cookie sheets with parchment paper.

2   In a mixing bowl, cream the butter with ⅓ cup (65 g) of the sugar and the lemon zest using a pastry scraper or a wooden spoon. (You can also make the dough in a stand mixer fitted with the paddle attachment.)

3   Add the salt, then add the flour a third at a time, mixing throughly after each addition.

4   Add ⅓ cup (35 g) of the coconut and mix to obtain a smooth dough; avoid overworking the dough. If the dough feels very soft and/or your kitchen is warm, wrap the dough in parchment or waxed paper and refrigerate for 30 minutes before continuing.

5 Roll the dough out about ⅛ inch (3 mm) thick between two sheets of parchment paper. Lift off the top sheet of parchment and cut out cookies using a 2-by-3-inch (5 by 7 cm) cookie cutter or a fluted pastry cutter (you can also cut out rectangular cookies, for authenticity, or another shape of your choice). Using a palette knife or metal spatula, transfer the cookies to the prepared cookie sheets. Combine the scraps and roll them out to make more cookies. Mix the remaining sugar and coconut, and lightly sprinkle the cookies with this mixture.

6 If you wish, using the tip of a small knife or a toothpick, write the word *NICE* in the center of each cookie.

7 Bake the cookies for 12 to 14 minutes, until just starting to brown. Remove from the oven and cool completely on a wire rack.

8 Store the cookies in a tin or other sealed container for up to a week.

FOUNDATIONS

In this chapter, you will find the building blocks for Niçoise cooking, each of which can be used in many different ways. Most of these preparations can be preserved or frozen, so that you have them on hand when you need them. But if you don't have time to make your own stock, tomato sauce, pastry, or bread dough, feel free to use store-bought substitutes; even the Niçois understand that the modern pace of life is not always compatible with their leisurely style of cooking.

COULIS DE TOMATES
Strained tomatoes

At the Cordon Bleu, any dish involving tomatoes would inevitably start with the chef bringing a pot of water to a boil, then making a small cross in the base of each tomato, removing the cores (*pédoncules*), and dipping them in the bubbling water until their skin came off easily. He (it was always a he) would then cut the tomatoes in half and squeeze them like sponges to remove the seeds before chopping them up.

During my early days in Nice, I noticed that when the locals cooked tomatoes, they simply cut them into rough chunks and threw them into the pot, skins, seeds, and all. And when I tasted the result, I realized that the chefs had actually been throwing away the most flavorful parts of the tomatoes before cooking them. I may still peel (but not seed) tomatoes for certain recipes where they are added to other ingredients, but most of the time I prefer to use this tomato coulis, an elixir of southern French cooking that serves as a base for many different dishes, from Bouillabaisse de Poulet (page 224) to Ratatouille (page 163).

In Nice, as in Italy, home cooks make big batches of tomato coulis at the peak of summer, when the tomatoes at the farmers' stalls are bursting out of their skins. Most farmers will put the ripest tomatoes aside–the ones that feel squishy to the touch–for this purpose, selling them at a discount; when I don't see them on display, some *tomates à cuire* (cooking tomatoes) may magically appear when I inquire about them. Just as with any fruit, the softer the tomato, the higher its concentration of sugar.

Although Italians often use the fleshy Roma or San Marzano tomatoes to make their coulis, which they call *passata*, these oval tomatoes are not commonly grown around Nice, so I choose whatever is ripest–usually a mix of different heirloom tomatoes. Because they can give off a lot of juice, it's hard to predict exactly how much coulis they will produce. It also depends on how thick you want your coulis–I like to reduce it until I can see the bottom of the pan when I scrape it with a flat wooden spoon, ensuring that the tomato flavor is concentrated to its essence.

I usually keep the flavor of my tomato coulis neutral: no oil, no onions or garlic, no herbs. This way, I can easily take it in different directions, adding basil for ratatouille, garlic and oregano for pizza sauce, or fennel and orange zest for chicken with Pastis. If you're making just enough tomato coulis for a particular dish, feel free to flavor it; I add basil stems as the tomatoes cook if I know that the finished sauce will contain the leaves. No matter how ripe the tomatoes, I add a small amount of sugar, as any Niçoise mamie or Italian nonna would, to balance their acidity as they cook.

And what about the skins and seeds? If you're serious about making tomato coulis, I encourage you to invest in a food mill, or *mouli-légumes*–a kind of sieve with a handle that separates the pulp from the skins (I use the disk with the larger holes, as I prefer a slightly chunky coulis and see no need to eliminate the seeds). This is a multipurpose tool that will also do a great job of pureeing root vegetables or cooked apples, and it will remove the seeds from fruits like raspberries or blackberries if you're making a sorbet or fruit coulis. In the absence of a food mill, you could simply cut the tomatoes in half before cooking, then fish out their skins using a fork at the end.

A final piece of advice: if you can't find perfectly ripe or overripe tomatoes, don't waste your time making coulis; an out-of-season supermarket tomato cannot escape its mediocre destiny. Instead, look for store-bought strained tomatoes, often sold in tall glass jars under the Italian name *passata*. Coulis de tomates will keep for about 3 days in the refrigerator, or in the freezer for several months, bringing the sweetness of summer to the winter months.

MAKES 3 TO 4 CUPS (750 ML TO 1 L)

4 pounds (1.8 kg) very ripe tomatoes (about 12 medium)
2 teaspoons sugar
2 teaspoons coarse sea salt

1 Cut the tomatoes into quarters (no need to core them, unless the core is particularly big and hard). Place them in a large nonreactive saucepan and add the sugar and salt.

2 Set the pan over medium-high heat and squash the tomatoes using a wooden spatula so that they release some juice. Once there is at least ½ inch (1 cm) of juice in the bottom of the pan, let the tomatoes bubble over medium heat for 45 minutes to 1 hour, scraping the bottom of the pan with the spatula every few minutes to prevent them from sticking. At the end of this time, the coulis should be thick enough that when you scrape the bottom of the pan, the juices only slowly fill in the space. Remove from the heat.

3 Strain the tomatoes through a food mill, using the disk with the largest holes, into a bowl, or remove the skins with a fork. Use immediately, or let cool to room temperature and store in the refrigerator or freezer.

SAUCE TOMATE RAPIDE

Quick tomato sauce

If you have tomato coulis on hand, whether homemade or store-bought, it's easy to make a quick tomato sauce, adding herbs and perhaps chile pepper, depending on its use. Harder to find than oregano, marjoram has a subtler, sweeter taste that works particularly well with southern French dishes.

MAKES 2 CUPS (500 ML)

1 tablespoon extra-virgin olive oil

2 garlic cloves, minced

¼ teaspoon chile flakes (optional, for a spicy sauce)

Sea salt

2 cups (480 ml) Coulis de Tomates (page 337) or store-bought passata (Italian strained tomatoes)

1 sprig fresh basil or ½ teaspoon dried marjoram or oregano

1 Heat the olive oil in a frying pan or sauté pan over medium heat. Add the garlic and chile flakes, if using, along with a pinch of salt, and cook for 1 to 2 minutes, until the garlic starts to turn golden around the edges. If using chile flakes, stand back, as the fumes can make your eyes sting.

2 Add the tomato coulis or strained tomatoes and the basil sprig or marjoram or oregano and bring to a boil. Lower the heat and simmer, partially covered, for 10 to 15 minutes. Adjust the seasoning and remove from the heat.

PIMENTS EN CONSERVE

Pickled chile peppers

If many farmers' stalls at the Cours Saleya market display a predictable array of produce for each season, Pierre and Anne Magnani's makes up for in originality what it lacks in size.

Famous for growing more than 100 tomato varieties at Le Potager de Saquier, among the vineyards of Bellet (see page 236), Pierre also cultivates dozens of different citrus fruits, from bright-tasting Tahiti lime to the "Buddha's hand" lemon, with its finger-like protrusions. A dreamer at heart, Pierre has turned a greenhouse into a tropical oasis, complete with banana trees, where he and Anne hold weekly Sunday lunches in summer with live music for up to thirty guests, and he always has a new project on the go. He is the only local farmer to plant a variety of hot chile peppers, and I snap up Pierre and Anne's homemade chile preserves as soon as I spot them at the market.

I particularly love their pickled chiles, because they are so versatile, bringing color and zip to a cheese board, sandwich, or sauce (see Semi-Salted Cod with Garlic Confit and Caper, Lemon, and Chile Sauce, page 78). They often pickle milder varieties, but this method, which I learned from them, is suited to any type of chile pepper, or even sliced bell peppers.

MAKES FIVE 12-OUNCE (360 ML) JARS

4 cups (1 l) water
1 cup (240 ml) white vinegar

⅔ cup (125 g) sugar
¼ cup (60 g) kosher salt
1 pound (450 g) chile peppers, any variety, with
  stems, washed

1 To sterilize the jars, follow the instructions in the recipe for Quince Jelly, page 57.

2 In a medum-large saucepan, combine the water, vinegar, sugar, and salt and bring to a boil, stirring to dissolve the sugar and salt. Add the chile peppers, stir, and cover with a lid slightly smaller than the pan, so that it sits directly on top of the peppers and keeps them immersed; if you don't have a lid this size, use a circle of parchment paper (see Cook's Note, page 62). Lower the heat to a simmer and cook for 5 minutes, removing the lid or paper to stir once or twice.

3 Using a slotted spoon, or tongs if the chiles are larger, remove the peppers from the brine and divide them among the jars. Fill each jar right to the top with the brine to submerge the peppers completely (you might not use all the liquid). Cover with the lids and seal tightly.

4 Turn the jars upside down on a kitchen towel and let stand until cooled to room temperature, then turn them right side up and let stand for at least 3 days before opening a jar; their flavor gets even better as the weeks go by. Unopened, the peppers will keep for at least a year; once opened, store in the refrigerator and use within 6 months.

Opposite: Pierre Magnani at his farm

POIVRONS MARINÉS À L'AIL ET AU THYM

Marinated bell peppers with garlic and thyme

At the farmers' stalls in Nice, bell peppers are not perfectly calibrated and uniform, but may instead be long and pointed or short and squat; twisted, curved, or straight; and red, yellow, green, purple, or striped. Before their season ends, I love to choose a variety of colors to make these marinated peppers, which can be served as a starter or snack on toasted baguette, topped with anchovy or crumbled fresh goat cheese. They may also appear alongside Eggplant Caviar (page 123), or in the filling for Turnovers Filled with Tomato, Pepper, and Onion (page 125). They will keep for several days in the refrigerator (and will improve with time), though I can't guarantee they will last that long.

SERVES 4

4 bell peppers, any combination of colors (6 to 8 ounces/150 to 200 g each)

2 teaspoons fresh thyme leaves

2 garlic cloves, shaved paper-thin with a sharp knife

1 tablespoon freshly squeezed lemon juice

About ½ cup (120 ml) extra-virgin olive oil

Fleur de sel or other sea salt for serving

1 Preheat the broiler. Line a baking pan with aluminum foil and arrange the peppers in it. Broil for 15 to 20 minutes, turning as needed, until the peppers are blackened all over. Transfer the peppers to a bowl and cover with a plate. Let them steam for at least 15 minutes so that the skin will release more easily, then remove the plate and let the peppers cool.

2 When the peppers are cool enough to handle, peel them and remove the cores and seeds. Cut into strips about ½ inch (1 cm) wide.

3 Place one third of the pepper strips in a wide-mouthed jar or other glass container large enough to hold all the peppers. Top with one third of the thyme and garlic. Repeat twice, until you have used all the peppers, thyme, and garlic.

4 Add the lemon juice to the jar, then add enough olive oil to just cover the peppers. Let marinate for at least 2 hours before serving as a starter or side dish (see headnote), sprinkled with fleur de sel or another sea salt.

PISTOU

Niçoise pesto

Pistou is not interchangeable with Italian pesto, even if this vivid green sauce made its way to Nice from the Ligurian capital, Genoa, in the Middle Ages. As with Italian pesto, the name *pistou* refers to the action of pounding in a mortar. When it comes to the ingredients, though, there are some surprising differences.

In the coastal region of Liguria, pesto consists of small-leaved basil, olive oil, pine nuts, some combination of Parmesan and pecorino, and garlic (which is actually optional). Across the border in Nice, cooks use large-leaved basil and a generous dose of garlic, and no pine nuts or pecorino. Cheese (which may be Parmesan, a Swiss cheese called Sbrinz, or Emmental) is added only when some extra creaminess is needed, as when serving the sauce with pasta. Pistou often has a slightly runnier texture than pesto, though this can vary according to its purpose.

At the market, I once heard a Niçois explaining why local cooks prefer a garlicky basil paste to the pine nut version: "Because we're cheap!" I'm not sure if this fully explains the difference, considering that pine nuts do appear in other dishes, like Sweet Swiss Chard Pie (page 317) and Swiss Chard Omelet (page 208). The basil grown around Nice has a stronger flavor than its sweet Genovese counterpart, and I think this might account for the bolder use of garlic.

The little bistro La Merenda is renowned for its pâtes au pistou, a simple dish of spinach tagliatelle tossed with chef Dominique Le Stanc's cheese-rich take on this sauce. I learned from him that, whether making pistou or pesto, it's crucial to select tender leaves. Greenhouse-grown basil is not only acceptable but occasionally even preferable.

Pasta and gnocchi are just the beginning when it comes to using pistou: I love to serve it drizzled over Ratatouille (page 163) or fish, and it's a key element in Soupe au Pistou (page 199), the local take on minestrone. Pistou also makes a bright topping for soft goat cheese, and it can be tossed with boiled new potatoes, sliced spring onions, and lightly cooked peas for a spring salad.

A marble mortar with a wooden pestle was the traditional tool used for making this sauce, and although most cooks have now switched to the food processor or blender, there is great pleasure to be had in pounding basil by hand if you have a large enough mortar. Smashing the leaves releases their fragrance, discolors them less, and creates a smoother texture—while simultaneously relieving stress! When using a machine, you can add an ice cube to counteract the heat that it creates and give the pistou a more vivid color.

Pistou keeps for up to 5 days in the refrigerator, and it can be frozen for several months (ice cube trays create convenient serving portions). To prevent discoloration, coat the surface with a thin layer of olive oil and store in an airtight container.

1 to 2 garlic cloves, smashed with the flat side of a
    knife and peeled, any green sprouts removed

2 cups (50 g) lightly packed basil leaves

½ teaspoon sea salt

About ⅓ cup (80 ml) extra-virgin olive oil

1 ice cube (if using a machine)

⅔ cup (50 g) freshly grated Parmesan or Emmental,
    or a combination (optional)

To make the pistou in a food processor or blender (see Cook's Note)

1 Combine the garlic, basil, and salt in the processor or blender and process until finely chopped,
then add the olive oil and ice cube and process until smooth.

2 Add the cheese, if using, and blend for a few seconds.

To make the pistou using a mortar and pestle

1 In a large mortar, crush the garlic with the salt to create a puree. Tear the basil leaves in half and
add a few at a time, pulverizing them completely with the pestle before adding more.

2 Add the olive oil bit by bit, stirring with the pestle to create a smooth paste. Finally, stir in the
cheese, if using.

Variation

When I can't find generous bunches of fresh basil, I
make a peppery winter version of pistou using half
baby spinach leaves and half arugula. It's especially
delicious with gnocchi (page 67).

Cook's note

This quantity of pistou is best made in a mini food
processor or a blender, rather than in a full-sized
food processor.

AÏOLI

A staple in the southern parts of Spain, France, and Italy, aïoli was originally a paste of garlic and oil (*ail* and *huile* in French), but it eventually came to include an egg yolk to help emulsify the sauce. In the French Mediterranean, it's common to use a cooked potato or a slice of day-old baguette as a neutral-tasting thickener; mustard has no place in aïoli, and it's preferable to use a mild-tasting olive oil (you can also cut stronger-tasting olive oil with vegetable oil, using equal quantities of each).

You might be surprised to see only one garlic clove in this recipe; I have learned to be cautious with the potent pink and purple garlic found in the South of France, so feel free to adapt the quantity according to the strength of your garlic. If you are sensitive to raw garlic but still want to enjoy aïoli, you can make it with garlic confit (see Semi-Salted Cod with Garlic Confit, Lemon, Capers, and Chile Sauce, page 78) using 3 to 4 cloves, since the flavor softens dramatically when garlic is cooked this way.

Aïoli is most often served as part of a grand aïoli (see page 85)—the spread of fish with cooked and raw vegetables—and is used as a thickener in the fish stew Bourride (page 82). It can also be spiced up with chile pepper and saffron to accompany Rockfish Soup (page 150) or Chicken with Pastis (page 224); in this case, its name changes to rouille, which means rust. I love either of these sauces in sandwiches, with French fries, tossed with steamed potatoes and herbs, as a dip for shrimp, and in maki rolls, to name just a few uses.

I prefer to make aïoli in a large mortar, the old-fashioned way, but once you have crushed the garlic and potato or bread, you can switch to a bowl and a whisk or to a stand mixer fitted with the whisk attachment. A Provençal superstition says that you must always stir aïoli in the same direction; I have not found that to be true, but the faster you stir, the thicker your aïoli will be. Aïoli will keep at cool room temperature for up to 2 hours, or in the refrigerator, covered, for up to 3 days.

MAKES ¾ CUP (200 ML)

1 slice dry baguette soaked in milk to cover for at least 15 minutes, or 1 baby potato (about 2 ounces/50 g), boiled and cooled to room temperature

1 garlic clove, cut lengthwise in half, any green sprout removed

Coarse sea salt

1 fresh free-range egg yolk, at room temperature

½ cup (120 ml) mild-tasting extra-virgin olive oil

2 to 4 tablespoons (30 to 60 ml) room-temperature water, if needed

½ lemon

Fine sea salt

To make the aïoli using a mortar and pestle

1 If using the bread, squeeze out the excess milk and discard any crust that has not softened. If using the potato, cut it into rough pieces and crush lightly with a fork.

2 Crush the garlic to a paste in the mortar with a large pinch of coarse salt. Add the bread or potato and pound until completely smooth. Add the egg yolk and stir to combine.

3 Stirring as fast as you can with the pestle, add the olive oil in a very thin drizzle (a helper is useful here!). It's okay to take a break if your arm starts to tire. If the aïoli becomes so stiff that it is difficult to stir, add room-temperature water a little at a time, as needed.

4 Once you have added all the oil, the aïoli should be so thick that the pestle will stand up in it. Adjust the flavor with lemon juice and a little fine salt, if needed.

To make the aïoli in a stand mixer

1 Squeeze any excess milk out of the bread, if using, and tear it into pieces with your fingers. If using the potato, mash it with a fork until smooth.

2 Crush the garlic to a paste and place it in the bowl of a stand mixer fitted with the whisk attachment. Add a pinch of coarse salt. Add the bread or potato and start mixing on low speed.

3 Add the egg yolk and mix thoroughly, then turn the speed to medium and add the oil in a very thin drizzle. Adjust the flavor with lemon juice and fine salt, if needed, and add a little of the room-temperature water if the aïoli is too thick.

Variation: Rouille

※

The authentic version of rouille contains saffron and chile pepper, but some cooks replace the saffron with paprika and/or tomato paste to save money and obtain a more "rusty" color. To make mine, I grind a few saffron threads in a small mortar, then add a tablespoon of water and soak them for at least 10 minutes. When the aïoli is ready, I add the saffron and its water, along with 1 teaspoon hot chile paste or ½ teaspoon chile powder (you can add more or less according to the strength of the chile and your taste).

Cook's note

※

It happens to everyone: one day, instead of forming a creamy emulsion, your aïoli looks like a curdled mess. This can be a result of adding the oil too quickly, using an egg yolk that is too cold, or more mystical reasons—some people blame the moon. There is no need to panic and throw it away; instead, start with a new egg yolk in a medium bowl, and whisk the curdled mixture into the egg yolk. Voilà, your aïoli is smooth and glossy again!

VINAIGRETTE

Everyday salad dressing

Salads are a simple affair in Nice, often featuring nothing more than the mixed greens known as mesclun, the subtle local olive oil, and a sprinkling of crunchy fleur de sel. My everyday vinaigrette is barely more complicated. I prefer sherry vinegar over balsamic, as to me it strikes the right balance of sweetness and acidity, but I also appreciate good wine vinegar. You can keep any leftover vinaigrette to use within 3 days (or up to a week if you have not added the shallot or spring onion). When using the vinaigrette to dress mesclun, I leave out the mustard, as it can make the dressing too heavy for the delicate greens. A small whisk is my favorite tool for mixing salad dressing, but you can also shake it up in a jar.

MAKES ABOUT ½ CUP (120 ML)

2 tablespoons sherry vinegar or wine vinegar

1 tablespoon finely minced shallot or thinly sliced spring onion (optional)

½ teaspoon Dijon mustard (optional)

Sea salt and freshly ground black pepper

6 to 8 tablespoons (90 to 120 ml) extra-virgin olive oil, or substitute 3 to 4 tablespoons (45 to 60 ml) toasted walnut oil plus 3 to 4 tablespoons (45 to 60 ml) mild-tasting olive oil

1 Place the vinegar in a small bowl or jar and add the shallot or spring onion, if using, mustard, if using, and salt and pepper to taste. Whisk until combined, or seal the jar and shake it well. If you have time, you can let the shallot or onion soak in this mixture for 15 to 30 minutes to soften its flavor.

2 Slowly add 6 tablespoons (90 ml) olive oil (or 3 tablespoons each walnut oil and mild-tasting olive oil), whisking to emulsify the vinaigrette, or add the oil all at once to the jar and shake until the vinaigrette looks smooth. Taste and add up to 2 tablespoons more olive oil (or 1 tablespoon each walnut and mild olive oil) if the vinaigrette tastes too acidic.

Mesclun, the Niçoise salad mix

If you know the word *mesclun*, then you speak a little of the Nissart language already. Like many Niçoise specialties, this mix of wild and cultivated salad greens was born of necessity. During the nineteenth century, the Franciscan monks of the Cimiez Monastery–founded in the ninth century on a hilltop next to the Roman arena–were said to have been so poor that they could not plant a row of salad greens with the same seeds. They cut the leaves before they reached full size and mixed them with wild arugula and dandelions from the hills around the monastery. To thank those who had given alms, they handed out bags of this mesclun (*mesclum* at the time), which was simply the word for "mix" in the local language.

Today no Niçoise meal is complete without a bowl of lightly dressed mesclun, and you will find many versions of this mix in the markets. Although it's rarely seen these days, an authentic mesclun contains no red leaves; it should have six types of greens plus chervil, which brings a hint of anise to the mix. The greens can vary according to the season, but the mix should always contain arugula (known as *roquette* if it is cultivated or *riquette* if it is the more peppery wild variety). During the hotter months, mesclun wilts easily, so be sure to check its freshness before buying, then wash it in a salad spinner, dry it thoroughly (I spread it out on a clean dish towel to air-dry), and store it in a covered container in the vegetable crisper. The bags of mesclun sold in supermarkets are convenient, but if you get a chance, try to find a mix of baby greens at your local farmers' market, and taste the difference.

When you are ready to make your salad, use a minimum amount of dressing and toss well–I like to use my olive wood "hands" for this. Add a little more dressing if necessary, but not too much, or your mesclun will quickly droop. For a Niçoise touch, toast thin slices of day-old baguette in a 325°F (160°C) oven for 5 to 10 minutes, until pale golden, then rub with a halved garlic clove before adding them to your salad, breaking them into pieces if you like.

If you would like to visit the birthplace of mesclun, the Franciscan monastery is now a museum that is open on weekday mornings.

VINAIGRE AUX FRUITS

Fruit vinegar

The Niçois have long thought of clever ways to preserve fruits, but this recipe comes from Eastbourne, the town on the southeast coast of England where my father was born and my parents retired. Here John and Mary Stratton, now retired, used fruits from their garden and the lush surrounding countryside to produce fruit vinegars under the label Stratta. They began selling their jewel-toned products at a local farmers' market, where I met them, and quickly expanded to supplying specialty shops around the country.

One summer I visited their Victorian house, where Mary explained to me that it all started with a recipe for red currant vinegar in an old British cookbook. Running out of bottles to give to friends and family, she began experimenting with other fruits, from mulberries to the underappreciated, apple-like medlar, a relative of rosehip. Known as *nèfle* in French, a type of medlar called loquat in America grows all over Nice, and I have followed Mary's lead in using it for vinegar. The size of a small plum, this orange-yellow fruit has a tangy flavor reminiscent of apricots. But this recipe works with any seasonal fruit at its peak, and vivid scarlet red currants remain a classic.

These vinegars are so good that you can use them as a dip for bread instead of olive oil, or combined with it, and they make a beautiful addition to salad dressings. You can also use them in marinades or to deglaze the pan when cooking seafood or chicken. Diluted with sparkling water, they make a refreshing drink similar to a shrub.

When making this vinegar, I choose a single fruit at its peak. Since many fruits, such as cherries, red currants, and blackberries, make only a brief appearance at the market, this is a way of savoring their flavor year-round. The vinegar will be ready to use in 2 to 3 weeks, depending on the fruit.

MAKES ABOUT 2½ CUPS (600 ML)

1 pound (450 g) fruit of your choice in season,
   such as red currants, raspberries, blackberries,
   strawberries, cherries, or pitted apricots, plums,
   or peaches, washed, dried, and pitted if applicable
   (no need to peel unless the fruit is blemished)

2 to 2½ cups (480 to 600 ml) white wine vinegar,
   preferably organic

½ to 1 cup (100 to 200 g) sugar, to taste

1 Place the fruit in a clean jar large enough to hold the fruit and the vinegar. Pour 2 cups (500 ml) vinegar over top. If the vinegar does not cover the fruit, add up to ½ cup (120 ml) more. To avoid making the finished product cloudy, I resist the urge to crush the fruit.

2 Place the jar in a dark place, such as a cupboard, for 2 to 3 weeks, "until the fruit has given up all its flavor," to quote Mary Stratton.

3 Preheat the oven to 350°F (180°C).

4 Sterilize three 7-ounce (200 ml) glass bottles by rinsing them with boiling water, placing them on a baking sheet, and drying them in the oven for 15 minutes.

5 Strain the vinegar into a medium saucepan, using a fine strainer if you have one. Add ½ cup (100 g) sugar and bring to a boil, stirring to dissolve the sugar. Remove from the heat. Taste to see if the vinegar is sweet enough for you, and add up to another ½ cup (100 g) sugar, stirring to dissolve it.

6 Using a funnel lined with cheesecloth, transfer the vinegar to the bottles (if you don't have cheesecloth, your vinegar may look a little cloudy, but it will still be delicious). Seal the bottles and store in a cool, dark place. The vinegar will keep for 1 year unopened; once opened, store it in the refrigerator and use within 6 months.

CHAPELURE À LA PROVENÇALE
Provençal breadcrumbs

Provençal breadcrumbs began as a way of using up stale bread, something that no self-respecting French cook would throw away. Baguette slices dry naturally when left out overnight, but if you don't have any day-old baguette on hand, you can dry slices of sourdough bread in the oven at 325°F (160°C). This will take 10 to 20 minutes, depending on the moisture content of the bread–it should feel completely dry but be no more than lightly toasted.

Although it's okay to use dried thyme here if that's what you have, the essential oils from fresh herbs give the crumbs an aroma that will make you want to dunk your head into the bowl and inhale deeply. Along with the garlic and oil, they will also allow the breadcrumbs to stick together slightly, so that the topping holds its shape.

I use these breadcrumbs on Rack of Lamb (page 233), Tomates Provençales (page 241), and Tian de Courge (page 201), but you can sprinkle them on anything you like. They store well in the freezer, so it's always a good idea to make more than you need. If you have some extra bread but don't have time to make the breadcrumbs right away, keep the sliced bread in the freezer until you're ready, then dry it in the oven before using.

MAKES ABOUT 1½ CUPS (180 G)

1 cup (20 g) packed flat-leaf parsley leaves

2 teaspoons fresh thyme leaves or ½ teaspoon dried thyme

1 tablespoon fresh rosemary leaves

2 garlic cloves, smashed with the flat side of a knife and peeled

⅓ baguette (about 3½ ounces/100 g), sliced ½ inch (1 cm) thick and dried (see headnote)

2 tablespoons extra-virgin olive oil

Sea salt and freshly ground black pepper

1 In a food processor or blender, process the parsley, thyme, rosemary, and garlic until finely chopped.

2 Break the dried bread into rough pieces and add it to the herb mixture. Using the pulse button, blend until you have coarse bright green breadcrumbs.

3 Add the olive oil, season well with salt and pepper, and pulse to combine.

4 Any leftover breadcrumbs can be stored in an airtight container in the refrigerator for up to 3 days or in the freezer for up to 3 months.

BOUILLON DE POULET

Chicken stock

When making soup and risotto, nothing can replace a good homemade chicken stock. A Jewish family friend taught me that a chunk of fresh ginger gives the stock a clean taste without dominating the flavor; adding the onion skins deepens the color. Any stock that you don't plan to use within 3 days will keep in the freezer for up to 6 months. You can make this in a pot on the stove, but I love to use my electric pressure cooker, which extracts all the goodness from the bones in far less time. To make **vegetable stock**, simply omit the chicken.

MAKES ABOUT 6 CUPS (1.5 L)

At least 2 pounds (about 1 kg) free-range chicken pieces (legs and wings, backbone, neck, etc.) or a roast chicken carcass

1 tablespoon extra-virgin olive oil if using raw chicken

8 cups (2 liters) water

1 onion, unpeeled, cut lengthwise in half

1 large carrot, scrubbed and cut into 2-inch (5 cm) lengths

1 celery stalk, with its leaves if possible, cut into 2-inch (5 cm) lengths

1 leek, including its dark green leaves, cut into 2-inch (5 cm) lengths

2 garlic cloves, unpeeled, smashed with the flat side of a knife

A few sprigs flat-leaf parsley

1 bay leaf

2 sprigs fresh or dried thyme

8 whole black peppercorns

A 1-inch (2.5 cm) piece fresh ginger, preferably organic, unpeeled, cut lengthwise in half

1 teaspoon coarse sea salt

1 If using raw chicken, heat the olive oil in a large pot over medium-high heat (or use the sauté setting on an electric pressure cooker) and brown it on all sides, which should take 10 to 15 minutes. If using a chicken carcass, just place it in the pot.

2 Cover the browned chicken or carcass with the water and bring to a boil over high heat (still on sauté in the pressure cooker). When the water boils, skim off any foam that has risen to the surface using a small ladle or slotted spoon. (You don't have to get every last bit.)

3 Add all the vegetables and herbs to the pot, along with the peppercorns, ginger, and salt. Bring the liquid to a boil, then lower the heat to a simmer, partially cover the pot, and cook for 2 hours at a slow but steady bubble. If you would like to use the meat from the chicken legs, remove them after 1 hour, separate the meat from the bones once they are cool enough to handle, and return the bones to the pot. (If using a pressure cooker, seal the lid and cook for 45 minutes on high. Remove the meat at the end of the cooking time.)

4 Strain the stock through a fine strainer into a large bowl or other container and let cool to room temperature. Transfer to storage containers if not using the stock immediately and chill in the refrigerator overnight. Remove the layer of fat that has formed on top of the stock before using it.

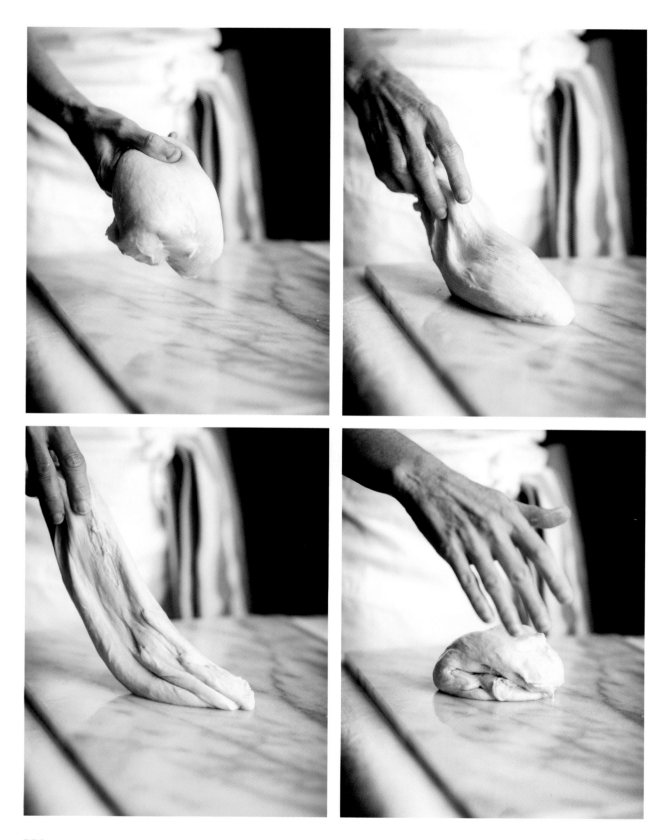

PÂTE À FOUGASSE

Olive oil bread dough

This versatile dough can be used as a base for many different toppings, most famously slow-cooked onions, anchovy, and olives for Pissaladière (page 191), or for Tarte à la Tomate, with vine-ripened tomatoes, garlic, and parsley (page 128). I also transform this dough into buns for the Niçoise sandwich Pan Bagnat (page 133), and sweeten it to make fougassettes; see the Variation. One of my favorite Old Town bakeries, La Fougasserie—which, sadly, no longer exists—offered a variety of vegetable toppings for fougasse, including a hearty version made with potato, bacon, and a light sprinkling of cheese. This dough becomes fougasse when it is shaped into an oval with diagonal slashes to represent an ear of wheat; it's similar to Italian focaccia, but the Niçoise version has a softer texture because of the addition of an egg.

   The dough might seems sticky to work with at first, but the more moisture it contains, the better the texture will be once it's baked, so add more flour a very small amount at a time until it becomes workable. If you use Italian 00 flour, you may need to add more flour. As you knead it, the dough should grow less sticky, though if your hands are naturally warm, you may have more trouble with it (this is one time when I am grateful for my cool extremities!). You can also make it in a food processor or in a stand mixer with a dough hook, but I find the silky dough particularly pleasurable to knead by hand.

MAKES ENOUGH FOR ONE 12-INCH-ROUND (30 CM) FLATBREAD OR 4 TO 6 BUNS

1½ teaspoons active dry yeast or 1 tablespoon fresh (brewer's) yeast

⅓ cup (80 ml) warm (not hot) water, plus more if needed

1 teaspoon sugar

1⅔ cups (200 g) all-purpose, bread, or Italian 00 flour, plus more if needed

1 teaspoon fine sea salt

2 tablespoons extra-virgin olive oil, plus more for kneading the dough

1 large egg, at room temperature

1 In a small bowl, dissolve the yeast in the water with the sugar; set aside for a few minutes, until the mixture starts to bubble.

2 In a mixing bowl, combine the flour and salt. Make a well in the center and add the olive oil, egg, and yeast-water mixture. Using a pastry scraper or a fork, break up the egg, then combine all the ingredients until you have a dough that is soft and slightly sticky but not wet, adding a little more flour or water as necessary (be careful to add just a little of either of these at a time).

3 Rub a little olive oil onto your hands and your work surface, turn out the dough, and knead for 3 to 4 minutes, until velvety. I like to use a kneading technique I learned at the Cordon Bleu: →

Hold the dough by one side, lift it high off the board, and slam the other end down on the work surface, without letting go; this will stretch the dough. Then fold it from the bottom up (folding the dough in your hand over the dough on the board), press it down very lightly, and grab the dough from the right side if you are right-handed, or from the left side if you are left-handed, giving it a quarter turn toward yourself. Repeat the process until the dough feels smooth and bouncy. When you press it with your finger, it should spring back. If the dough is too sticky to knead, add a little more oil to the work surface and your hand; if it remains impossibly sticky, sprinkle with a little more flour. A plastic pastry scraper is useful for scraping up any dough that has stuck to the work surface.

4 Shape the dough into a ball by cupping both hands and squeezing the base as you turn it a few times on your work surface. Transfer it to a bowl, cover with a plate or plastic wrap, and set aside in a warm place to rise for at least 45 minutes, until doubled in size. At this stage, you can refrigerate the dough, covered, for up to 2 days; remove it 30 minutes before proceeding with your chosen recipe.

Variation: Fougassettes

To make fougassettes, which are associated with Christmas in Nice and may be eaten for breakfast or as a sweet snack, replace 2 tablespoons of the water with orange flower water, and add 3 tablespoons sugar to the dry ingredients (omit the sugar for the yeast). After the dough has doubled in size, divide it in half, shape into 2 balls, and flatten each one on an oiled baking sheet into an oval about ½ inch (0.5 cm) thick. Make 3 diagonal slashes all the way through each piece of dough with a dough razor (called a *lame*), a small knife, or a pastry scraper, then pull the dough apart with your fingers to widen the holes. Cover with a dish towel and set aside to rise in a warm place for another 20 minutes while you preheat the oven to 375°F (190°C).

Before baking, spritz the fougassettes with water or, even better, orange flower water (mine comes in a spray bottle). Bake for 15 to 20 minutes, until puffed and browned. Let cool on a rack, and sprinkle with confectioners' sugar.

PÂTE À L'HUILE D'OLIVE

Olive oil pastry

Butter is a recent addition to the Niçoise diet, having become common only in the past few decades; in the mountains, many cooks still use it rarely, if at all. Before butter pastry became the norm thanks to the availability of dairy products from other parts of France, both sweet and savory tarts were made with olive oil pastry.

When I began making this pastry, I was surprised at how quickly it came together and how flaky it is. I now use it for most of my savory pies and quiches (see Coca Frita, page 125, and Tourte de Blettes Salée, page 73). I had a revelation when I realized that using hot water improves the dough, helping the oil to blend in more thoroughly without compromising the flakiness. This pastry lends itself well to the use of more rustic flours like spelt or whole wheat. If you use cake flour or Italian 00 flour, the texture will be especially tender.

MAKES ENOUGH FOR ONE 10-INCH (25 CM) ROUND TART SHELL

1⅔ cups (200 g) all-purpose, cake, or Italian 00 flour, plus more if needed

1 teaspoon fine sea salt

⅓ cup (80 ml) olive oil

⅓ cup (80 ml) hot water

1 Place the flour in a large mixing bowl and stir in the salt with a pastry scraper or fork.

2 Add the olive oil and mix it in until the mixture forms coarse crumbs.

3 Add the hot water all at once and mix with a pastry scraper or fork until the dough comes together in a ball. If it seems sticky, add a little more flour to coat the outside of the ball.

4 Turn the dough out onto a lightly floured work surface and knead it lightly for about 20 seconds, until it is soft and smooth. Flatten the ball into a disk about 1 inch (2.5 cm) thick.

5 Wrap the dough in plastic wrap and let it rest in the refrigerator for at least 30 minutes, and up to 24 hours, before using.

PÂTE SABLÉE

Quick basic pastry

At the Cordon Bleu, I watched the pastry chefs make pâte sucrée, or sweet pastry, directly on the countertop using room-temperature butter and a plastic pastry scraper to mix the ingredients. The dough then needed to be chilled for at least an hour before it could be rolled out.

Although I loved to watch their hands-on method, in my classes I try to eliminate any time-consuming steps in the pastry-making process. For this dough, which is known as *pâte sablée*, because its texture is shortbread-like, I start with cold butter so that we can roll out the dough after the shortest possible resting time. Using a food processor or mixer rather than working by hand keeps the ingredients cool as they are mixed. I also add a secret ingredient that makes the pastry tender even when you hurry the process along.

First, a little kitchen science: gluten, the protein in wheat flour, becomes elastic when it is activated by water. After mixing a pastry dough, bakers traditionally let it rest not just to cool the butter but also to allow the gluten to "relax," resulting in a dough that does not shrink or toughen as it bakes. I replace the water with cream, whose high fat content reduces the risk of creating too much elasticity. My first choice is crème fraîche, which also adds a slight acidity to the dough, but heavy cream works too.

You will still want to be careful not to overwork the dough or let it get too warm, but after years of teaching this recipe, I can confidently say that it makes the idea of buying packaged pastry seem pointless (not to mention the dubious fats that often go into the industrial version). For a savory pastry dough, simply eliminate the sugar.

MAKES ENOUGH FOR ONE 9-INCH (23 CM) ROUND TART SHELL

1½ cups (180 g) all-purpose flour

¼ cup (25 g) confectioners' sugar, sifted

¼ teaspoon fine sea salt

6 tablespoons (90 ml) cold unsalted butter, cut into pieces)

1 large egg yolk, cold from the refrigerator

¼ cup (60 ml) very cold crème fraîche or heavy cream

To make the dough in a food processor

1 Place the flour, confectioners' sugar, and salt in the bowl of a food processor and pulse a couple of times to combine. Add the butter and pulse until the mixture forms coarse crumbs.

2 Add the egg yolk and crème fraîche or heavy cream and pulse just until the dough starts to gather together around the blade. →

3 Remove the dough from the bowl, shape into a ball, and flatten into a disk about 1 inch (2.5 cm) thick. Roll out right away if it is not too soft, or wrap in plastic wrap and chill for at least 15 minutes, and up to 24 hours.

To make the dough in a stand mixer

1 Place the flour, confectioners' sugar, and salt in the bowl of a stand mixer fitted with the paddle attachment and mix on low speed to combine. Add the butter and mix until the mixture resembles coarse crumbs, about 1 minute.

2 Add the egg yolk and cream and mix on low speed until the dough forms a ball, 15 to 20 seconds. Be careful not to overmix, but do let the dough come together.

3 Remove the dough from the bowl, shape into a ball, and flatten into a disk about 1 inch (2.5 cm) thick. Roll out right away if it is not too soft, or wrap in plastic wrap and chill for at least 15 minutes, and up to 24 hours, before using.

RECIPES BY CATEGORY

SEASONAL MENUS

Spring

MENU 1
Artichokes stewed in white wine

Fish fillets with aïoli and spring vegetables

Strawberry and cream tart

MENU 2
Asparagus with yogurt dressing and egg

Fisherman's stew from Sète

Spring strawberry cake in a jar

MENU 3
Niçoise salad

Spiced meatballs with chickpeas and yogurt

Cherry clafoutis

Summer

MENU 1
Eggplant caviar with goat cheese and yogurt

Stuffed sardines

Lavender crème brûlée

MENU 2
Anchovy dip

Little stuffed vegetables

Rustic plum tart

MENU 3
Stuffed zucchini blossoms with Niçoise "salsa"

Rockfish soup

Peaches roasted with olive oil and honey

Fall

MENU 1
Caramelized onion tart with anchovies and olives

Chicken with pastis and chile-saffron aïoli

Pears poached in red wine with spices

MENU 2
Squash soup with orange

Duck breast with honey and aniseed

Chickpea fries

Fig tart with honey-almond cream

MENU 3
Beet flans with lamb's lettuce and walnut dressing

Rack of lamb with mustard-herb crust

Upside-down apple tart with lemon and olive oil

Winter

MENU 1
Orange salad with olives and mint

Beef stew cooked in red wine with porcini and orange zest

Chocolate mousse with olive oil

MENU 2
Rustic green pasta with walnut sauce

Stuffed beef rolls cooked in red wine

Lemon soufflé

MENU 3
Warm anchovy and garlic dip

Semi-salted cod mashed with potatoes, preserved lemon, and herbs

Sweet Swiss chard pie

ADDRESS BOOK

In this section, you will find the restaurants and food shops mentioned in this book, and a few places where you can try Niçoise cuisine in other parts of the world. The list is by no means comprehensive, but many of these places are like a second home to me. Armed with this *carnet d'adresses*, you will be able to enjoy much of the best food and drink that Nice has to offer.

Restaurants

BANH MEI
6 rue Rossetti, 06300 Nice
Vietnamese-Mediterranean food
and natural wines

BISTROT D'ANTOINE
27 rue de la Préfecture, 06300 Nice
Armand Crespo's flagship
modern bistro

CAFÉ DE LA FONTAINE
4 avenue du Général de Gaulle,
06320 La Turbie
www.hostellerie-jerome.com/le-café
-de-la-fontaine
Down-to-earth bistro offshoot of the
renowned Hostellerie Jérôme

LE CANON
23 rue Meyerbeer, 06000 Nice
lecanon.fr
Produce-driven bistro and
natural wines

CHEZ PALMYRE
4 rue Droite, 06300 Nice
restaurantchezpalmyre.eatbu.com
Superb-value set menu

LA MERENDA
4 rue Raoul Bosio, 06300 Nice
lamerenda.net
Classic haunt for Niçoise specialties

OLIVE ET ARTICHAUT
6 rue Sainte-Reparate, 06300 Nice
oliveartichaut.com
Sophisticated bistro

OLIVIERA
8 bis rue du Collet, 06300 Nice
oliviera.com
Olive oil shop and
Mediterranean restaurant

RESTAURANT JAN
12 rue Lascaris, 06300 Nice
janonline.com/restaurantjan
High-end dining with a South
African touch

LA TABLE ALZIARI
4 rue François Zanin, 06300 Nice
Family-run Niçoise bistro

LA TABLE DU CHEF
5 rue Jean Daumas, 06400 Cannes
latableduchefcannes.com/en
Modern bistro with a changing
seasonal menu

Street Food

LOU PELANDROUN
4 boulevard Joseph Garnier,
06000 Nice
Exemplary pissaladière and
pan bagnat

PIPO SOCCA
13 rue Bavastro, 06300 Nice
chezpipo.fr
Crispy socca, including versions
with toppings

SOCCA TRAM
6 bis avenue Alfred Borriglione,
06100 Nice
Socca and other local specialties

Markets

MARCHÉ COURS SALEYA
Cours Saleya, 06300 Nice
Tuesday–Sunday, 8 a.m.–1 p.m.

MARCHÉ LIBÉRATION
Place du Général de Gaulle and
avenue Malaussena, 06100 Nice
Tuesday–Sunday, 8 a.m.–1 p.m.

Food Shops

**BOUCHERIE CARLICCHI
ZELINO**
3 rue Flaminius Raiberti,
06100 Nice
Family-run butcher selling
heritage meats

CAFÉS INDIEN
35 rue Pairolière and 2 bis rue
Sainte-Réparate, 06300 Nice
cafes-indien.com
Coffee roaster and café

CHARCUTERIE POTTIER-GHIBAUDO
10 boulevard Jean Jaurès,
06300 Nice
maisonghibaudopottier.com
Local pork specialties,
including porchetta

CHARCUTERIE NATHALIE
6 boulevard Joseph Garnier,
06100 Nice
Female-run pork butcher
specializing in free-range meat

FROMAGERIE MÉTIN
13 rue Pairolière, 06300 Nice
fromageriemetin.fr
Cheese shop with its own
aging cellar

MAISON AUER
7 rue Saint-François de Paule,
06300 Nice
www.maison-auer.com
Sixth-generation candied fruit and
sweets shop

MAISON BARALE
7 rue Sainte-Réparate, 06300 Nice
www.maison-barale.fr
Family-run fresh pasta shop
since 1892

NICE ORGANIC
24 rue Pairolière, 06300 Nice
herboristeriebio.com/en
Organic herbs, spices, and
essential oils

Wine Shops/Wine Bars

APERITIV
11 avenue Malaussena, 06100 Nice,
and 4 rue Cassini, 06300 Nice
Wines, spirits, and snacks

CAVES CAPRIOGLIO
16 rue de la Préfecture, 06300 Nice
www.caprioglio.fr
Family-run Old Town institution

CAVE DE LA TOUR
3 rue de la Tour, 06300 Nice
cavedelatour.com
Wine shop and bar featuring
local wines

LA PART DES ANGES
17 rue Gubernatis, 06000 Nice
lapartdesanges-nice.com
Wine bar and bistro specializing in
natural wines

Ice Cream

ARLEQUIN
9 avenue Malaussena, 06100 Nice
www.arlequingelati.com
Creative Italian-run gelato shop

FENOCCHIO
Main shop at 2 place Rossetti,
06300 Nice
www.fenocchio.fr
A Nice institution since 1966

OUI JELATO
5 rue de la Préfecture, 06300 Nice
https://www.ouijelato.fr/
Classic Italian gelato and
frozen desserts

Bakeries

**MAISON JEAN-MARC
BORDONNAT**
19 rue Barla, 06300 Nice
Baguettes and specialty breads that
change daily

**LA BOULANGERIE PAR
MICHEL FIORI**
19 boulevard Raimbaldi,
06000 Nice
Outstanding baguettes,
croissants, and flans

**PAINS ET PÂTISSERIES
CARABACEL**
9 rue Pastorelli, 06000 Nice
Baguettes, croissants, and
seasonal treats

Cooking Classes

**LES PETITS FARCIS COOKING
STUDIO**
12 rue Saint Joseph, 06300 Nice
www.petitsfarcis.com
My school, offering cooking and
pastry classes, wine tastings, and
food tours

For a Taste of Nice
Outside of Nice

LES NIÇOIS
7 rue Lacharrière, 75011 Paris
lesnicois.com
Popular Nice-themed bistro
and épicerie

LPM
lpmrestaurants.com
Offshoots of the fashionable
Niçoise restaurant La Petite Maison
throughout the world, including
London, Miami, and Dubai

NICE MATIN
201 West 79th Street, New York, NY
nicematinnyc.com
Updated Niçoise cuisine

ACKNOWLEDGMENTS

First, I would like to thank David Lebovitz for convincing me over a lunch in Paris that Niçoise cuisine was not too niche a subject for an American publisher. David also introduced me to his agent, Bonnie Nadell, who shared his faith in the idea and encouraged me to tell my story. Bonnie found a perfect match in my editor, Melanie Tortoroli, whose warmth and enthusiasm have kept me going throughout this project. Her assistant, Annabel Brazaitis, has also been a joy to work with, and I couldn't have hoped for a better copy editor than Judith Sutton, who brought her deep knowledge of French cuisine (and of English grammar!) to these pages.

Writing the proposal for this book was a drawn-out process, and I would especially like to thank Susan Herrmann Loomis and Stephanie Williams for their invaluable guidance and editing skills in the early stages.

Many thanks to Jan Hendrik van der Westhuizen for making our photography sessions feel so relaxed and fun, and for his willingness to see the local cuisine through my eyes. I would also like to thank all my kitchen helpers during the photo shoots: Peter Newbury, Sophia Olson, Jasmina Ristic Mukha, Alexandra Abashmadze, and Karine Brun. Without their cheerful efficiency, it could all have spiraled into chaos!

Dozens of volunteer testers helped make this book as useful as it is beautiful; I loved receiving their thoughtful feedback. Special thanks to Shelley Dobyns, Kelly Arno, Lara Patil, Caroline Crawford, Shizuka Hashimoto, John Hendrix, and Jocelyne Parent, a few of my most loyal students and cheerleaders.

Viktorija Todorovska propped me up in all sorts of ways as I worked on this book; I feel very lucky to have her as a friend and fellow teacher at Les Petits Farcis. Pastry chef Sophie Lim and administrative assistant Damaris Cacciabue also saved the day when I needed extra help running my cooking school.

I am grateful to all the cooks and purveyors who took the time to share their stories and recipes, particularly Michel Alziari, Dominique Le Stanc, Hélène Albou, Vincent Verneveaux, Franck Bermond, Nathalie Barale, Jean-François Torre and Hansley Rose, Sebastien Perinetti and Elmahdi Mobarik, Thi-hieu Nguyen, →

Pierre and Anne Magnani, Flavien Falchetto, Carine Dalmasso, Thomas Métin, Nazih Borghol, Nadim Beyrouti, Armand Crespo, Louis Berthon, Claude Aschani, John and Mary Stratton, Bruno Cirino, and Fouad Zarrou. I will forever appreciate chef Franck Cerutti for taking me under his wing when I first arrived in Nice.

Ceramicist Mounia Guenatri convinced me to make my own tableware for the photo shoots; my weekly class with her has opened up a whole new world.

Fellow food and drink writers and cooking school owners Lucy Vanel, Jane Bertch, Dorie Greenspan, Judy Witts Francini, Emily Monaco, Allison Zinder, Kate Hill, Forest Collins, Guy Dimond, Susan Low, and Paule Caillat have provided endless support over the years; it's wonderful knowing that I can turn to any of you at any time. I also treasure my longtime friends and Edible Paris colleagues Stephen Mudge and Claude Cabri. James Pouliot, who convinced me to spend a month down the street from him in Palermo working on this book, never fails to make me laugh in my moments of despair.

Every student who enters my kitchen at Les Petits Farcis reminds me why I chose this unique and rewarding profession: many thanks to all of you for your curiosity and good spirits. My loyal newsletter readers also motivate me each month to keep writing.

I am lucky to have friends and family throughout the world, and nothing makes me happier than sharing a meal with those I love. A special mention to my ever-supportive son, Sam: I owe you a lifetime's worth of lemon tarts!

INDEX

Note: Page references in *italics* indicate photographs.

Jan Hendrik van der Westhuizen

ROSA JACKSON has been a France-based food writer since 1995, when she moved to Paris to pursue her love of cooking. In 2004 she made the leap from Paris to Nice, lured by its vibrant food market and colorful Mediterranean cuisine. Jackson edited several editions of the *Time Out Paris Eating and Drinking* guide, has contributed to publications such as *Food & Wine*, *Eating Well*, *The Financial Times*, and *Australian Gourmet Traveller*, and was a columnist for *France Magazine*. Her company, Edible Paris, offers custom guided tours of Paris, and at her studio, Les Petits Farcis, in the heart of Old Nice, Rosa teaches cooking and pastry classes that focus on the city's unique culinary traditions.